GLENVIEW PUBLIC LIBRARY

3 1170 00821 4540

DEC 2 8 2009

☆☆☆ Forbes

TRAVEL GUIDE

CHICAGO

GLEN
1
G

D1507734

ACKNOWLEDGMENTS

We gratefully acknowledge the help of our representatives for their efficient and perceptive inspections of the lodgings listed. Forbes Travel Guide is also grateful to the talented writers who contributed to this book.

Copyright © 2010 The Five Star Travel Corporation. All rights reserved. This publication may not be reproduced in whole or in part by any means whatsoever without written permission from Forbes Travel Guide, 200 W. Madison St., Suite 3950, Chicago, IL 60606; info@forbestravelguide.com

Some of the information contained herein is derived from a variety of third-party sources. Although every effort has been made to verify the information obtained from such sources, the publisher assumes no responsibility for inconsistencies or inaccuracies in the data or liability for any damages of any type arising from errors or omissions.

Neither the editors nor the publisher assume responsibility for the services provided by any business listed in this guide or for any loss, damage or disruption in your travel for any reason.

Front and Back Cover images: ©Almay and ©istock
ISBN: 978-1-936010-05-9
Manufactured in the USA
10 9 8 7 6 5 4 3 2 1

CONTENTS

CHICAGO STAR PROPERTIES

STAR ATTRACTIONS

If you've been a reader of Mobil Travel Guide, you will have heard that this historic brand partnered with another storied media name, Forbes, in 2009 to create a new entity, Forbes Travel Guide. For more than 50 years, Mobil Travel Guide assisted travelers in making smart decisions about where to stay and dine when traveling. With this new partnership, our mission has not changed: We're committed to the same rigorous inspections of hotels, restaurants and spas—the most comprehensive in the industry with more than 500 standards tested at each property we visit—to help you cut through the clutter and make easy and informed decisions on where to spend your time and travel budget. Our team of anonymous inspectors are constantly on the road, sleeping in hotels, eating in restaurants and making spa appointments, evaluating those exacting standards to determine a property's rating.

What kinds of standards are we looking for when we visit a proprety? We're looking for more than just high-thread count sheets, pristine spa treatment rooms and white linen-topped tables. We look for service that's attentive, individualized and unforgettable. We note how long it takes to be greeted when you sit down at your table, or to be served when you order room service, or whether the hotel staff can confidently help you when you've forgotten that one essential item that will make or break your trip. Unlike any other travel ratings entity, we visit each and every place we rate, testing hundreds of attributes to compile our ratings, and our ratings cannot be bought or influenced. The Forbes Five Star rating is the most prestigious achievement in hospitality—while we rate more than 8,000 properties in the U.S., Canada, Hong Kong, Macau and Beijing, for 2010, we have awarded Five Star designations to only 53 hotels, 21 restaurants and 18 spas. When you travel with Forbes, you can travel with confidence, knowing that you'll get the very best experience, no matter who you are.

With our new City Guide series, you can also count on a local perspective, in the form of a fresh, witty, insider voice. We employ local writers and inspectors who are well-connected in their respective cities to give you the very latest information on what's going on around town. As you are reading these pages, we hope you get a real flavor of the city and that you feel even more inspired to visit and take it all in. All of our books in the City Guide series include vibrant photos and easy-to-use maps to help you find your way to the city's best attractions. We understand the importance of making the most of your time. That's why the most trusted name in travel is now Forbes Travel Guide.

STAR RATED HOTELS

Whether you're looking for the ultimate in luxury or the best value for your travel budget, we have a hotel recommendation for you. To help you pinpoint properties that meet your needs, Forbes Travel Guide classifies each lodging by type according to the following characteristics:

★★★★★These exceptional properties provide a memorable experience through virtually flawless service and the finest of amenities. Staff are intuitive, engaging and passionate, and eagerly deliver service above and beyond the guests' expectations. The hotel was designed with the guest's comfort in mind, with particular attention paid to craftsmanship and quality of product. A Five-Star property is a destination unto itself.

★★★★These properties provide a distinctive setting, and a guest will find many interesting and inviting elements to enjoy throughout the property. Attention to detail is prominent throughout the property, from design concept to quality of products provided. Staff are accommodating and take pride in catering to the guest's specific needs throughout their stay.

★★★These well-appointed establishments have enhanced amenities that provide travelers with a strong sense of location, whether for style or function. They may have a distinguishing style and ambience in both the public spaces and guest rooms; or they may be more focused on functionality, providing guests with easy access to local events, meetings or tourism highlights.

★★The Two Star hotel is considered a clean, comfortable and reliable establishment that has expanded amenities, such as a full-service restaurant.

★The One Star lodging is a limited-service hotel or inn that is considered a clean, comfortable and reliable establishment.

For every property, we also provide pricing information. All prices quoted are accurate at the time of publication; however, prices cannot be guaranteed.

STAR RATED RESTAURANTS

Every restaurant in this book has been visited by Forbes Travel Guide's team of experts and comes highly recommended as an outstanding dining experience.

★★★★★Forbes Five-Star restaurants deliver a truly unique and distinctive dining experience. A Five-Star restaurant consistently provides exceptional food, superlative service and elegant décor. An emphasis is placed on originality and personalized, attentive and discreet service. Every detail that surrounds the experience is attended to by a warm and gracious dining room team.

★★★★These are exciting restaurants with often well-known chefs that feature creative and complex foods and emphasize various culinary techniques and a focus on seasonality. A highly-trained dining room staff provides refined personal service and attention.

★★★Three Star restaurants offer skillfully-prepared food with a focus on a specific style or cuisine. The dining room staff provides warm and professional service in a comfortable atmosphere. The décor is well-coordinated with quality fixtures and decorative items, and promotes a comfortable ambience.

★★The Two Star restaurant serves fresh food in a clean setting with efficient service. Value is considered in this category, as is family friendliness.

★The One Star restaurant provides a distinctive experience through culinary specialty, local flair or individual atmosphere.

Because menu prices can fluctuate, we list a pricing range rather than specific prices. The pricing ranges are per diner, and assume that you order an appetizer or dessert, an entrée and one drink.

STAR RATED SPAS

Forbes Travel Guide's spa ratings are based on objective evaluations of more than 450 attributes. About half of these criteria assess basic expectations, such as staff courtesy, the technical proficiency and skill of the employees and whether the facility is clean and maintained properly. Several standards address issues that impact a guest's physical comfort and convenience, as well as the staff's ability to impart a sense of personalized service. Additional criteria measure the spa's ability to create a completely calming ambience.

★★★★★Stepping foot in a Five Star Spa will result in an exceptional experience with no detail overlooked. These properties wow their guests with extraordinary design and facilities, and uncompromising service. Expert staff cater to your every whim and pamper you with the most advanced treatments and skin care lines available. These spas often offer exclusive treatments and may emphasize local elements.

★★★★Four Star spas provide a wonderful experience in an inviting and serene environment. A sense of personalized service is evident from the moment you check in and receive your robe and slippers. The guest's comfort is always of utmost concern to the well-trained staff.

★★★These spas offer well-appointed facilities with a full complement of staff to ensure that guests' needs are met. The spa facilities include clean and appealing treatment rooms, changing areas and a welcoming reception desk.

BEST BETS

TASTE OF CHICAGO

SWEET HOME CHICAGO

Things change fast in the Windy City, with new restaurants, shops and even multi-million dollar sights (as anyone who's seen the incredible Millennium Park can attest) opening every day. Whether it's your first time in Chicago or your fiftieth, there's certain to be a new skyscraper, celeb chef creation or cutting-edge art gallery you need to experience. Here, a short list of the very best to see, do and taste in Chicago right now.

WHAT ARE THE TOP HOTELS?

Don't be surprised if the **Four Seasons Hotel Chicago** *(page 97)* has a file on you. The staff meets every morning to go over who's arriving that day and what they might need, whether it's something you requested prior to your visit or something they know by scrolling through their huge database of guests. It's this flawless service that makes a stay here feel exquisitely relaxing. It also doesn't hurt that the hotel recently underwent a thorough revamp, and is just steps from the city's best shopping.

The **Peninsula Chicago** *(page 98)* mixes Old World opulence with modern-day ease. The hotel's graceful service befits the dignified atmosphere of this gem. But the Peninsula's crown jewels are also its most delicious. While the trendy Shanghai Terrace serves inhalable Asian-inspired fare and cocktails, the reputable Avenues is still a force to be reckoned with in the city's fine-dining scene.

You might be confused when you walk into **Trump International Hotel and Tower** *(page 106)*. Is it a hotel? Is it a condo building? Well, it's both, and the understated but upscale lobby is a precursor to everything else this well-done hotel has to offer: A sophisticated but relaxed lounge; a gorgeous, fine dining restaurant; lavish rooms where every detail has been taken into consideration (down to the Sub-Zero refrigerators); and amazing views from everywhere.

WHAT ARE THE CAN'T-MISS SIGHTS?

When **Millennium Park** *(page 35)* opened in the summer of 2004, it was several years overdue and millions of dollars over budget. But for Chicagoans, it's hard to stay miffed about the delays and cost after seeing the park's tremen-dous role as a civic center. Throughout the year, tourists and locals mix and mingle over the park's weekly concerts (many of them free), and public art exhibitions and expos. The park is also home to the lovely, peace-inducing Lurie Garden; the interactive, wet-and-wild Crown Fountain; and everyone's favorite reflective bean-shaped sculpture, Cloud Gate.

Other cities might vie for the title of skyscraper capital of the country, but the truth is, these awe-inspiring structures were invented in the Windy City at the turn of the century after the Chicago Fire. If you're mad for Mies (van der Rohe, that is), all you have to do is walk through Chicago's Loop and look up; or take a tour, like the **Chicago Architecture Foundation's Architecture River Cruise** *(page 49)*, which winds through the Chicago River and gives you a rundown of the city's most significant buildings.

Likewise, Chicago is peppered with public art, beyond the confines of Millennium Park. A walk through the **Loop** *(page 33)* showcases the city's wealth in public art, as would a trek to the city's neighborhoods (for example, the West Loop has The Haymarket Memorial on Desplaines Street between Lake and Randolph streets, and the South Loop has Arris at Cermak Road and Calumet Avenue). Even the El can bring you closer to public art: Many

NAVY PIER

of the city's CTA stations feature mosaic murals and pieces by local artists, such as Juan Chavez and Corinne Peterson's *Hopes and Dreams* (Roosevelt station on the Red Line, South Loop).

From the observation deck at the 103rd floor of the **Willis Tower** *(page 35)*, formerly the Sears Tower, you can see up to 40 miles out in either direction on a clear day. The **John Hancock Observatory** *(page 31)* is no slouch, either. Take the elevator to the 95th floor Signature Room Lounge, where you can get vistas for the cost of a slightly sugary cocktail. (Ladies, check out the view from the bathroom.)

You've seen *Ferris Bueller's Day Off* and the spoofs of the farmer couple in the *American Gothic* painting—now experience the **Art Institute of Chicago** *(page 33)* in the flesh. The new Renzo Piano-designed Modern Wing, opened in 2009, is simply stunning, and is one of the city's best new attractions. Whatever you do, set aside an afternoon to take in this massive museum, which boasts an impressive collection of Impressionist and post-Impressionist pieces, plus 20th century classics.

WHAT ARE THE TOP EXPERIENCES?

If you enjoy the great outdoors, there's nothing like summer in Chicago. The season ignites three months of celebration, during which Chicagoans cram in every outdoor activity possible before they have to hibernate again for the winter. The city's many street festivals are alfresco shindigs held every weekend, celebrating everything from folk music (Chicago Folk and Roots Festival at Welles Park) to local eats at the massive **Taste of Chicago** *(page 165)*. The hot weather also ushers in another only-in-Chicago experience: **Lollapalooza** *(page 165)*. The three-day music extravaganza brings big-name acts such as Radiohead and hometown heroes Wilco to Grant Park and, of course, fans from all over the country follow them. For a real taste of Chicago in the summer, head to **Green City Market** *(page 50)*, the city's only sustainable market, where you can shop alongside the area's top chefs for the freshest-of-the-fresh fruit and vegetables.

WHERE IS THE BEST SHOPPING?

Until you have walked the **Magnificent Mile**, you won't really know just how huge of a shopping destination this section of Michigan Avenue is. Walk north on Michigan between the Chicago River and Oak Street, and your closet will lack for nothing. From reliable chains like Gap, Guess and Aldo; to high-end department stores such as Neiman Marcus and Bloomingdale's; to niche shops like the Apple Store and Niketown, you'll be hard-pressed to go home empty-handed.

If you're searching for something homegrown, break away to buzzing neighborhoods like **Wicker Park**, where you can often buy local designers' goods at boutiques such as **Habit** *(page 124)* and **Eskell** *(page 129)*.

When it comes to shopping for clothes, girls might prefer to hit **American Girl Place** *(page 127)* to outfit their dolls instead. Aside from the new wardrobe, girls can pamper their Samanthas and Kayas with a cut at the doll hair salon, afternoon tea at the café and family portraits at the photo studio—all are available at the massive Chicago shop, the company's first flagship store.

A short trek from downtown to Wrigleyville is a small distance to go for a bit of history—a visit to **Wrigley Field** *(page 158)*. The home of the Chicago Cubs baseball team was built in the early 1900s, and it remains one of the city's most beloved landmarks; possibly more beloved than the ill-fated Cubbies themselves, who haven't won a single World Series in 100 years and counting. Win or lose, games at Wrigley are a cherished part of Chicago summers, and it's not hard to see why: It's a thrill to sit with the loyal Cubs bleacher bums, chow down on a ballpark dog and watch Derrek Lee hit one out of the park. A huge highlight is seeing which celebrity guest will pop in to sing *Take Me Out to the Ball Game*—it could be anyone from Bill Murray to Vince Vaughn stepping up to the mic. Can't get tickets? Head to Wrigley anyway and watch the game from one of the watering holes surrounding the park; the neighborhood setting is half the fun.

If baseball isn't your thing, go see the one daytime diva everyone seems to adore. Oprah is bigger than life, so if you want to see her in action at **Harpo Studios** *(page 35)*, plan ahead to snag those hard-to-get tickets.

When day turns into night, the city just gets hotter. One place in particular that heats up is the area in the Gold Coast where Division, Rush and State streets come together. Here, a mix of locals and tourists crowd the pricey restaurants, bars or clubs. Another nightlife hub that's growing in popularity is the six-corner intersection in Wicker Park where Milwaukee, North and Damen avenues meet. All sorts of party people roam the neighborhood, ducking into clubs, music venues and hotter-by-the-minute restaurants.

Ready-for-primetime comedy is a Chicago legacy. **The Second City** *(page 153)* and **iO Chicago** *(page 152)* have turned out some of the best jokesters around, including Tina Fey and Steve Carell. At Second City, you'll get top-notch topical sketch shows, while iO will give you laugh-out-loud improv, an art form invented in Chicago.

WHAT ARE THE BEST FOOD EXPERIENCES?

Chicago has come a long way from the days when it was known as the "Hog Butcher for the World." Nowadays, the city's dining scene is known much more for its role in the molecular-gastronomy movement—hot spots like **Alinea** *(page 83)* and **Moto** *(page 80)* give Ferran Adrià a run for his money. Meanwhile, stalwarts like **Charlie Trotter's** *(page 84)* confidently remain at the very top of the country's contemporary American list.

EMPTY BOTTLE

Of course, if you've come for the fulfilling, gooey goodness of deep-dish pizza, you won't be disappointed. Just pack your patience when you visit the legendary **Pizzeria Uno** *(page 72)*; the waits are usually long (Uno claims to have invented deep-dish pizza in the '40s), but the pie is worth the wait. If you simply cannot stick it out, then try other deep-dish spots like **Gino's East** *(633 N. Wells St., River North, 312-943-1124; www.ginoseast. com)* and **Giordano's** *(Prudential Plaza, 135 E. Lake St., 312-616-1200; www.giordanos.com)*.

Though the city has plenty of outstanding vegetarian options—from the upscale **Green Zebra** *(page 89)* to the Indian food counters on the Far North Side's Devon Avenue—Chicago is still largely a carnivore's paradise. Witness the city's famous steakhouses, which are always packed cheek to jowl. You can't go wrong whether you chow down at classics like **Gibsons** *(page 60)*, where you can expect a lively atmosphere and full-flavored steaks, or at old-time joints like **Gene & Georgetti** *(page 67)*.

On the other end of the spectrum—but no less delicious—are Chicago's renowned Italian beef sandwiches. These messy sandwiches (thinly sliced roast beef and au jus served on an Italian-style roll with giardi-niera or sweet peppers on top) are said to have originated in the city in the 1930s. Nowadays, you can try this drippy, delicious throwback at **Al's #1 Italian Beef** *(169 W. Ontario St., River North, 312-943-3222; www. alsbeef.com)* and **Portillo's** *(100 W. Ontario St., River North, 312-587-8910; www.portillos.com)*. Another Depression-era classic that's still as popular as ever is the hot dog. But not just any frank will do—locals line up for the gourmet dogs at **Hot Doug's** *(page 63)*, which offers a Chicago-style hot dog with all the trimmings, with a side of addicting duck fat frites.

WHAT'S THE BEST NIGHTLIFE?

Chicago nightlife suffers from bipolar disorder. On one hand, you have the Midwest's famous no-nonsense, pragmatic attitude, which manifests itself in dive bars, come-as-you-are live-music hubs—such as **Smartbar** *(page 156)*. On the other hand, you have an irrepressible appetite for drinking and dancing the night away. (It's not for nothing that house music was born here.) You could go from lounging with the hip-and-hot at **J Bar** *(page 138)* to cutting a rug at **Sound-Bar** *(page 148)* to sipping the city's best-mixed cocktails at **The Violet Hour** *(page 134)*, all in one night.

If you're looking for that beloved local institution known as the dive bar, you won't have to look far. These holes-in-the-wall are usually tucked into any residential neighborhood, and many sport generic Old Style beer signs out front and the words "Zimne Piwo" or "Cerveza Fria" (cold beer in Polish and Spanish, respectively). Here, beer is cheap and plentiful, and the crowd varies from blue-collar regulars to hipsters, all seeking a low-key spot to drink and congregate with friends. Some, such as **Empty Bottle** *(page 154)* and **The Hideout** *(1354 W. Wabansia Ave., Bucktown, 773-227-4433; www.hideoutchicago.com)* have turned into destinations for music aficionados. By and large, many remain no-frills: perfect for when all you need is a cold one, and no pretense.

If it's summer, you don't want to be holed up—and for that, Chicago teems with beer gardens and bars with patios from which you can tipple and people watch under the sun to your heart's content. Popular spots include **Sheffield's** *(page 140)* and **Nick's Beergarden** *(1516 N. Milwaukee Ave., Wicker Park, 773-252-1155; www.nicksbeergarden.com)*. Chances are that if you simply walk around neighborhoods like Lakeview or Wicker Park, you'll practically trip over an alfresco patio down any street.

BUCKINGHAM FOUNTAIN

WHAT'S THE EARLY HISTORY OF THE CITY?

Tucked in the heartland of the country, Chicago holds its own on both a national and international level. As the home of the skyscraper and an always-thriving cultural scene, this jewel by the lake is both gritty and cosmopolitan at once. Its short and storied history reflects the city it has become today: The Haymarket Riot of 1886 demanding legalized workers' rights happened here, and to this day, Chicago has a reputation as a hardworking, blue-collar town. The skyline, one of the most recognizable anywhere, continues to make global headlines by pushing forward with some of the world's most boundary-shattering architecture.

Centuries before buildings jutted into the sky, Chicago's lakeside location proved auspicious. The first Native Americans who found the spot recognized its strategic positioning long before French explorers Marquette and Joliet "discovered" it in the 1670s. The Chicago River, around which the city grew, was relatively small, but it provided the shortest portage from the Great Lakes—the largest body of fresh water on Earth—to the river systems connecting with the Mississippi, making it an ideal port for trade. The first permanent European settler of record here was Jean Baptiste Pointe DuSable, a Frenchman whose mother had been a slave taken from Haiti. (The DuSable Museum of African American History, in the Bronzeville neighborhood on the city's South Side, is named after him.) DuSable established a trading post on the north side of the river in the 1790s, but was driven away for a time by the Indian wars that followed the Revolutionary War. Not long after came the Fort Dearborn Massacre of 1812, a brutal battle resulting in the killing of more than 50 U.S. soldiers, women and children by indigenous Indian tribes seeking to reclaim the land. Walk just south of the Michigan Avenue Bridge today, and you'll see the spot where the fort—abandoned by the soldiers and civilians who only made it a mile and a half away before the Indians caught up with them—once stood. The tribe's victory was short-lived, as Fort Dearborn was rebuilt and Europeans continued their mass migration here. By the 1830s, Native Americans had been driven across the Mississippi and forced out of the area, and the settlers started taking over. Chicago soon became the hub of a new national rail system, and the rest of the country's connection to the prairie, where both goods and people of all kinds came and went.

HOW DID THE CITY REBUILD AFTER THE FIRE?

Just as Chicago was establishing itself as an important city, the Great Fire of 1871 set the city ablaze. Most historians now doubt that the inferno began as legend has it, by Mrs. O'Leary's cow kicking over a kerosene lamp. (Theories of the actual cause range from someone knocking the lamp over while trying to steal milk or while playing a craps game in Mrs. O'Leary's barn. Some aerospace scientists have even argued that the fire was caused by a meteor shower.) Regardless of how the fire started, it blazed on October 8, and three days later, driven by strong winds, had burned three and a half square miles—virtually all of Chicago—to the ground. Among the few buildings left standing was the Water Tower at Chicago and Michigan avenues, a then-modern sandstone structure containing a 135-foot-high standpipe that was constructed just two years earlier. The fire was considered one of the greatest U.S. disasters of the 19th century, but the almost immediate rebuilding that followed transformed Chicago from a poorly planned city into a bigger and better international hub of commerce. Between 1872 and

MILLENNIUM PARK

1879, more than 10,000 construction permits were issued here. With land in short supply and prices for lots at a premium, architects started thinking vertically. Wooden structures were banned within city limits by then, so they turned to steel, and by 1882 Chicago was home to the steel-framed, 10-story Montauk Building—the first to be called a skyscraper.

There was plenty of work in rebuilding the city after the fire, but a growing rift was deepening between business- and working-class segments of the population. Calls for legalized workers' rights, including a maximum eight-hour workday, started to flare. In 1886, the infamous Haymarket Riot took place at the corner of Randolph and Desplaines streets. A melee sparked by protesters resulted in the killing of 11 people and eventually led to the creation of May Day, a workers' holiday still observed the first day of May through much of Europe. (The eight-hour workday, however, is but a dream for many of Chicago's modern-day workers.)

Toward the end of the 19th century, Chicago began to earn a more cosmopolitan reputation. In 1893, with a new metropolis in place, the Chicago World's Fair (also known as the World's Columbian Exposition) gave the city a chance to strut its stuff. (One of several legends has it that a journalist who wanted New York to host the fair made a statement to "pay no attention to that windy city," earning Chicago its most popular nickname.) More than 27 million people from all parts of the world came to visit during the fair's six-month run, getting a firsthand look at new inventions like the Ferris wheel.

It was 200 new architectural gems built for the fair and designed in large part by local greats Daniel Burnham and Frederick Law Olmsted in the beaux arts style that gave Chicago a new level of international prestige. Still, the picturesque setting also provided a backdrop for tragedy: H.H. Holmes, considered the country's first serial killer, lured victims to his "World's Fair Hotel," which he built just for the expo. Inside was a gas chamber, dissection table and crematorium to dispose of bodies. Holmes admitted to 27 murders, though only nine were ever confirmed. (You can read more about how the lives of Holmes and Burnham horribly intertwined in Erik Larson's best-selling book *The Devil in the White City*.)

After the turn of the century, the city's racial makeup began to shift. Previously, the population predominantly consisted of white immigrants from Germany, Ireland, Poland and Scandinavia. But during World War I, African-Americans from the South began arriving in search of wartime industrial jobs. There was work to be had (in his 1916 poem *Chicago*, Carl Sandburg referred to the city as both "Hog Butcher for the World" and "City of the Big Shoulders" because of the thriving meatpacking industry and the strong willingness of the people here to bear the burden of this work). But for many African-Americans, jobs were not as plentiful as they had hoped. Tensions brewed and ethnic groups established strong territorial boundaries throughout the city. The eight-day Chicago Race Riot of 1919 was sparked by conflict between working-class whites and African-Americans—many of them war veterans who felt they deserved equal pay and the better housing they saw their white counterparts getting. By the riot's end, 38 people were dead, and more than 500 injured.

HOW DID MODERN CHICAGO TAKE SHAPE?

By the 1920s, Prohibition-era gangsters like Al Capone had made Chicago synonymous with crime and corruption. Bootleggers made money hand over fist while police looked the other way, thanks to their handsome payoffs. Violence reached a peak when the rivalry between South Sider Al Capone and North Side gangster George "Bugs" Moran led to the St. Valentine's Day Massacre in 1929, when seven men—several from Moran's gang—were shot to death in a garage on Clark Street, presumably on Capone's orders. Today, there is no historical marker of the site, just an inconspicuous patch of grass. But the Biograph Theater—another landmark that became infamous in that era as the site where notorious bank robber John Dillinger was killed by the FBI in 1934—is still standing not far away and is now home to the renowned local Victory Gardens Theater.

One of the good things to come from the illegal speakeasies of the '20s was the birth of Chicago's jazz scene. (One of Al Capone's henchmen had a 25 percent stake in the legendary Green Mill Jazz Club at one time.) Louis Armstrong made his name in Chicago, coming up from New Orleans in 1919 to be a part of Joe "King" Oliver's band. Piano player Earl Hines soon joined him, and the records they made together revolutionized jazz.

In the early '40s, at the height of World War II, scientists secretly worked in an underground bunker beneath a football field on the University of Chicago campus, conducting experiments that led to the creation of the atomic bomb. That invention in turn led to the abrupt mushroom-cloud end to World War II in August 1945, when nuclear bombs were dropped by the United States on the Japanese cities of Hiroshima and Nagasaki.

The World War II years also produced another surge of movement north by Southern African-Americans, but this time, more found work. At the same time, music legends like Howlin' Wolf and Muddy Waters brought the blues to the South Side. When Elvis Presley duplicated their sound in the '50s, rock 'n' roll earned a spot in mainstream culture. In 1955, Chuck Berry recorded *Maybelline* at Chess Records, located at 2120 South Michigan Avenue—later immortalized in the Rolling Stones' song named for that address. (In 1965, the Stones again used the studio to lay down the basic tracks of *Satisfaction*, one of that era's biggest hits, just a year after Frank Sinatra sang about Chicago being *My Kind of Town*.)

CHICAGO THEATER DISTRICT

The '50s saw the expansion of nearby suburbs, and protests over Vietnam and civil rights hit Chicago hard during the '60s. Local riots following the assassination of Martin Luther King, Jr. left fires burning for days on the city's West Side. The 1968 National Democratic Convention was overshadowed by a battle between protesters and the police, augmented by the National Guard. Mayor Richard J. Daley (father of current mayor Richard M. Daley; *page 19*) promised that "law and order would be maintained," but protestors chanted, "The whole world is watching!" while violent street conflicts were broadcast on the newly powerful medium of television. Eight of the protestors—national figures Abbie Hoffman, Jerry Rubin and Bobby Seale among them—were charged with conspiracy in connection with the protests that eventually led to the notorious "Chicago Seven" trial. (Seale wound up being tried separately; the others were acquitted on the charge of conspiring to incite a riot, though five were convicted of incitement as individuals.)

WHAT IMPACT DID URBAN RENEWAL HAVE?

Gentrification—and in some cases, a lack thereof—has been a significant part of Chicago's more recent history. Notorious public housing projects like Cabrini Green—built near downtown between two affluent neighborhoods over a 20-year period ending in the 1960s—represented a model of "urban renewal" upon its completion. But Cabrini Green became a synonym for everything that could go wrong with this idea. "White flight" heightened the segregation of public housing, and almost simultaneously, factories providing the majority of work in the neighborhood closed and laid off thousands of people. Furthermore, the budget-crunched city cut back on services like transit, police presence and regular maintenance of the area. Vandalism and crime rose, leading law-abiding residents with any financial means to move away and leave the area to the poorest citizens, ripening it for increased problems. By the 1980s, the complex was so crime-riddled that even police were said to fear Cabrini Green.

But the project's prime location made it a diamond in the rough during the housing boom that began in the '90s. In 1995, the federal Department of Housing and Urban Development took over management from the city and demolished many of the buildings to create a new, mixed-income approach in the neighborhood. New construction now includes everything from rental apartments and condos to a seniors-only complex and swanky single-family homes. Crime is down, but only time will tell if what's officially called the "Plan for Transformation" will improve things in the long term.

Meanwhile, other neighborhoods throughout Chicago continue to experience rapid change. The Southwest neighborhood of Pilsen—originally home to Czech immigrants and more recently to the city's largest Mexican-American community—became a haven for starving artists in the '90s because of its proximity to downtown and as an alternative to more expensive gallery districts. Developers soon caught on to the prime locale, and now families who have lived in the area for decades face moves from what is now an unaffordable neighborhood. Similar situations are occurring in other parts of the city, including longtime German neighborhood Lincoln Square on the Far North Side and Ukrainian Village on the near Northwest Side.

HOW LONG HAVE THE DALEYS RULED CHICAGO?

Mayoral Term Limits? Not here. Chicago—a city known for a "vote early, vote often"-style of politics, is the largest U.S. city without them. Due to this, someone with the last name Daley has held the office here during 41 of the last 55 years.

The first, Richard J. Daley, was elected in 1955 and remained mayor until his death in 1976. Considered the last of the bosses of big-city politics, Daley was known as tough and hard-nosed even by loyalists, and racist, corrupt and cruel by his harshest critics. His son, Richard M. Daley (not-so-affectionately dubbed Richard II), was elected in 1989 and remains in office today despite his own brushes with corruption. The father-son combo are the only Chicago mayors to serve more than five terms. They're also the most influential duo to shape the city's modern political history.

During what many consider his "reign," Richard J. Daley was one of the most powerful politicians in the United States. His Chicago Democratic machine—a tightly run ship of controlled patronage positions—was pivotal in getting John F. Kennedy his narrow victory in Illinois during his 1960 run for president. (Chicago and the state of Illinois have always had a reputation for crooked politics, the most famous recent example being ex-Governor Rod Blagojevich's Senate-seat-selling scandal.) The Sears Tower, McCormick Place and O'Hare International Airport were all built during his tenure, as were some controversial expressways that critics said divided the city along racial lines. When the 1968 Democratic Convention came to Chicago and thousands of Vietnam War protesters came along with it, the infamous violent conflicts that ensued between police and the public were blamed on Daley. His own party criticized him during the convention for the "Gestapo-style" tactics police used, but his image managed to recover and he won re-election again in 1971.

Though his years in office were tumultuous, Richard J. is still credited with helping Chicago avoid the decline many other American cities endured during the 1960s and 1970s. Before his death from a heart attack in 1976, his efforts to revitalize downtown and largely keep the city's middle class from fleeing to the suburbs helped Chicago escape the fate of places like Cleveland, Detroit and New York.

It was 13 years later when Richard M. took the helm as the head of the city, and he's had his own stronghold on it ever since. He tends to run largely unopposed—mayoral elections seem barely noticed in Chicago, and he garnered more than 70 percent of the vote in 1999, 2003 and 2007. If "Da Mare" completes his current term, he'll beat his father's record of 21 years in office. Charges of bid-rigging, a corruption investigation by high-powered U.S. District Attorney Patrick Fitzgerald and even the covert destruction of small lakefront airport Meigs Field in the dark of night seem to be easily forgiven by voters. (Though the recent loss of the 2016 Olympic bid may leave the mayor, who staked his legacy on it, bruised.) They'd rather think about the fact that the Mayor has given them treats like lush Millennium Park and how he has revived just about every part of the city, from the South Loop to the notorious Cabrini Green projects (where you will now find beautiful mixed housing).

WHAT TIES DOES BARACK OBAMA HAVE TO CHICAGO?

Barack Obama first came to Chicago in 1985, at the age of 24, to work as a community organizer in poor neighborhoods. He left to attend Harvard Business School and then returned to work as an associate intern in Chicago with the country's oldest law firm, Sidley Austin. It was here that he met the future First Lady, then Michelle Robinson, who was assigned to be his

CITY SKYLINE

mentor. By 1992, the two were married and had set up permanent residence on the South Side of Chicago and had two daughters, Malia and Sasha. Obama went to work practicing law as a civil rights attorney, teaching at the University of Chicago Law School and heading up Project Vote in Illinois, registering almost one-half of the 400,000 African-Americans in the state. In 1997, he ran for the Illinois State Senate and served seven years, leaving to become the third African-American to be elected to the U.S. Senate.

Obama first announced his plan to run for president in early 2007. His national headquarters occupied the 11th floor of a building located in Chicago at 233 North Michigan Avenue. He received many endorsements from fellow politicians, including Chicago Mayor Richard M. Daley, but one of his biggest supporters was Chicago talk show host Oprah Winfrey. After Obama defeated Senator Hillary Clinton to become the Democratic presidential nominee, Oprah headlined a $2300-a-person fundraising event for him at the Sheraton Hotel & Towers.

On November 4, 2009, Barack Obama's election night celebration was held in Chicago at Grant Park. When the gates opened at 8:30 p.m., over 200,000 people (including, famously, a teary-eyed Oprah Winfrey and Jessie Jackson) poured into Hutchinson Field to hear him give his acceptance speech. It was an unforgettable night in the city and one that locals and people from all over the world will never forget. Banners were put up all over the city celebrating Chicago's hometown hero.

The Obamas still keep their residence in Hyde Park and the First Family still makes time for their city. In July, the President—a die-hard White Sox fan—took time out of his busy schedule to travel to Busch Stadium in St. Louis to throw out the ceremonial first pitch at the MLB All Star Game.

In October, the President and Mrs. Obama both traveled to Copenhagen to represent Chicago when the International Olympic Committee met to choose the sight for the 2016 Olympic games. Unfortunately, the games went to Brazil, but both spoke passionately about the city they love.

WHAT ARE CHICAGO'S NICKNAMES?

Chicago has more nicknames than P. Diddy, including the Windy City, the City of the Big Shoulders and the City of Neighborhoods. The reason is that Chicago is all of these things and more—so here's how to keep the names straight.

Windy City

The origins of the Windy City moniker are unclear, but the most widely accepted theory is that it was a jab at the city's boastful, long-winded politicians. Nowadays, people use it to refer to the city's cutting winter winds that blow off Lake Michigan.

The Second City

The population of Los Angeles has surpassed that of Chicago, but the Second City nickname remains. The nickname is usually used to signify Chicago's second-billing status to New York, but don't mention that to proud Chicagoans—they'll insist that their hometown is second to none.

City on the Make

Nelson Algren's 1951 essay is a love letter—a booze-soaked, beautifully imperfect love letter—to the city. In it, he famously wrote that "like loving a woman with a broken nose, you may well find lovelier lovelies. But never a lovely so real."

City of the Big Shoulders

Poet Carl Sandburg gave Chicago this nickname as a nod to the hard-working people who toiled away in its industrial heyday. (In the same poem, Sandburg gave the city another nickname, "Hog Butcher for the World.")

Chi-Town

Chi-Town is simply a slang way of saying Chicago. Chicago native Kanye West raps, "Two words, Chi Town, South Side…" in his 2004 song *Two Words*. Many local radio DJs use the nickname, and some businesses include it in their names.

WHAT ARE THE CITY'S GREEN INITIATIVES?

Say what you will about Mayor Richard M. Daley—and plenty of his critics do—but one thing most Chicagoans seem pleased with is his initiative to make the Windy City one of the greenest places in America.

More than half a million trees have been planted amidst the asphalt, highways and miles of concrete here since 1989, when Daley was first elected. In warmer months, workers seem to sprout up everywhere planting trees, pruning bushes and potting flowers. At different times during the growing cycle, an army of gardeners hits the city overnight to transform the planters with tulips in spring, lush greenery and flowers in summer, and mums and hardier plants in fall. You'll find greenery along roadsides, over underpasses, and in all kinds of high-traffic and high-profile places about town, plus a few of the less tony neighborhoods, too.

There's always been an attention to greenery in Chicago, whose official motto became "Urbs in Horto" (Latin for "City in a Garden") in 1837 when the city incorporated. In 1909, famed architect Daniel Burnham developed a

WATERTOWER AT NIGHT

URBAN GARDENS

plan for a string of parks connected by wide boulevards dubbed Chicago's "Emerald Necklace," akin to similar green-space plans in Boston and New York City.

Daley's plans go beyond keeping the city looking pretty. Environmental efforts include an extensive green roof program, started with a lush garden planted atop City Hall (consisting of more than 100 species of indigenous plants)—it's the first municipal green roof in the country. Today, it's estimated that there are more than four million square feet of high-in-the-sky gardens completed or under construction here, thanks to the Chicago Green Roof Grants Program. The roofs—which work as natural insulators, improve air quality and reduce rainwater runoff—dot Chicago atop everything from McDonald's locations and the Apple store to new office towers and private residences, many planted with the city's financial assistance or incentive.

Daley has said his goal is to see Chicago eventually use renewable energy for a quarter of all municipal operations. To do that he's lured solar-panel manufacturers to move to the city and ordered local government departments to do more things like buy energy-efficient vehicles and forbid them from idling for more than five minutes, as well as repave alleys with asphalt that better absorbs water. Though it ironically sits on a former illegal dump site, the Chicago Center for Green Technology offers free seminars to the public, distributes rain barrels, and is home to organizations and businesses with an environmental bent. (Greencorps Chicago, the city's community gardening and job-training program, is here.)

There's still plenty of room for improvement. The city's recycling program—launched by beloved late Mayor Harold Washington in the late 1980s—is considered a giant flop, with the overwhelming majority of garbage still not being fully recycled. (The city is trying to rectify the problem by launching new initiatives, including the Blue Cart program.) And Daley's blind eye to the high air pollutants coming from coal-burning power plants on the Southwest Side has raised eyebrows for years. Just mention the CTA to a local, and they're likely to launch into a tirade on what a dilapidated mess that system is (slow trains, buses that run on diesel). Daley's solution is to encourage people to bike everywhere, adding 25 miles of new bicycle lanes on various city streets, 200 miles of signed routes and 2,500 new bicycle racks.

AT A GLANCE

DOWNTOWN EL TRAIN

CHICAGO STYLE

The nation's third largest city is notorious for its harsh winters and its love of sports. But there's much more to Chicago than subzero temperatures and professional sports. The city is headquarters for major international businesses from Boeing to Sears, and is home to a thriving media industry as well as finance and insurance hubs. Scores of ethnic neighborhoods make up the fabric of the city, and a rich history of scrappy (and sometimes unscrupulous) political figures give it a gritty edge. So what makes Chicago so unique? Read on for a snapshot of the Second City.

WHAT KIND OF BUSINESSES MAKE CHICAGO THEIR HOME?

No longer the epicenter of the nation's meatpacking industry, Chicago now keeps its economy humming in other ways. One of the city's main sectors is food processing, which includes confections. Although big-time brands such as Brach's and Fannie May have stopped producing sweets in the city, the chocolaty aroma in River West comes from the nearby **Blommer Chocolate Factory** (*600 W. Kinzie St., River West, 800-621-1606*), confirming that the city still retains the "national candy capital" title.

Chicago is also a hub for the printing and publishing industries. It's the source for nationally distributed magazines, catalogs, educational materials, encyclopedias and specialized publications, ranking it second only to New York in the publishing industry.

The city's location in the middle of the country makes it a national transportation and distribution center, thanks to a substantial industrial base and a major inland port. Chicago also gets a boost from the finance and insurance sectors, as it is home to the Federal Reserve Bank, the Chicago Board of Trade and the Chicago Mercantile Exchange.

WHERE ARE THE ETHNIC NEIGHBORHOODS?

Chicago's many ethnic enclaves retain their distinct character in a way that doesn't happen in other metropolises. Pilsen and Little Village, for example, are home to a vibrant Mexican-American community. Located on the Southwest Side, these conjoined neighborhoods are peppered with taquerías and bakeries—get a slice of tres leches cake from **Bombon Bakery** (*3748 W. 26th St., Little Village, 773-277-8777*). The **National Museum of Mexican Art** (*1852 W. 19th St., Pilsen, 312-738-1503*), as well as the numerous galleries that dot the area—especially around the Chicago Arts District (18th and Halsted streets in East Pilsen)—make the area an artists' hub.

A few blocks east of Pilsen is Chicago's **Chinatown** (*Wentworth Avenue and Cermak Road*). All along Wentworth and Archer avenues, you can find shops literally brimming with tchotchkes and wares, such as paper umbrellas, lanterns, jade statuettes and woks. Dining options are just as diverse—head for **Lao Szechuan** (*page 77*) for tongue-singeing Szechuan fare, or **Phoenix Restaurant** (*2131 S. Archer Ave., Chinatown, 312-328-0848*) for Sunday dim sum.

For a taste of Swedish heritage, head to the North Side's Andersonville. Locals wait on Soviet-era long lines at the **Swedish Bakery** (*5348 N. Clark St., Andersonville, 773-561-8919*) to snatch up goodies like streusel and flourless chocolate cake. Crowds also pack **Ann Sather** restaurant (*5207

N. Clark St., Andersonville, 773-271-6677) for a traditional breakfast of Swedish pancakes with tart lingonberries.

WHAT'S THE BEST WAY TO BLEND LIKE A LOCAL?

If you want to fit in with the natives, you have to talk the talk. The city has words of its own for everyday things. Say "soda" and "sneakers" and you will probably be met with blank looks; instead use "pop" and "tennis shoes" (or "gym shoes"), respectively. The greater Chicago area is called Chicagoland in news broadcasts, but natives just refer to the outskirts as "the 'burbs." And Chicagoans don't refer to highways by their numbers, but by their names, such as the Kennedy (I-90), the Eisenhower (I-290) and the Dan Ryan (I-90/I-94).

Be sure to note that Chicago-ese has detailed diction: "Da Mare" (Chicagoan pronunciation of "the mayor") and "Hizzoner" ("his honor") are both nicknames for Mayor Daley. "Sassage" refers to the meaty pizza topping, while "sammitch" is a sandwich.

Beef up on Chicago-specific vocab, too. An "Italian beef" is roast beef cooked in its own juices and served on an Italian roll. You can order it "hot," with spicy giardiniera sauce; "wet," dunked in meat juice; or "sweet," with peppers. "The El" is what everyone calls the train system. Though it's short for "elevated train," the underground El trains get the same moniker. The "Friendly Confines" is another name for Wrigley Field. "Trixies" are native to Lincoln Park, and the twenty- or thirty-something ladies can be recognized by their bleach-blond hair and preppie attire, and are usually seen flirting with overgrown frat-boy types. (They're called Chads, by the way.)

WHICH MOVIES HAVE BEEN FILMED IN CHICAGO?

The city has long been a destination for filmmakers to shoot movies, and was the backdrop for Hitchcock's *North by Northwest* (1959), and *A Raisin in the Sun* (1961) starring a young Sidney Poitier. The '80s ushered in a made-in-Chicago film renaissance led by teen-flick king, the late John Hughes, who grew up in nearby Northbrook, Illinois. Hughes' *Ferris Bueller's Day Off*, *The Breakfast Club* and *Sixteen Candles* all were shot in the Windy City.

Meanwhile, another iconic '80s film, *The Blues Brothers*, showed the nitty-gritty city, including Maxwell Street Market. And *The Untouchables*

WHAT IS THE FASHION IN CHICAGO?

The Windy City's residents have never been known for their fashion sense. But that's changing. In 2006, Mayor Richard M. Daley, himself a fan of fedoras and rumpled suits, appointed a director of fashion arts and events and formed the Mayor's Fashion Council, a group of designers and industry leaders brought together to help promote local designers and boutiques. The council hosts the yearly **Fashion Focus Chicago**, the city's answer to New York's Fashion Week, and maintains **Chicago Fashion Resource** *(page 124)* to connect well-dressed consumers with the city's designers and independent shops. Even though you'll see many locals decked out in not-so-flattering orange and navy Bears gear, with all of these initiatives, Chicago is aiming to become a major player on the fashion stage.

PILSEN STOREFRONT

relived Chicago's gangster past of Al Capone in the Brian de Palma film. Today, the tape keeps on rolling in Chicago. Jennifer Aniston and Vince Vaughn filmed *The Break-Up* (2006); Angelina Jolie shot *Wanted* (2008); and Christian Bale donned the Batsuit for *Batman Begins* (2005) and *The Dark Knight* (2008). Part of the movie *Public Enemies* (2009), starring Johnny Depp in the role of gangster John Dillinger, were also filmed here and the movie had its world premiere downtown.

★ WHAT TO SEE

CHICAGO SKYLINE

SIGHTS TO SEE

No matter how old you are or what you like to do, you won't have a dull moment in Chicago. The city has world-class museums (the Art Institute of Chicago and Field Museum among them); inviting parks; amazing architecture; and colorful neighborhoods inhabited by famously friendly Midwesterners. Add to that the sparkling, expansive Lake Michigan, and you've got a magical place.

GOLD COAST/STREETERVILLE

The name speaks for itself. The Gold Coast shines with world-class retail (the gilded northern edge of Michigan Avenue and Oak Street) and gorgeous mansions (especially along Astor Street). Homeowners in this tony residential neighborhood know the area's pedigree and oblige by maintaining gorgeous homes north of Division Street and east of State Street, while ladies who lunch gather at old-fashioned hang-outs like the Drake Hotel and shop at Chanel. Streeterville, the neighborhood just south of the Gold Coast, is a gentrifying mish-mash of chains and shops along Michigan Avenue and '70s-era hole-in-the-wall bars, with graduate schools for Northwestern University, University of Chicago and Loyola University thrown into the mix.

JOHN HANCOCK CENTER

875 N. Michigan Ave., Gold Coast, 312-751-3681, 888-875-8439; www.hancock-observatory.com

It may not be the first or even the second or third tallest building in Chicago, but the world-famous Hancock, which towers over the city at 1,127 feet, still holds the record for being the world's highest residence (condos begin on the 49th floor). Zoom up to the always-packed 94th-floor observatory for a view that can extend to four states on a clear day. Then check out the city's only open-air skywalk to feel the famous Chicago wind. Don't worry about taking a plunge; though the skywalk is windowless, NASA-tested stainless-steel screens will prevent you from falling. Before you leave, be sure to skim the wall murals to read about how the city went from the ashes of the Great Chicago Fire to a booming metropolis. For a less-touristy option, visit the 95th-floor Signature Room's bar (*www.signatureroom.com*) to enjoy the same stunning vista of the city as you sip a cocktail.

Admission: adults $15, children 3-11 $10, children under 3 free. Daily 9 a.m.-11 p.m.

MUSEUM OF CONTEMPORARY ART

220 E. Chicago Ave., Gold Coast, 312-280-2660; www.mcachicago.org

Housed in a rather uninspired building between Lake Michigan and the Water Tower, the MCA is home to 2,345 pieces in its permanent collection, including work by Dan Flavin and Lee Bontecou. The interior space can be daunting, with wide hallways and an unusual eyelid-shaped staircase with a fish pond at the bottom that is worth viewing on its own. But despite its size, the MCA won't take long to see (perhaps an hour or two to review the museum's first-rate contemporary experimental works) before you'll want to grab some lunch at the museum's café, operated by chef Wolfgang Puck of Spago fame. If you're around on the first Friday of the month, the museum holds a happening event where, for a $16 admission, you can check out the museum's latest exhibit, enjoy live entertainment, nibble on tasty Wolfgang

NAVY PIER

Puck hors d'oeuvres and sip cocktails (you can purchase extra drink tickets). Local singles pack the joint on First Fridays, which has become a meat market for culture vultures on the prowl.

Admission: adults $12, seniors and students $7, children 12 and under free. Free Tuesday. Tuesday 10 a.m.-8 p.m., Wednesday-Sunday 10 a.m.-5 p.m. First Fridays: $16; first Friday of the month 6-10 p.m.

NAVY PIER
600 E. Grand Ave., Streeterville, 312-595-7437, 800-595-7437; www.navypier.com

Nearly 200 navy planes remain submerged in Lake Michigan as a result of the training once done at Navy Pier. Reborn in 1995 after years of disuse, the tourist-packed pier and lakefront area have become as emblematic of Chicago as deep-dish pizza. The pier contains a mall (nothing notable there) as well as a 3-D IMAX theater (which sold out the latest Batman film, *The Dark Knight*, for weeks and weeks), a small ice-skating rink, the Chicago Shakespeare Theater, the Smith Museum of Stained Glass Windows (seriously, it's a lot better than it sounds), and the Chicago Children's Museum (head here quickly, as the museum is planning to move into its own 100,000-square-foot structure in Daley Bicentennial Plaza at 337 E. Randolph St. in the next few years). The museum has plenty of hands-on but not-so-messy exhibits for the kids, including Dinosaur Expedition, which re-creates a trip to the Sahara to dig for fossils. There is also an urban "neighborhood" for toddlers to practice driving a city bus or shopping for groceries. Adults can have fun at the outdoor beer garden or on any number of dinner cruises that leave from the docks, which offer a lakeside view of the pier's 150-foot-high Ferris wheel and the Chicago skyline beyond.

Memorial Day-Labor Day, Sunday-Thursday 10 a.m.-10 p.m., Friday-Saturday 10 a.m.-midnight; Labor Day-November, Monday-Thursday 10 a.m.-8 p.m., Friday-Saturday 10 a.m.-midnight; November-March, Monday-Thursday 10 a.m.-8 p.m., Friday-Saturday 10 a.m.-10 p.m., Sunday 10 a.m.-7 p.m.; April-Memorial Day, Sunday-Thursday 10 a.m.-8 p.m., Friday-Saturday 10 a.m.-10 p.m.

OLD CHICAGO WATER TOWER AND PUMPING STATION
806 N. Michigan Ave., Gold Coast, 312-742-0808

After the Great Chicago Fire of 1871 roared through the city, the Old Chicago Water Tower and Pumping Station were the only public structures left unscathed. The Water Tower now houses City Gallery (*Monday-Saturday 10 a.m.-6:30 p.m., Sunday 10 a.m.-5 p.m.*), which features Chicago-themed photography exhibits. The Pumping Station is now the base of the Chicago Water Works Visitor Center and the Lookingglass Theatre Company (*312-337-0665; www.lookingglasstheatre.org*), which was co-founded by David "Ross from *Friends*" Schwimmer (who also writes and directs here). Try to catch a Lookingglass production by Tony Award-winning director Mary Zimmerman. Her visually stunning shows, such as *The Arabian Nights* and *Argonautika*, set the place on fire (metaphorically speaking, of course).

LOOP/WEST LOOP

Chicago's heart is in the Loop. It's home to the city's government, commerce and civic cultural venues. Visitors typically start their tour of the city in the shadows of the Loop's towering skyscrapers, sometimes from inside an El train, which lumbers through it. Keep in mind that after 5:30 p.m., office drones head home and the area becomes a bit desolate, despite recent efforts by the city (Millennium Park, Theater District revitalization) to lure locals and tourists after dark. The West Loop encompasses the area west of the Loop across the Chicago River, including Greektown; the Randolph Row restaurant stretch; and the gritty-trendy Fulton Market, Chicago's answer to New York's Meatpacking District. The greatest draw in this neighborhood is perhaps the Big O—*The Oprah Winfrey Show*, which films right off Washington Boulevard.

THE ART INSTITUTE OF CHICAGO
111 S. Michigan Ave., Loop, 312-443-3600; www.artic.edu/aic

The Art Institute is best known for its vast stock of Impressionist works. But with the spring 2009 opening of the Modern Wing, it may become known for its contemporary art expansion, which will house collections of modern art, photography, and architecture and design. With this addition of 264,000

WHAT ARE THE CAN'T-MISS FIRST VISIT SIGHTS?

Lake Michigan *(page 51)* One of the city's biggest surprises is its great beaches. Locals love hitting Lake Michigan's 26 miles of free lakefront during summers. On a typical sunny Saturday, you'll see hundreds of Chicagoans at the beach, baking on towels, playing volleyball, running and barbecuing.

Millennium Park *(page 35)* Millennium Park is fast becoming synonymous with Chicago, home to the Frank Gehry-designed Jay Pritzker Pavilion, Crown Fountain and stainless-steel sculpture Cloud Gate, which acts as a fun-house mirror from underneath and reflects the city's skyline on the outside.

Willis Tower Skydeck *(page 40)* The Sears Tower may have a new name, but it is the tallest building in America (and currently the second tallest in the world).

CLOUD GATE AT MILLENNIUM PARK

square feet, the Art Institute will be the second-largest art museum (in square feet) in the United States at approximately 1.2 million square feet. Among the museum's permanent collection of approximately a quarter million pieces (in ten curatorial departments) are iconic works such as *American Gothic*, *A Sunday on La Grande Jatte* and *Nighthawks*.

Admission: adults $18, children, seniors and students $12; children under 14 free. Labor Day-Memorial Day, Monday-Wednesday, Friday 10:30 a.m.-5 p.m., Thursday 10:30 a.m.-8 p.m., Saturday-Sunday 10 a.m.-5 p.m. Free Thursday after 5 p.m.; free February; Memorial Day-Labor Day, Monday-Wednesday 10:30 a.m.-5 p.m., Thursday-Friday 10:30 a.m.-9 p.m., Saturday-Sunday 10 a.m.-5 p.m. Free Memorial Day-Labor Day on Thursday-Friday 5-9 p.m.

CHICAGO CULTURAL CENTER

78 E. Washington St., Loop, 312-744-6630; www.cityofchicago.org

While locals head to the Cultural Center for the free art exhibits, daily concerts and other performances, visitors go to gape at its magnificent Tiffany stained-glass dome, which is the biggest in the world. If you zoom your camera in on the center of the 1897 dome, which was refurbished in 2008, you might be able to make out the signs of the zodiac. After craning your neck to see the dome, make like a native and see if any of the art offerings are worth a gander—or just escape the downtown crowds with a quick bite at the center's Randolph Café.

Monday-Thursday 8 a.m.-7 p.m., Friday 8 a.m.-6 p.m., Saturday 9 a.m.-6 p.m., Sunday 10 a.m.-6 p.m.

GRANT PARK

337 E. Randolph St., Loop

Grant Park's Buckingham Fountain is best known for its role in the opening credits for the TV show *Married...With Children*, but don't dismiss the beloved Chicago site as a tourist trap. Come on the hour to see one of the world's largest fountains and its elaborate 20-minute water display (Daily 8 a.m.-11 p.m., the last starting at 10 p.m.), which features colored lights and music at dusk and a water jet stream at the center that shoots 150 feet high (mid-April to mid-October, weather permitting). Grant Park also hosts many popular outdoor festivals in the summer, including the Taste of Chicago *(page 165)*, a massive annual event that offers samples from hundreds of the city's restaurants, and Blues Fest *(page 164)*, a yearly celebration featuring preeminent blues artists. Music fans also flock to Grant Park for Lollapalooza *(page 165)*, a three-day extravaganza that's featured big-name acts such as The Killers and Kings of Leon. And film fans tote blankets and picnic baskets to the free Outdoor Film Festival *(page 165)* to see classics such as *Tootsie* and *Sunset Boulevard*.

MILLENNIUM PARK
Michigan Avenue near Randolph Street, Loop;
www.millenniumpark.org
Widely regarded as one of the best public works projects in the city's recent memory, Millennium Park is fast becoming synonymous with Chicago. Once an eyesore filled with railroad tracks and parking lots, it's now home to the Frank Gehry-designed Jay Pritzker Pavilion (which displays the architect's well-known style of curved steel), and Crown Fountain, which is a set of two large faces (the likenesses of 1,000 Chicagoans rotate through the display) opposite one another that spit water into a play area. In fact, today the park is one of the city's most popular attractions, especially its stainless-steel sculpture Cloud Gate, which acts as a fun-house mirror from underneath and reflects the city's skyline on the outside. Just don't ask locals about the sculpture by name (they won't have any idea what you're talking about)—everyone calls it "The Bean."
Daily 6 a.m.-11 p.m.

MONADNOCK BUILDING
53 W. Jackson Blvd., Loop, 312-922-1890;
www.monadnockbuilding.com
It's funny that the Monadnock Building is considered a masterpiece in the Chicago School of architecture, because it's like two very separate buildings in one: John Wellborn Root designed the northern section, the tallest commercial building to be supported primarily by brick walls; and firm Holabird & Roche designed the southern section, which uses steel-frame construction. There's also the seemingly incongruous design mix of Chicago School simplicity with Egyptian elements. But put it all together, and you have a visual representation of one building tradition's end and the beginning of another. Today in the Monadnock you'll find a mix of tenants, including old-school Frank's Barber Shop, the city's finest cup of joe at Intelligentsia and women's boutique Florodora.

THE OPRAH WINFREY SHOW
1058 W. Washington Blvd., West Loop, 312-591-9222; www.oprah.com
Oprah moved to the Windy City in 1984 to be on TV morning show *AM Chicago*, and the city has considered her as one of its own ever since. If you're an Oprah fan, you'll likely be on the hunt for tickets to her show. And most likely, you'll have to wait at least a year. The season runs from August to November and then January to May; you must be 18 years or older to attend a taping and have a valid photo ID. Still want those tickets? Here are some tips: Call the Audience Department, but have your dialing finger

WHAT ARE THE CITY'S BEST PUBLIC ART WORKS?

Some of the city's most famous artwork is spread out across parks and plazas, making Chicago widely acclaimed for its commitment to public art. What's better than free art? The fact that you can reach all of these by foot in an afternoon stroll.

❶ Start with the **The Four Seasons** (*JPMorgan Chase Tower, Dearborn and Monroe streets, Loop*). Russian artist Marc Chagall is known for his paintings, but Chicagoans know him for his 14-foot-high, 10-foot-wide and 70-foot-long mosaic mural. This is a bright spot among downtown's business offices; the piece is adorned with hand-chipped stone and glass pieces in more than 250 pastel colors. Chagall used elements from his surrealist paintings to depict six city scenes in the mural, with couples embracing, suns shining and birds flying.

❷ Walk north on Dearborn Street three blocks until you hit Washington Street, where the **Picasso** (*Daley Plaza, 50 W. Washington St., Loop; www. thedaleycenter.com*) stands tall. When this 162-ton, 50-foot-high steel sculpture by Pablo Picasso was unveiled in 1967, residents scratched their heads. They couldn't figure out what the heck it was. (Picasso didn't help by leaving it untitled.) Your reaction will likely depend on your own love or hate for modern art. Though many at the time deemed it an eyesore, "The Picasso" jump-started an interest in public art and prompted the city to add more pieces to its outdoor gallery. People still wonder what the abstract sculpture is supposed to be—a woman? A horse? A woman who looks like a horse?

❸ Head west on Washington Street for about five blocks and when you get to Michigan Avenue, **Cloud Gate** (*Millennium Park, 55 N. Michigan Ave., Loop; www.millenniumpark.org*) won't even need an introduction. Millennium Park, just across Michigan Avenue, is home to this 66-foot-long, 33-foot-high stainless-steel kidney bean-shaped installation, whose official title is Cloud Gate. To locals, it's "The Bean." Gaze at the 110-ton behemoth to see Michigan Avenue's buildings and the blue skies above them reflected brightly in seamless silver. Or walk under its 12-foot-high arches to see your own reflection (and that of those around you) stare back like a kaleidoscopic mishmash on the Bean's shiny underbelly. This marks British artist Anish Kapoor's first site-specific installation in the U.S. and it's one of the city's newest works. Completed in 2004, "The Bean" is an essential part of an art lover's diet.

❹ Make your way a few steps southwest of Cloud Gate, and you'll practically trip over **Crown Fountain** (*Millennium Park, 55 N. Michigan Ave., Loop; www.millenniumpark.org*). This pair of 50-foot glass blocks project gigantic faces across from one another as they "spit" water into a shared shallow reflecting pool. Instead of using traditional gargoyles for his modern 2004 fountain, Spanish artist Jaume Plensa decided to feature the faces of 1,000 Chicagoans, each appearing one by one on large LED screens. The water is on from mid-spring through mid-fall (weather permitting), when kids splash around in the pool, while the faces peer from the towers all year long.

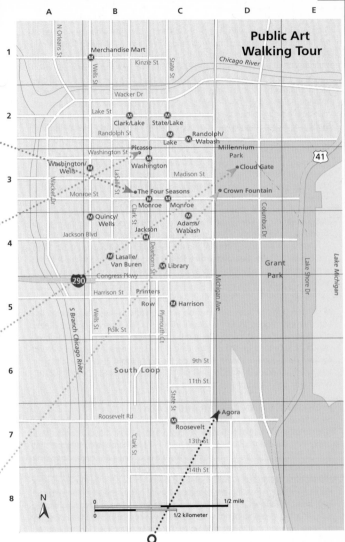

Public Art Walking Tour

❺ In ancient Greece, people met at the Agora, or marketplace. Polish artist Magdalena Abakanowicz's installation, **Agora** (*Grant Park, Michigan Avenue at Roosevelt Road, South Loop*) is also a meeting place, where you can interact with the 106 nine-foot-tall headless, armless humanoid figures. The work represents the relationship of Chicago's people to its city, with the figures dwarfed by the high-rise buildings behind them. From afar the headless "people" look all the same, but up close the iron-case figures show individuality in their wrinkled and tree bark-like surfaces.

WHAT IS THE BEST WAY TO SEE CHICAGO IN ONE DAY?

Start your day early with a cup of Chicago's own **Intelligentsia** coffee at the **Monadnock Building** (*53 W. Jackson Blvd., Loop, 312-922-1890; www. intelligentsiacoffee.com*), then head to **Millennium Park** *(page 35)* to see your reflection in "The Bean" and check out the "spitting" faces at Crown Fountain. Next-door neighbor the **Art Institute of Chicago** *(page 33)* will give you a chance to look at more works. See the man behind the sunflowers in Vincent van Gogh's *Self-Portrait*, and you'll notice the artist's seemingly mismatched dirty-blond hair and red beard. Also take a gander at Monet's *Stacks of Wheat* series, which depicts the eponymous wheat through different seasons. Be sure to leave some time to peruse the excellent first-floor Museum Shop.

If your stomach is growling, grab some pub grub directly across from Millennium Park at **The Gage** *(page 79)*. Snack on a Scotch Egg or chips (that'd be fries) with curry gravy before digging into a juicy burger or locally crafted sausages. Then head south to the **Field Museum** *(page 42)* to meet Sue the T. rex, the largest and most complete Tyrannosaurus rex ever discovered. Or to see some live animals, make your way to the nearby **Shedd Aquarium** *(page 43)* to see the beluga whales in the Oceanarium.

Head back north and stroll along the **Magnificent Mile** *(page 127)*. Stop in the Hancock Center's **Signature Room** *(page 31)* for a drink and some of the best views in the city before catching dinner in any of the **Gold Coast** restaurants *(page 60)*.

ready and don't let busy signals stop you. The phone lines close during the summer but reopen in early August. Also, call the reservation line during off hours, as it's most busy after a broadcast. You can also try getting last-minute tickets through the show's Web site—screeners are always looking for people to attend shows based on the day's topic. If all else fails, you can simply check out The Oprah Store (*37 N. Carpenter St., 312-633-2100*) where you can take home O's favorite things.

RICHARD J. DALEY CENTER AND PLAZA
50 W. Washington St., Loop

Named after the city's former mayor (who was current mayor Richard M.'s father), the building is literally rusting away—it's built from a compound that uses rust to strengthen the building's façade and give it its brown color. You won't want to go in the building, given the traffic courtrooms and civic offices inside, but outside is a plaza dominated by an untitled 50-foot sculpture by Pablo Picasso (*page 36*), the artist's personal gift to the city. The plaza is kept busy by farmers' markets in the warmer months and festivals in winter, including the perennial Christkindlmarket (*www.christkindlmarket.com*), an alfresco German market leading up to Christmas, which is a great place to sip hot apple cider and eat potato pancakes as you admire the tall, sparkly Christmas tree in the plaza.

Farmers' Market: May-October, Thursday 7 a.m.-3 p.m. Christkindlmarket: November 27-December 24, times vary.

ROOKERY
209 S. LaSalle St., Loop

The Rookery is the city's oldest high-rise and widely considered the master-piece of famed architects John Wellborn Root and Daniel Burnham, who

LAKEFRONT RECREATIONAL PATH

FIELD MUSEUM OF NATURAL HISTORY

housed their offices in this grand 1886 building. The structure represents a transition between the use of masonry and metal construction techniques, with the outer walls supported mostly by masonry piers and the inner frame built of steel and iron. In 1905, Frank Lloyd Wright injected some of his trademark Prairie School design into the building when he remodeled its gorgeous glass-domed, two-story lobby. He added white marble and gold-leaf trim and let more light seep through the dome, all of which make it a bright, airy space that gleams when the sun hits it.

WILLIS TOWER
233 S. Wacker Drive, Loop, 312-875-9696; www.theskydeck.com
No other building says Chicago more than the Sears Tower, er, Willis Tower. The name may have recently changed but this iconic building is still the tallest building in America (and currently the second tallest in the world) and defines the city's skyline at 1,450 feet and 110 stories high. The Skydeck on the 103rd floor gives a view of 40 to 50 miles out on a clear day, enabling you to see Michigan, Indiana, Illinois and Wisconsin. It also offers interactive multi-language kiosks and exhibits. Although there are displays on the building's history to keep you busy while waiting to snag an elevator to get to the Skydeck, avoid the long, long lines by heading here before the observation deck opens, or after 5 p.m., when it tends to be less crowded.
Admission: adults $14.95, children 3-11 $10.50, children under 3 free. April-September, daily 9 a.m.-10 p.m.; October-March, daily 10 a.m.-8 p.m.

SOUTH LOOP/PRINTERS ROW
The South Loop is a condo-riddled neighborhood that, up until about fifteen years ago, was a no man's land of abandoned warehouses. Rapid gentrification in the form of new restaurants and slick new buildings led to its current status as some of the hottest blocks in city real estate (even Mayor Richard Daley lives in the neighborhood). Printers Row is a small portion of the South Loop—technically, it's just the stretch of Dearborn Street between Congress Parkway and Polk Street. But this two-block area was

WHAT IS THE BEST WAY TO SEE CHICAGO IN THREE DAYS?

Begin your second day in Chicago at the **Willis (Sears) Tower** *(page 40)*, arriving before it opens at 10 a.m. to get a jump on the lines to zip up to the observatory. At 1,353 feet, the observatory offers a view of Michigan, Wisconsin and Indiana when the clouds are at bay. After seeing Chicago by land, look at it by sea—or rather, river. Hop on a riverboat tour along the **Chicago River** *(page 9)* to see the city's famous architecture. Grab lunch at River North pizzeria **La Madia** *(page 70)*, which often has great specials.

After lunch take a walk through the **Lincoln Park Zoo** *(page 50)*, one of the country's only free zoos. There you can see the usual bears and lions and the not-so-usual snow leopards and sloths. You'll have time to kill before seeing a nighttime improv show at the legendary **Second City** *(page 153*; be sure to purchase tickets in advance because shows consistently sell out). Spend your waiting time wandering through the great nearby neighborhoods of **Lincoln Park** and **Old Town**. Armitage Avenue is an excellent independent-boutique thoroughfare in Lincoln Park. While you're in Lincoln Park, stop by **1154 Lill Studio** *(904 W. Armitage Ave., Lincoln Park, 773-477-5455; www.1154lill. com)* to customize your own purse. For a Chi-Town souvenir, forget tacky tchotchkes and instead head to **Art Effect** *(934 W. Armitage Ave., Lincoln Park, 773-929-3600; www.arteffectchicago.com)*, an eclectic shop that carries everything from clothing to ibride trays to a parking meter alarm. Stop at **Adobo Grill** *(1610 N. Wells St., Old Town, 312-266-7999; www.adobogrill. com)*, a Mexican eatery next door to the Second City theater that has delicious guacamole and margaritas. You'll want to arrive at Second City early to wait in line for a table or even just a chair; seating is first-come, first-served, so early fans of comedy will get the best tables. But don't jet out once the show is over; the jokesters put on a free improv set after the last performance every night but Friday.

For your last day, plan ahead and get tickets for bleacher seats at **Wrigley Field** *(page 158)*. As you cheer on the Cubbies, resist the urge to order a ballpark dog—save your appetite instead for authentic Chicago hot dogs with the works at the **Wieners Circle** *(2622 N. Clark St., Lincoln Park, 773-477-7444)*. Be sure to ask nicely; the sassy staff is known to dish out insults with the cheese fries (no doubt their patience was strained long ago by drunken Cubs fans and the area's weekend revelers).

To see a less-touristy side of the city, travel southwest to **Bucktown** and **Wicker Park**. Fashionistas will point their Choos in the direction of **p.45** *(page 133)* to browse racks of clothing from 3.1 Phillip Lim and local designer Lara Miller. For dinner, try **Coast Sushi Bar** *(2045 N. Damen Ave., Bucktown, 773-235-5775; www.coastsushibar.com)* for some of the city's best sushi (bring your own booze); or **Restaurant Takashi** *(page 93)* for immaculately prepared contemporary American/Japanese fare. Then head to **HotChocolate** *(1747 N. Damen Ave., Bucktown, 773-489-1747; www. hotchocolatechicago.com)* for delicious hot chocolate with housemade marshmallows. The Black & Tan (one part hot fudge, two parts medium hot chocolate) is so rich, it'll count as dessert.

Try to reserve tickets for a show at the renowned **Steppenwolf Theatre** *(page 163)* or a production from the city's many storefront troupes (ones to check out: in-your-face **Profiles Theatre***, 4147 N. Broadway, Uptown, 773-549-1815, www.profilestheatre.org;* or the rockin' **House Theatre of Chicago***, page 161)*.

the Midwest's printing hub in the late 1800s, and it boasts some architectural fan's dreams: The Dearborn Street Station and Pontiac and Donohue buildings are all beauties.

ADLER PLANETARIUM
1300 S. Lake Shore Drive, South Loop (Museum Campus), 312-922-7827; www.adlerplanetarium.org

If you're still mourning the fact that a fear of flying took you out of contention for a career as an astronaut, then head to the Western Hemisphere's first planetarium. Interactive exhibits like Shoot for the Moon, which features Apollo 13 astronaut Jim Lovell's fully restored Gemini 12 spacecraft and some of his effects, will let you envision what your life might have been like. Stargazers should make their way to the Doane Observatory for a look through the largest public telescope in the area, but to appreciate the heavenly Chicago skyline instead, step onto the North and South terraces.

Admission: adults $10, Chicago residents $8, children 3-14 $6, Chicago residents 3-14 $5. Labor Day-mid-June, Monday-Friday 10 a.m.-4 p.m; mid-June-Labor Day, daily 9:30 a.m.-6 p.m.

FIELD MUSEUM OF NATURAL HISTORY
Roosevelt Road and Lake Shore Drive, South Loop (Museum Campus), 312-922-9410; www.fieldmuseum.org

Lurking in the grand Stanley Field Hall that greets visitors at this historic museum is Sue—at 42 feet long and 13 feet high at the hips, it is the most complete, best-preserved and largest Tyrannosaurus rex fossil ever discovered. Unearthed in South Dakota in 1990, Sue (named after the woman who found her) is no plastic replica (though the creature's skull is so heavy the real thing is housed upstairs while a stand-in graces the actual body), and the skeleton's placement near the entry is a reminder of the museum's commitment to displaying authentic remnants from nature's past. Spread out over 400,000 square feet, the museum also holds popular exhibits on ancient Egypt as well as artifacts and wilderness scenes from all parts of the globe. It's the holy grail of Chicago museums.

Admission: adults $15, children 3-11 $10, seniors and students $12. Daily 9 a.m.-5 p.m. Additional charge for special exhibits.

PRAIRIE AVENUE HISTORIC DISTRICT
1800 and 1900 blocks of South Prairie Avenue, South Loop

Chicago's wealthiest denizens set up mansions in this South Side neighborhood after the Great Chicago Fire of 1871. Biz whiz Marshall Field and inventor George M. Pullman were among a select few who had Prairie Avenue

---

WHAT ARE THE BEST PLACES FOR FAMILY FUN?

Adler Planetarium *(page 42)* A visit here is a must, if only because it is the Western Hemisphere's first planetarium. Interactive exhibits include a fully restored Gemini 12 spacecraft, which allow you to envision what it would be like to fly to the moon.

Navy Pier *(page 32)* The tourist-packed pier and lakefront area have become as emblematic of Chicago as deep-dish pizza. All kinds of events take place here year-round, and kids will love the hands-on museum and Ferris wheel.

SHEDD AQUARIUM

addresses. Many of the houses were demolished in the 20th century, but a few remain. The Glessner House (*1800 S. Prairie Ave., 312-326-1480; www. glessnerhouse.org*), built by Henry Hobson Richardson for businessman John J. Glessner, has a Romanesque Revival-style façade and is one of the last remaining Prairie Avenue mansions. Walk around inside to see more than 6,000 artifacts, including Arts and Crafts Movement furniture and rare art glass. Built in 1836, the Clarke House Museum (*1855 S. Indiana Ave., 312-326-1480*) is the city's oldest building and it keeps chugging, having survived fires and two moves. The Greek Revival structure was owned by hardware dealer Henry B. Clarke and shows what life was like for a middle-class family in Chicago before the Civil War.

Single-house admission: adults $10, seniors and students $9, children 5-12 $6, children under 5 free; combo tour admission: adults $15, seniors and students $12, children 5-12 $8, children under 5 free. Free Wednesday. Glessner tour: Wednesday-Sunday 1 p.m., 3 p.m. Clarke tour: Wednesday-Sunday noon, 2 p.m.

SHEDD AQUARIUM
1200 S. Lake Shore Drive, South Loop (Museum Campus), 312-939-2438; www.sheddaquarium.org

More than 32,000 animals swim, slither or crawl around this underwater wonderland, which is one of the largest and best indoor aquariums in the world. You can't miss the Caribbean Reef, a circular 90,000-gallon habitat filled with sea turtles, moray eels, sharks, rays and plenty of colorful fish, where you can watch a diver feed the sea creatures while speaking to guests. Head over to Wild Reef, where only five inches of glass separate you from more than two dozen sharks. Don't miss the new Fantasea water show where you can see dolphins, belugas and penguins perform stunts.

Admission: adults $24.95, children 3-11 $17.95. Labor Day-Memorial Day, Monday-Friday 9 a.m.-5 p.m., Saturday-Sunday 9 a.m.-6 p.m. Memorial Day-Labor Day, daily 9 a.m.-6 p.m.

WHERE IS CHICAGO'S GREATEST ARCHITECTURE?

The Great Fire of 1871 leveled nearly everything in Chicago, so the city had to rebuild from scratch. It needed a new architectural vision and construction technique (wood buildings weren't so resilient the last time around), all of which set the stage for innovation. The ensuing building boom in the 1880s attracted creative architects, and that's when the city's reputation as an architectural hub started.

Almost 130 years later, Chicago maintains that reputation. The world's best architects, including Ludwig Mies van der Rohe, Frank Lloyd Wright and Frank Gehry, passed through the city, leaving their marks in the form of towering structures of steel, glass and concrete. The city continues to be at the forefront with architects like Santiago Calatrava, who hopes to bring to the lakefront his 2,000-foot Chicago Spire.

FRANK GEHRY: PRITZKER PAVILION
Millennium Park, 55 N. Michigan Ave., Loop; www.millenniumpark.org
Gehry's 2004 Pritzker Pavilion is a remarkable sight. The 120-foot-high outdoor bandshell shows the architect's trademark use of bright steel to make buildings look like free-form sculpture. The stainless-steel layers curl upward from the stage like shaved chocolate, and a steel criss-crossed trellis covers the venue seating and lawn below. Known for his contorted steel structures, Gehry made this one of his most accessible and functional buildings. His adjacent BP Bridge echoes the unique design.

BURHAM & ROOT: RELIANCE BUILDING
32 N. State St., Loop
Chicago became the birthplace of skyscrapers because of buildings like this Burnham & Root 1890 masterpiece. Its glass-covered exterior makes it a precursor to today's glass-and-steel skyscrapers. The exterior looks like it's all windows, but between them you'll see narrow piers, mullions and spandrels, all covered with cream terra cotta and Gothic ornamentation. It's a prime example of the Chicago School of architecture; it combines columns of steel to house airy façades of glass. Today, the building houses the Hotel Burnham and Atwood Café, and is often sketched by students from the nearby Art Institute.

HOLABIRD & ROOT: CHICAGO BOARD OF TRADE
141 W. Jackson Blvd., Loop
Holabird & Root created this imposing Art Deco behemoth in 1930, an unapologetically vertical structure marking an abrupt end to LaSalle Street. Head into the two-story lobby to really see its Art Deco beginnings, with its clean lines forming intricate yet orderly geometric designs. If you're wondering what is on top of the building, it's Ceres, the Roman goddess of agriculture—a symbol of the exchange's beginnings in the agricultural commodities business.

LOUIS SULLIVAN: SULLIVAN CENTER
1 S. State St., Loop
The former Carson, Pirie, Scott and Company Building has changed its name to honor its architect, Louis Sullivan. The 12-story structure was constructed for the Schlesinger and Mayer Department Store between 1898

PRITZKER PAVILION

and 1904 and is considered one of Sullivan's most important. After Carson's took over the building in 1904, a 12-story south addition by Daniel Burnham was made and an eight-story south addition followed by Holabird and Root in 1961—a succession of great Chicago architects competing and complementing each other's styles in one building. The white terra cotta façade is most remarkable for Sullivan's amazing intricate, curvy cast-iron ornamentation. Renovations are expected to be completed in 2010 to make room for new tenants in the months to follow, including FlatTop Grill and—no doubt to take advantage of the locals' lust for Lake Michigan's three-inch waves— surf-shop chain Billabong.

LUDWIG MIES VAN DER ROHE: CROWN HALL
3360 S. State St., Bronzeville
One of the Modernist architect's masterpieces is a literal lesson to the people who work and study inside of it, as it's the location for the Illinois Institute of Technology's College of Architecture. Mies had the foresight to accommodate the changing needs of the students. He created a 120-foot-long, 220-foot-wide and 18-foot-high clear-span building without any columns, a flexible space where temporary partitions can be changed as needed (though school officials nixed student requests to use the space for keggers). Mies, who was head of the school's architecture program in 1938, also designed nearly 20 campus structures for the Illinois Institute of Technology, the largest collection of the architect's buildings.

FRANK LLOYD WRIGHT: ROBIE HOUSE
5757 S. Woodlawn Ave., Hyde Park; www.gowright.org
In 1910 Frank Lloyd Wright, the grandfather of American architecture, created this home in his signature Prairie style. Named for the prairie landscape of his Midwest youth, this style is characterized by sweeping horizontal lines, dramatic overhangs, art glass windows and an open floor plan—all of which can be seen at the Robie House (entry is by guided tour only; to reserve a spot, visit *www.gowright.org*).

OLD TOWN/RIVER NORTH/RIVER WEST

River North lies just west of Streeterville, and in spirit, it's not much different: the area is a tourist's haven for its preponderance of deep-dish pizza places like Pizzeria Uno, but it's also home to more upscale restaurants and lounges, boutique hotels, dress-code-enforcing clubs and tons more shopping. On the western edge of River North—under the El train tracks, on Franklin Street between Chicago Avenue and Kinzie Street—major chains give way to established art galleries. In-the-know Chicagoans take it across the river to River West for a more urban setting and less crowded but chic eats at spots like Japonais, though the neighborhood is largely residential. Old Town, which is north of River North, is also a residential area with some historic gems and includes the Second City improv theater, the Chicago History Museum, and plenty of neighborhood restaurants.

CHICAGO HISTORY MUSEUM
1601 N. Clark St., Old Town, 312-642-4600; www.chicagohs.org
As Chicago's oldest cultural institution, the Chicago History Museum predates the Great Chicago Fire of 1871. And the CHM gets better with age. A major 2006 renovation provided new galleries, which feature shows such as Chicago: Crossroads of America. The comprehensive permanent exhibit looks at the city's many neighborhoods, and its disasters and innovations. The CHM tries to go beyond stuffy historical documents with past exhibits like Chicago@40: The Band and Its City, an homage to the legendary soft-rock band, and Chic Chicago: Couture Treasures from the Chicago History Museum, a collection of dazzling gowns worn by local fashionistas, including the first couture dress designed for an uncorseted woman as well as modern designer pieces by the likes of Versace.
Admission: adults $14, seniors and students $12, children 12 and under free. Free Monday. Monday-Saturday 9:30 a.m.-4:30 p.m., Sunday noon-5 p.m.

CHICAGO TRIBUNE TOWER
435 N. Michigan Ave., River North, 312-222-3232, 800-874-2863; www.chicagotribune.com
When the Chicago Tribune needed a bigger space in 1922, the newspaper held a contest challenging architects to create the world's most beautiful office building for the prosperous paper. The unanimous winning entry: A

WHAT ARE CHICAGO'S TOP MUSEUMS?

The Art Institute of Chicago *(page 33)* The Art Institute has always been known for its vast stock of Impressionist works, but the spectacular new Modern Wing will no doubt put it on the contemporary art map (and make it the second-largest art museum in the United States).

Field Museum of Natural History *(page 42)* The Field Museum houses the best-preserved and largest Tyrannosaurus rex fossil ever discovered. Spread out over 400,000 square feet, the museum also holds popular exhibits on ancient Egypt as well as artifacts and wilderness scenes from all parts of the globe.

Museum of Contemporary Art *(page 31)* The MCA is home to 2,345 pieces in its permanent collection and includes first-rate contemporary experimental works.

MICHIGAN AVENUE BRIDGE

AIR SHOW ON THE LAKEFRONT

distinctive 36-story Gothic skyscraper topped with dramatic floodlights from New York City architects John Mead Howells and Raymond M. Hood. To ensure the tower's grandeur, embedded into its lower elevations are fragments from well-known buildings throughout the world, including a chunk of the Great Wall of China. Although you can't tour inside the tower, which now serves as the Tribune Company's headquarters, its ground-level radio room lets the public peek at live broadcasts of WGN talk radio, and you can peruse the Chicago Tribune Store *(312-222-3080)* to buy an authentically Chicago trinket (like the Tribune logo mug etched with an image of the top of the tower, or a framed poster of the front page of the *Chicago Tribune* announcing Barack Obama's presidential victory).
Store hours: Monday-Friday 9 a.m.-5:30 p.m., Saturday 10 a.m.-4 p.m.

HOLY NAME CATHEDRAL
735 N. State St., River North, 312-787-8040;
www.holynamecathedral.org
Built in the 1870s to replace a church destroyed in the Great Chicago Fire of 1871, the cathedral's gothic architecture sits uneasily against the Magnificent Mile's modern skyline. But Holy Name Cathedral has grown up with Chicago and has been a spiritual home to the city's growing Roman Catholic population. It is the seat of the Roman Catholic Archdiocese of Chicago and was host to a mass by John Paul II in 1979. Open the 1,200-pound bronze doors (don't worry, they open easily thanks to a finger-touch hydraulic system) and peek inside the church to see five galeros—the red, broad-brimmed hats worn by cardinals—suspended from the ceiling. A galero used to be raised to the ceiling of a cardinal's cathedral upon his death and left there until it decayed as an example that all earthly glory passes. Also check out the stained-glass windows; made in Milan, they tell a story of humankind's movement from darkness into light. The western windows are dominated by dark shades of blue and red, but lighten up until they become primarily white and gold behind the altar and crucifix. The cathedral is also a part of Chicago's macabre lore, since it was the site of a

WHAT ARE THE BEST TOURS?

If you're going to do one sightseeing activity in Chicago, make it a tour. These options will help you cover the city in just a few hours.

There's nothing like seeing the city from the river, which flows through downtown. Board the **Chicago History Museum**'s *(465 N. McClurg Court, River North, 312-527-2002; www.chicagoline.com)* 90-minute architecture tour, where you'll see Mies van der Rohe's last major Chicago project (IBM Building) and learn about Chicago's tie to the Ferris wheel. Obviously the CHM is all about history, but the tour also looks at Chicago's future, showing plans for Santiago Calatrava's 2,000-foot lakefront Chicago Spire.

If you're more interested in hearing about the city's sordid past, go on the **Chicago Architecture Foundation**'s *(224 S. Michigan Ave., Loop, 312-922-3432; www.architecture.org)* 3.25-hour Devil in the White City Companion Tour. First you'll get a slide show of photos taken during the 1893 Chicago World's Fair. Then you'll travel around by bus to the various sites mentioned in Erik Larson's best-selling nonfiction book of the same name about one of the nation's first serial killers, who struck during the fair.

Mob lore fans enjoy the **Untouchable Tours** *(Clark and Ohio streets, River North, 773-881-1195; www.gangstertour.com)*, which delves into Al Capone-era Chicago gangland. The two-hour tour takes you around the city explaining who got whacked by whom. And while it's a bit cheesy—the guides dress in fedoras and adopt Italian accents—it's a fun time, and you get to see the sites of such grisly events like the St. Valentine's Day Massacre.

Chicago History Museum: For days and times, visit www.chicagoline.com. Tickets: adults $36, seniors $31, children 7-18 $21, children 6 and under free. Chicago Architecture Foundation: For days and times, visit www.architecture.org. Tickets: adults $55, seniors and students $50. Untouchables Tour: For days and times, visit www.gangstertour.com. Tickets: $28.

battle between Al Capone-era mobsters over turf. Bullet holes remain in a Philippians inscription, now covered by stairs.

Mass schedule: Weekdays 6 a.m., 7 a.m., 8 a.m., 12:10 p.m., 5:15 p.m.; Saturday vigil 5:15 p.m., 7:30 p.m.; Sunday 7 a.m., 8:15 a.m., 9:30 a.m., 11 a.m., 12:30 p.m., 5:15 p.m. The building is open a half hour before the first Mass of the day through 7 p.m.

MICHIGAN AVENUE BRIDGE
At the Chicago River between Michigan and Wabash avenues, River North

Motorists drive on Michigan Avenue Bridge daily, but they're too busy cursing the traffic to stop and appreciate the striking gateway to the Magnificent Mile, which connects the North and South Sides of the city. Built in 1920 by Edward Bennett, the bridge was designed not just for better transportation but also to enhance the waterfront as part of architect Daniel Burnham's 1909 Plan of Chicago. The landmark bridge later got an esplanade in 1926 and sculptures in 1928. The southwest bridge tower houses the McCormick Tribune Bridgehouse & Chicago River Museum *(376 N. Michigan Ave., River North, 312-977-0227; www.bridgehousemuseum.org)*. Not atmospheric enough for you? There's often street performers playing saxophones or drums on either side of the bridge, adding a fitting soundtrack to the hustle and bustle.

McCormick Tribune Bridgehouse and Chicago River Museum: adults and children 5-18 $3, children under 5 free. May-October, Thursday-Monday 10 a.m.-5 p.m.

WRIGLEY BUILDING
400 N. Michigan Ave., River North, 312-923-8080; www.wrigley.com
Sitting on the north bank of the Chicago River, the Wrigley Building signals the start of the Magnificent Mile. The white terra-cotta building with its distinctive clock tower is particularly stunning when it stands in contrast against the night sky. Built to house the headquarters of William Wrigley, Jr.'s chewing gum empire, the building is actually two structures connected by ground-level and third-floor walkways. To create the building, Graham, Anderson, Probst and White used the Seville Cathedral's Giralda Tower in Spain as a template for its shape while employing French Renaissance-style ornamentation. Inside there's not much to see, because it's mostly business offices, and unfortunately, there are no free samples of Wrigley's gum or tours to be had.

LINCOLN PARK
Pretty does it in the LP—this mainly residential neighborhood is home to some of the most gorgeous two- and three-flats in the city and picture-perfect tree-lined streets, as well as acclaimed restaurants like Alinea and Charlie Trotter's. Culture is not far behind (Lincoln Park is home to Steppenwolf Theatre Company), and shopping won't be outdone here, either—Barneys Co-Op, local chocolatier Vosges Haut-Chocolat, Kiehl's and more dot the landscape along Halsted Street and Armitage Avenue.

LINCOLN PARK
2400 N. Stockton Drive, Lincoln Park, 312-742-7529
Lincoln Park, also the name of the neighborhood in which it is located, is the largest of Chicago's parks. On its grounds, which reach from North Avenue to Hollywood Avenue, you'll find numerous beaches and the lakefront jogging/biking trail. It's also the home of the Lincoln Park Zoo *(2200 N. Cannon Drive, 312-742-2000; www.lpzoo.org)*. At only 35 acres, it's not as big as its suburban Brookfield counterpart, but its park surroundings make it a scenic place to visit, plus it's free and open year-round. Check out ZooLights in the wintertime, when the zoo puts out Christmas lights in animal shapes and serves warm drinks while kids visit Santa. Just past the zoo's north border is the Lincoln Park Conservatory *(2391 N. Stockton Drive, 312-742-7736; www.chicagoparkdistrict.com)*. The free botanical garden offers four houses within its glass-domed structure: the Palm House, Fern Room, Orchid House and Show House, which hosts annual flower shows. If you head to the south end of the park, you'll see Green City Market *(www.chicagogreencitymarket.org)*, Chicago's only sustainable green market. The market features more than 40 vendors hawking everything from baked goods (get a slice of whatever pie is in season at Hoosier Mama Pie Co.) to produce (buy juicy peaches from Mick Klug Farms) and flowers (pick up lilies from The Flower Garden). After you gather your ingredients, watch the chef demos to learn how pros from noted restaurants like West Town Tavern whip up culinary masterpieces. In winter, the outdoor market sets up shop indoors at the Notebaert Nature Museum *(page 51)*.
Lincoln Park Zoo: Admission: Free. April-May, daily 9 a.m.-5p.m.; Memorial Day-Labor Day, Monday-Friday 10 a.m.-5 p.m., Saturday-Sunday 10

GRACELAND CEMETERY

a.m.-6:30 p.m.; September-October, daily 10 a.m.-5 p.m.; November-March, daily 10 a.m.-4:30 p.m. Lincoln Park Conservatory: Daily 9 a.m.-5 p.m. Green City Market: Mid-May-October, Wednesday and Saturday 7 a.m.-1 p.m.; November-late December, Wednesday and Saturday 8 a.m.-1 p.m.; January-April, days and times vary.

LAKE MICHIGAN
Lakefront, Lincoln Park, 312-742-7529; www.chicagoparkdistrict.com
One of the city's biggest surprises is its great beaches. Locals love hitting Lake Michigan's 26 miles of free lakefront for a respite during the scorching summers. On a typical sunny Saturday, you'll see hundreds of Chicagoans baking on towels, playing volleyball, running in the sand, barbecuing in designated grassy areas and, of course, swimming. Although there are tons of entry points to the beach in various neighborhoods, the hub is North Avenue Beach, which has a boat-shaped beach house; a restaurant *(Castaways Bar & Grill, 1603 N. Lake Shore Drive, 773-281-1200; www.stefanirestaurants.com)*, complete with live music from cover bands on weekends; and an outdoor gym. Fitness fiends also will find that the lakefront is a great place to work out; the 18-mile trail is perfect for jogging, rollerblading or biking. If group sports are more your thing, try to pick up a game at the sand volleyball courts and tennis courts that line the trail. In the summer, the best of Chicago's local theater companies put on Theater on the Lake, at Fullerton Avenue and Lake Michigan.

THE PEGGY NOTEBAERT NATURE MUSEUM
2430 N. Cannon Drive, Lincoln Park, 773-755-5100; www.chias.org
Be one with nature at the hands-on Notebaert. Watch more than 75 species of colorful butterflies set the Judy Istock Butterfly Haven aflutter year-round in the 2,700-square-foot greenhouse. Kids love the interactive River Works, a permanent exhibit where they can splash around while learning

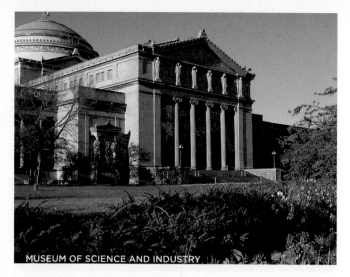

MUSEUM OF SCIENCE AND INDUSTRY

the mechanics of a river. For some fresh air, take a walk in the museum's gardens or watch the Lincoln Park action from the rooftop. The Notebaert also houses the Green City Market *(page 51)*, the city's only sustainable green market, during early winter, so that you can get your fill of nature along with its bounty.

Admission: adults $9, seniors and students $7, children 3-12. $6, children under 3 free. Free Thursday. Monday-Friday 9 a.m.-4:30 p.m., Saturday-Sunday 10 a.m.-5 p.m. Green City Market: November-late December, Wednesday and Saturday 8 a.m.-1 p.m.; January-April, days and times vary.

LAKEVIEW/WRIGLEYVILLE

Lakeview is the umbrella neighborhood that encompasses Wrigleyville—the surrounds of Wrigley Field—and Boystown, Chicago's main gay neighborhood. The area just off the Belmont El station is where Lakeview's heady mix of artsy and sporty happily collide in a blast of hip clothing stores, reliable neighborhood restaurants and raucous sports bars.

GRACELAND CEMETERY TOUR
4001 N. Clark St., Lakeview, 773-525-1105;
www.gracelandcemetery.org
Graceland is called "The Cemetery of Architects" for being the final resting place for such acclaimed architects as Daniel Burnham, William Le Baron Jenney, Louis Sullivan and Ludwig Mies van der Rohe. But many of early Chicago's major players have their permanent home here as well, including businessman Marshall Field and power couple Potter (the business mogul who came up with the idea of store sales and policies such as money-back guarantees for any reason) and Bertha Palmer (the socialite trumped her hubby's accomplishments; she claimed to have invented the brownie). The cemetery, which is on the National Register of Historic Places, is also known for its artistry. A popular site on the grounds is *Eternal Silence*, a 1909 sculpture by Lorado Taft. Also called the Statute of Death, the haunting

work features a black slab of granite fronted by a hooded bronze figure that menacingly covers his mouth and chin with his long robe. While the cemetery doesn't offer tours, it provides a free map for those who want to have a go at it by themselves, and the Chicago Architecture Foundation *(312-922-8687; www.architecture.org)* and the Chicago History Museum *(312-642-4600; www.chicagohistory.com)* offer walking tours. Try planning a fall visit, when the colorful leaves make for a beautiful backdrop.

MUSIC BOX THEATRE
3733 N. Southport Ave., Lakeview, 773-871-6604;
www.musicboxtheatre.com

Built in 1929, the Music Box Theater was originally planned with an orchestra pit, in case "sound" films (new at the time) failed. They haven't, and neither has the Music Box. The theater has shown everything from Arabic feminist films exploring the oppression of women to *Sound of Music* sing-alongs. But for the last 20 years, the Music Box has been the premier Chicago spot to see independent and experimental films. Over the years, the theatre has also hosted movie premieres, such as *The Break-Up* and *(500) Days of Summer*, with the stars walking the red carpet beforehand. In 1991, the Music Box added a second, smaller theater, which sweetly tries to reproduce a small Italian garden with shabbily painted stars and clouds above and plaster side walls. You'll be quite close to the dozen or so people in the audience, but also likely to watch a great indie movie that you can name-drop at your next dinner party.

SOUTH SIDE

The South Side is really the expansive region below the city center, which stretches from the South Loop all the way to the Indiana border. The area, which is vastly residential, has some of Chicago's most historically important and culturally diverse pockets, including Bronzeville *(35th Street and South King Drive)*, the center of Chicago's black renaissance; Hyde Park *(55th Street and Stony Island Avenue)*, home to the University of Chicago and the former site of the World's Columbian Exposition of 1893; Chinatown *(Cermak Road and Wentworth Avenue)*, the city's main Chinese enclave; Bridgeport *(35th and Halsted streets)*, the stomping grounds of both the Chicago White Sox and the powerful Daley family; and Pilsen *(18th and Halsted streets)*, the gateway to the city's formidable Mexican-American community and a burgeoning arts area.

DUSABLE MUSEUM OF AFRICAN-AMERICAN HISTORY
740 E. 56th St., Hyde Park, 773-947-0600; www.dusablemuseum.org

The DuSable Museum was created in 1961 when a local art teacher cleared out her living room furniture, replaced it with a collection of African-American art and artifacts, and hung a modest sign labeled simply "African-American Museum." Since then, it's grown quite a bit. Now in a building on the eastern side of Washington Park, the museum doesn't have the resources of, say, the Field Museum, but it holds a remarkable collection of more than 13,000 paintings, photographs and other artifacts. A large part of its collection focuses on local artists and history, with one wing dedicated to Chicago's first African-American mayor, Harold Washington. The exhibit, Red, White, Blue & Black: A History of Blacks in the Armed Forces, looks at how African-American military men struggled with enemies abroad and racism back home. The museum also hosts ongoing events, such as jazz

EL TRAIN IN THE LOOP

concerts, poetry readings and film screenings.

Admission: adults $3, seniors and students $2, children 6-12 $1, children under 6 free. Free Sunday. Monday-Saturday 10 a.m.-5 p.m. (closed Mondays June-January 2), Sunday noon-5 p.m.

MUSEUM OF SCIENCE AND INDUSTRY

57th Street and Lake Shore Drive, Hyde Park, 773-684-1414, 800-468-6674; www.msichicago.org

Opened in 1933, the MSI is the largest science museum in the Western Hemisphere—and it needs to be. It houses a full-size 727 airplane (board the plane and buckle up for a fake San Francisco-Chicago flight, complete with banter from an automated pilot); a full-scale coal mine, one of the museum's oldest displays with a great simulated trip into the depths of the mine; a refurbished Burlington Pioneer Zephyr train with interactive exhibits; the U-505 German submarine, which was captured in 1944 and has been given a new indoor arena that brings that era of American history to life; as well as farming, Internet and fairy castle-themed collections among its 2,000 exhibits. As if that weren't enough, there's the recently renovated Henry Crown Space Center in addition to its collections highlighting the history of space exploration.

Admission: adults $13, seniors $12, children 3-11 $9. Memorial Day-Labor Day, Monday-Saturday 9:30 a.m.-5:30 p.m., Sunday 11 a.m.-5:30 p.m.; Labor Day-late May, Monday-Saturday 9:30 a.m.-4 p.m., Sunday 11 a.m.-4 p.m.

THE UNIVERSITY OF CHICAGO

5801 S. Ellis Ave., Hyde Park, 773-702-1234; www.uchicago.edu

You don't need to have high SAT scores to gain admittance to the grounds of one of America's premier universities. The Hyde Park campus features lovely collegiate buildings, in any number of which scholars are working to increase the U. of C.'s already large number of Nobel Prize winners. It was on these grounds that the Enrico Fermi first sustained a nuclear reaction, that

Milton Friedman created a generation of students championing his brand of economics, and that REM sleep was first discovered. The U. of C.'s Oriental Institute, devoted to art from the Near East, holds an outstanding collection of Ancient Egypt artifacts (like the gigantic 17-foot red quartzite statute of King Tut and the *Book of the Dead*, a collection of spells, hymns and prayers intended to secure for the deceased safe passage to the other world). And nearby is Frank Lloyd Wright's Robie House *(5757 S. Woodlawn Ave.)*, a Prairie-style house with dramatic overhangs and wide horizontal lines that, despite its design 90 years ago, revolutionized American architecture and looks as modern today as it did then.

CHINATOWN
Cermak Road and Wentworth Avenue, Chinatown; www.chicagochinatown.org
The Midwest's largest Chinatown is just a quick El ride from the Loop, and just seeing its architecture is worth the trip. The Chinatown Gate (Cermak Road and Wentworth Avenue) greets visitors with a hand-painted message that translates to "The world belongs to the commonwealth," reflecting the determination of the people—this 10-block commonwealth has more than 8,000 residents. Across from the gate, see the ornate "Nine Dragon Wall," a reproduction of the original in Beijing. Both dragons and the number nine are considered sacred among the Chinese, and the wall's vibrant gold, red and blue signify good fortune. The traditional Chinese design of the Pui Tak Center Building *(2216 S. Wentworth Ave., 312-328-1188; www.puitak.org)* makes for an interesting juxtaposition against the looming Willis (Sears) Tower. Be sure to check if any seasonal events (January/February: Chinese New Year; fall: Dragon Boat Races) are taking place during your trip, but the main reason you'll want to visit Chinatown is to chow down. Eat dim sum at the always-packed Phoenix *(2131 S. Archer Ave., 312-328-0848; www.chinatownphoenix.com)*. For dessert, you can queue up for sweet, fruity bubble tea at Joy Yee's Noodle Shop *(2139 S. China Place, 312-328-0001; www.joyyee.com)* inside Chinatown Square, or grab some moon cakes from one of the many bakeries in the Square or along Wentworth Avenue and head to Ping Tom Memorial Park *(300 W. 19th St.)*, where you can get a view of the Chicago River and stroll through the Chinese-style landscaping. Afterward, buy some souvenirs. Ten Ren Tea & Ginseng Co. *(2247 S. Wentworth Ave., 312-842-1171, 888-650-1047; www.tenren.com)* offers a great selection of exotic teas and unusual teapots such as the whimsical ones modeled after Chinese zodiac animals. If you browse the many shops in the neighborhood, you can find hand-painted paper fans, jade plants and more only-in-Chinatown treats.

SUBURBS
Chicagoans poke fun at the suburbs, but believe it or not, there are great reasons to venture beyond the city limits. For one, the suburbs offer an alternative to the faster pace of Chicago without necessarily forsaking the great things about Chicago: Oak Park on the West Side drips with culture and architecture (Ernest Hemingway was born here; Frank Lloyd Wright spent the first 20 years of his career here and plenty of his structures remain), while just north of the city, Evanston boasts amazing Lake Michigan vistas, Northwestern University and acclaimed restaurants. The western suburb Brookfield has the respected Brookfield Zoo, while Glencoe, on the North Shore, hosts the breathtaking Chicago Botanic Gardens.

ROBIE HOUSE

ARLINGTON PARK
2200 W. Euclid Ave., Arlington Heights, 847-385-7500;
www.arlingtonpark.com

With horse names like "Smack Daddy," "Heckofanacttofollow" and "Pass the Brandy," you don't need to be a gambler to enjoy thoroughbred racing in this six-story grandstand racetrack. Located in Chicago's northwest suburb, Arlington Heights, and only a 45 minute train ride outside the city, Arlington Park generates a diverse crowd of onlookers, from tranquil families soaking up a summer day to betters caught in the adrenaline rush of the race. With more than 50,000 seats and stables for over 2,000 horses, the dirt oval turf first made its appearance in 1927, thanks to founder Harry D. "Curly" Brown. The park received national attention in 1981 when the winner of the Arlington Million purse race, legendary "John Henry," had a thrilling come-from-behind win over 40-1 long-shot "The Bart." The statue, "Against All Odds," located in the paddock, reveals the horse and his jockey, Bill Shoemaker, edging out "The Bart" by a nose. Stop by the paddock shortly before a race to see the horses being groomed

See Web site for race schedules.

BROOKFIELD ZOO
3300 Golf Road, Brookfield, 708-688-8000, 800-201-0784;
www.brookfieldzoo.com

West-suburban Brookfield Zoo has the pioneering Midwestern spirit. It was the first zoo in the U.S. to have a mostly cageless facility—instead it uses natural barriers such as moats—and it was the first to exhibit giant pandas. The zoo also created Tropic World, the first indoor simulated rainforest in North America, where you see monkeys amid the treetops as waterfalls cascade nearby and fake thunderstorms growl overhead. If you're not a landlubber, check out the daily indoor dolphin shows, which star bottle-nose dolphins doing Flipper-like feats (this exhibit is closed until Summer 2010 due to renovations). Set on 216 acres, the zoo is Chicagoland's largest and is home to more than 2,000 animals, including lions and tigers and binturongs.

Admission: adults $12, seniors and children 3-11 $8. Free October-December, Tuesday and Thursday. Mid-May-Labor Day, Monday-Friday 9:30 a.m.-6 p.m., Sunday 9:30 a.m.-7:30 p.m.; Labor Day-mid-October and April-mid-May, Monday-Friday 10 a.m.-5 p.m., Saturday-Sunday 10 a.m.-6 p.m.; mid-October-March, daily 10 a.m.-5 p.m.

CHICAGO BOTANIC GARDEN
1000 Lake Cook Road, Glencoe, 847-835-5440;
www.chicago-botanic.org

Despite its name, the Chicago Botanic Garden is north of the city in Glencoe, but it is definitely worth the 20-mile car ride if you have a green thumb. (Just hop on I-94 W; you can't miss it.) Never the same on any two visits given the various blooms of its flowers, the garden is spread over 385 acres with 23 display gardens, along with small lakes, a prairie area and a woodland. Be sure to visit the Japanese Garden's three islands, where you can follow the curvy paths and find some Zen underneath the pruned trees. The garden also has a great café and offers a nice respite for those seeking a relaxing walk after several days of touring the city.

Admission: Free. Labor Day-June, daily 8 a.m.-sunset; mid-June-Labor Day, daily 7 a.m.-9 p.m.

ILLINOIS HOLOCAUST MUSEUM AND EDUCATION CENTER
9603 Wood Drive, Skokie, 847-967-4800;
www.iholocaustmuseum.com

Opened in April 2009, the Illinois Holocaust Museum and Education Center is the largest one of its kind in the Midwest. The museum was originally housed in a small Skokie storefront in 1981, but with the large number of Holocaust survivors living in Skokie after World War II and the personal accounts and artifacts they willingly provided to the museum, more space was needed—65,000 square feet to be exact. Today, the sprawling museum is both somber and hopeful. In the Zev and Shifra Karkomi permanent exhibition, you can trace the Holocaust from pre-war Germany all the way to post-war life in Skokie. The walls of the Room of Remembrance are inscribed with names of some of the victims who died during the Holocaust, homage to the six million Jews who lost their lives. In addition to several interactive exhibits, artifacts like ghetto work permits, work camp uniforms and discarded luggage are also on view. Adopting the slogan "Remember the Past, Transform the Future," the museum is dedicated to preserving the memory of all those lost, while teaching younger generations about the need to prevent future genocides by fighting hatred and intolerance all over the world.

Monday-Friday 10 a.m.-5 p.m., Saturday-Sunday 11 a.m.-4 p.m.

★ WHERE TO EAT

NOMI

TASTES OF CHICAGO

Meat and potatoes rank right up there with Al Capone on the list of hardest to beat Chicago stereotypes. And that's not for lack of trying by the city's stellar culinary community. Everyone knows that some of the country's best, most innovative restaurants call Chicago home—Charlie Trotter's, Alinea, Moto. The list goes on. But not everyone knows about the tucked-away gems in cozy neighborhoods like Lincoln Square or Wicker Park, nor the modest but mind-bending pet projects of superstar chefs such as Rick Bayless, Paul Kahan and Shawn McClain. So although Chicago is proud of its "low-brow" dining history—deep-dish pizza and hot dogs are staples throughout the city—you'll never go hungry for award-winning and fine dining options. And neither will locals, who are more than happy to live in a place where dining comes in second to none.

GOLD COAST/STREETERVILLE

★★★GIBSONS

1028 N. Rush St., Gold Coast, 312-266-8999;
www.gibsonssteakhouse.com

Pinky rings and massive steaks are the hallmark of Gibsons, a Gold Coast fixture since 1989. The walls are adorned with pictures of celebs ranging from Muhammad Ali to Clint Eastwood, but the restaurant is just as well-known as the haunt of local powerbrokers who make their deals over Gibsons' fishbowl-sized martinis and then celebrate with a gargantuan 24-ounce porterhouse. Big spenders go for the surf and turf, which features a huge Australian lobster tail served with a massive fillet. You could save room for dessert, but we're guessing you won't get too far into the famed macadamia turtle pie.

Steak. Lunch, dinner. Reservations recommended. Bar. $36-85

★★★LE COLONIAL

937 N. Rush St., Gold Coast, 312-255-0088;
www.lecolonialchicago.com

Chicago's Rush Street is a loud, bombastic avenue, often filled with rowdy revelers and tipsy tourists. But that's not the only reason the restrained elegance of Le Colonial stands out here. With its slowly rotating ceiling fans and potted palm trees, Le Colonial serves French-Vietnamese fare in a space that vividly evokes the feel of French colonial Southeast Asia. The authentic Vietnamese fare starts with pho, the popular beef soup with rice noodles and flavorful slivers of ginger and chilies. Then it's on to entrées like Ca Chien Saigon, a seared snapper in a sweet, spicy sauce, and Bo Bitet Tom Nuong, a grilled filet mignon with shrimp and tomato rice pilaf. Afterward, enjoy a cocktail in a high-backed rattan chair, which is a pleasant way to savor the last drop of atmosphere before heading back out into the boisterous night.

French, Vietnamese. Lunch, dinner. Bar. $36-85

★★★★LES NOMADES

222 E. Ontario St., Streeterville, 312-649-9010; www.lesnomades.net

From its location in a former townhouse to the fresh flowers placed throughout the restaurant, Les Nomades is nothing but low-key elegance. And despite being a mere croissant's throw from nearby Michigan Avenue, the serene

SEASONS

spot is secluded and intimate for those seeking a romantic getaway within the city. That's not to say the French haute cuisine is an afterthought, though. From rack of lamb in a delicate mushroom soubise to perfectly roasted venison loin with puréed parsnips, Les Nomades' prix fixe French fare is expertly prepared and perfectly fits the restaurant's elegant atmosphere. In keeping with the formal feel, jackets are required for men, and cell phones are strictly prohibited.

French. Dinner. Closed Sunday-Monday. $86 and up

★★★NOMI

Park Hyatt Chicago, 800 N. Michigan Ave., Gold Coast, 312-239-4030; www.nomirestaurant.com

When you first arrive at NoMI, you have to go through a glass-encased wine "cellar" and take several turns before entering the main dining room. It's almost as if they want to reward you for your efforts—and what a reward it is. The beautiful space, which offers stunning views of Michigan Avenue and the Water Tower across the street, matches executive chef Christophe David's cuisine: simple, unpretentious and elegant. Sushi makes up much of the menu, with à la carte pieces and larger plates of several rolls offered. David also presents entrées such as slow cooked salmon with mushrooms,

---

WHAT ARE THE BEST OVERALL RESTAURANTS IN CHICAGO?

Alinea *(page 83)* Alinea burst onto the scene a few years back with some of the most wildly creative dishes in the country, and the complex meals here continue to blow us away.

Charlie Trotter's *(page 84)* There's not much about internationally renowned chef Charlie Trotter that hasn't already been said. His exactingly prepared food is always a treat.

yellow curry and coconut, and a duet of beef with petite ribeye and braised veal cheek. After your meal, the outdoor garden's gently pulsing lounge music, comfortable tables and spectacular view make a perfect environment for a relaxing after-dinner drink.

French, Asian. Breakfast, lunch (Sunday-Thursday), dinner, Sunday brunch. Reservations recommended. Bar. $36-85

★★★★SEASONS
Four Seasons Hotel Chicago, 120 E. Delaware Place, Gold Coast, 312-649-2349; www.fourseasons.com

Let other restaurants try to impress you with a stark, minimalist atmosphere. Seasons, located within the Four Seasons Hotel, goes the other way and spoils you with old-school luxury. How so? For starters, there's the marble fountain, armchair seats and deep mahogany wood trim. Then there are French-leaning prix fixe menus of four, five or six courses as well as a vegetarian option. The fare constantly changes to reflect availability of ingredients, but past favorites include Tasmanian sea trout filled with slow-cooked Kobe short ribs, and rack of Colorado lamb wrapped in eggplant and scented with toasted cumin. After a day of Mag Mile shopping, no other place in the Gold Coast feels quite as decadently classic.

Contemporary American, French. Breakfast, lunch, dinner (Tuesday-Saturday), Sunday brunch. Reservations recommended. $86 and up

★★★SPIAGGIA
980 N. Michigan Ave., Gold Coast, 312-280-2750; www.levyrestaurants.com

Any talk of Chicago's high-end Italian restaurants begins (and arguably ends) with the gorgeous Spiaggia. How many restaurants have their own cheese cave? Exactly. The elegant setting matches the caliber of the food: The multi-tiered restaurant, appropriately perched at the outset of the city's famed Magnificent Mile, offers a view of Lake Michigan and the city's most famous street. James Beard award-winning chef and partner Tony Mantuano offers an à la carte menu that includes hand rolled potato gnocchi with ricotta sauce and black truffles. There's also a tasting menu inspired by the island of Sicily, which includes items such as pasta sheets with wood-roasted sardines, fennel pollen and black currants, and desserts such as the fig cake with Sambuca gelato.

Italian. Dinner. Jacket required. $86 and up

★★★TABLE FIFTY-TWO
52 W. Elm St., Gold Coast, 312-573-4000; www.tablefifty-two.com

Art Smith will likely forever be known as Oprah's chef, although that's probably not such a bad thing. After all, it's given him the chance to open TABLE fifty-two, which provides a perfect outlet for his Southern-inflected cuisine. Each table begins the meal with piping hot, fluffy buttermilk biscuits pulled fresh from the oven. The menu boasts Smith's upgraded take on Southern classics, including fried green tomatoes layered with goat cheese, bacon and greens and cornmeal-crusted catfish with cheese grits and bacon-braised collard greens. Housed in a 19th century carriage house and featuring an open-hearth oven, Smith's restaurant is as cozy and comforting as his cuisine.

American, Southern. Lunch, dinner. Reservations recommended. $36-85

CHICAGO-STYLE HOT DOG

LET'S BE FRANK

The origins of the classic Chicago-style hot dog are somewhat fuzzy, but one thing's clear—don't dare order it with ketchup on top.

Chicago cuisine isn't just about deep-dish pizza. For a taste of the real Windy City, order up a Chicago-style hot dog. But what does that mean, exactly? For starters, the base is a poppy seed-studded bun and a boiled or steamed (not grilled nor charred) all-beef frank. Then come the seven key toppings: mustard, chopped onions, neon-green relish, sport peppers, tomato wedges, a quarter of a pickle cut lengthwise, and a sprinkling of celery salt. Woe to the vendor who squirts ketchup on it in the presence of a Chicago dog purist (and the city is crawling with them)—many believe that the tart sweetness of the red stuff clashes with the other toppings.

Yet as strongly as Chicagoans feel about their unique dog, nobody's really sure how it originated. Legend has it that the first vendor to serve it up was Fluky's (now called U Lucky Dawg), in the old Maxwell Street Market during the Depression. The toppings are said to have developed from the city's various ethnic groups at the time—namely Greek (tomatoes, onions) and Italian (relish, peppers) vendors trying to add more value to their product during a nose-diving economy.

To sample this classic Chicago invention, try **U Lucky Dawg** (*6821 N. Western Ave., 773-274-3652*), the disputed originator of the formula; **Hot Doug's** (*3324 N. California Ave., 773-279-9550; www.hotdougs.com*), which on Saturdays and Sundays offers the wildly popular duck-fat fries; **Jim's Original** (*1250 S. Union Ave., 312-733-7820; www.jimsoriginal.com*), where you can also get a mean Polish sausage; and **Superdawg** (*6363 N. Milwaukee Ave., 773-763-0660; www.superdawg.com*), a truly old-fashioned drive-in where uniformed servers bring your order out to your car.

TRU

★★★★TRU

676 N. St. Clair St., Streeterville, 312-202-0001;
www.trurestaurant.com

If you want a stellar dining experience in a large, beautifully understated room with perfectly attuned service, make a reservation at Tru, the partnership of chef Rick Tramonto and executive pastry chef Gale Gand. The gorgeous surroundings include an original Andy Warhol, and the food is equally inspiring. Tru offers different ways to take advantage of Tramonto's work, including a three-course prix fixe and a six- or nine-course "collections" tasting menu. The offerings include a delicate roasted day boat halibut with heirloom tomato and fennel, and prime beef ribeye with grilled foie gras, chanterelle mushrooms and parsley. Practically anything at Tru will delight, but we especially recommend the caviar staircase appetizer, which serves several different types of roe on an elegant glass spiral stairway. Even the bathrooms here, with their sinks made up solely of large slanted glass panels, are a sight.

Contemporary French. Dinner. Closed Sunday. Reservations recommended. Jacket required. $86 and up

OLD TOWN/RIVER NORTH/RIVER WEST
★★★★AVENUES

The Peninsula Chicago, 108 E. Superior St., River North, 312-573-6695;
www.chicago.peninsula.com

Forget the plain name, and overlook the fact that the intimate Avenues is in a hotel (though the hotel is the Peninsula, one of the best in the city). You might have to tolerate a setting that's a little more staid than luxurious. Instead, try to focus on the food, as chef Curtis Duffy offers cuisine that manages to be both simple and extravagant. Duffy succeeded acclaimed toque Graham Elliot Bowles (who left to start his own eponymous River North restaurant; *page 64*). But Duffy, who was Grant Achatz's right-hand man at Alinea, has made Avenues all his own. He favors unusual pairings that work despite seeming contradictory: A grilled Wagyu steak comes with smoked coconut and African blue basil, and lamb is poached in tangerine oil with mint blossom. The best bet might be to take a seat at the bar in front of the open kitchen and watch Duffy work his magic.

Contemporary American. Dinner. Closed Sunday-Monday. Reservations recommended. Bar. $86 and up

★★BIN 36
339 N. Dearborn St., River North, 312-755-9463; www.bin36.com
Most restaurants serve food and enhance the experience with wine. At the cavernous Bin 36, it's the other way around. You'll see that love of the grape from the many wine flights served with dinner to the wine store on the premises that will sell you that wine you really liked with your dinner. "Wine Director" Brian Duncan—he refuses to be called a sommelier—offers more 50 wines by the glass, and about 300 bottles to choose from. But despite the hullabaloo about vino, the menu is hardly an afterthought. Chef John Caputo's seafood-oriented fare includes a seared ahi tuna with herb-ricotta dumplings, and peppercorn-crusted blue marlin with mashed potatoes, onion rings and bordelaise sauce. Bin 36 offers three different dining areas, depending on your mood: the bar, the cheese bar or at a standard table in the dining room. The wine list in the downstairs trattoria, A Mano, which the owners opened in late 2007, focuses on small producers. Take a seat here on a Thursday after 5 p.m. for the $5 pizzas, and then grab a gelato from the gelato and sorbet bar on our way out. A sophisticated environment with options galore? We'll drink to that.

Contemporary American. Breakfast, lunch, dinner. Bar. $36-85

★★BRASSERIE JO
59 W. Hubbard St., River North, 312-595-0800; www.brasseriejo.com
High ceilings and Art Deco accents aren't the only archetypal French elements at this River North fixture. With whimsical French accordion music constantly playing in the background, chef/owner Jean Joho's bistro has been a Chicago favorite since it opened in 1996, drawing adoring crowds with a casual Alsatian menu that features classics such as coq au vin and a juicy cut of steak topped with a heaping mound of frites. The value-conscious, however, don't need to venture beyond the tartes flambées, delicious pizzas topped with everything from pears, blue cheese and walnuts to spinach, mushroom and Gruyère. A large beer and wine selection (including the restaurant's own Hopla brew) makes this the next best thing to being in Paris.

French. Dinner. Bar. $36-85

★★★CHICAGO CHOP HOUSE
60 W. Ontario St., River North, 312-787-7100;
www.chicagochophouse.com
It's hard to capture authenticity—some places have it, while other spots feel like a couple of marketing majors drummed up a concept. But the Chop House has authenticity to spare, from the classic green awnings on the Victorian façade to the 1,400 pictures of Chicago icons on the walls. Of course, old-school charm is irrelevant if the food doesn't work—but the reasonably priced steaks here are wet-aged and perfectly prepared. The menu is light on perks, so don't expect anything fancy. Just start out with the prosciutto-wrapped asparagus before going for the massive New York strip (or the 64-ounce porterhouse, if you're up to it). The award-winning wine

list features more than 600 bottles, from Oregon pinot noirs to renowned French cabs. Just be sure to leave the baseball caps and T-shirts at home; the dress code, while relatively relaxed, encourages smart attire.

Steak. Dinner. Reservations recommended. Bar. $36-85

★★★CROFTON ON WELLS

535 N. Wells St., River North, 312-755-1790; www.croftononwells.com

In a city that features such renowned chefs as Charlie Trotter and Grant Achatz, it's telling that Suzy Crofton's eponymous River North restaurant has survived—thrived, actually—since 1997. By leaving the foam and froth to others, Crofton has earned a truckload of awards for her elegant contemporary cuisine. The restaurant's muted gray-and-white décor mirrors Crofton's French-tinged cooking: elegant and thoughtful, without pretense. She puts as much thought into her appetizers—including the crab cake and sautée of wild mushrooms with bacon, cracked peppercorn and brioche—as she does on her Amish chicken and smoked pork belly topped with her famous smoked-apple chutney. Vegetarians aren't relegated to a cursory dish at the corner of the menu—Crofton puts out a separate vegetarian menu, as well as several vegan options.

Contemporary American. Dinner. Closed Sunday. Bar. $36-85

★★★DAVID BURKE'S PRIMEHOUSE

The James Hotel, 616 N. Rush St., River North, 312-660-6000; www.davidburke.com

Sure, many Chicago restaurants claim to be serious about their steaks, but we're guessing not many of them go as far as David Burke's Primehouse, which boasts its own salt-tiled aging room, in which the owners dry-age their own beef. Even more impressive: David Burke owns a stud steer in Kentucky whose offspring produce the meat for his aged steaks. These are just two of the reasons this spot stands apart from the herd. The room is a veritable ode to all things bovine: The chairs are a deep brown leather and the tables are wrapped in red leather. The steaks are the main draw, from the "South Side" bone-in filet to the châteaubriand for two. There is a respectable number of non-steak options as well, including a seared Alaskan king salmon and a grilled ahi tuna mignon. They're not bad, but when else will you have a chance to trace the family tree of your prime rib?

Steak. Breakfast, lunch (Monday-Saturday), dinner, Sunday brunch. Bar. $36-85

★★★FRONTERA GRILL

445 N. Clark St., River North, 312-661-1434; www.rickbayless.com

If you can't quite spring for the upscale offerings of Topolobampo next door—or maybe you want to save your money for Rick Bayless' acclaimed margaritas (we don't blame you)—you won't feel cheated if you opt for Frontera Grill. The always-popular spot has a festive atmosphere with colorful walls and hanging papier-mâché animals, which provides a perfect environment to enjoy the PBS chef's housemade moles and freshly ground corn tortillas. The menu features such mouthwatering fare as Puerco Al Chipotle, a grilled pork loin in a red-bean chipotle sauce, and carne Asada a la Oaxaquena, a grilled Angus rib steak marinated in red chile and served with black beans and plantains. Be forewarned: The restaurant takes reservations only for a limited number of tables, which explains the lines that form well before the doors open for dinner.

AVENUES

Mexican, Southwestern. Lunch, dinner, Saturday brunch. Closed Sunday-Monday. Bar. $36-85

★★★GENE & GEORGETTI

500 N. Franklin St., River North, 312-527-3718;
www.geneandgeorgetti.com

Chicago's famed stockyards officially closed in 1971, but the city's carnivorous tradition is still going strong—and perhaps no stronger than at this timeless Italian steakhouse that's resided in the shadow of the El since 1941. From the pictures of Frank Sinatra and Bob Hope on the walls to the red vinyl chairs, G&G (as it's known) is old-school through and through. The waiters have as much character as the classic environs, and they're not exactly known for their geniality, but you'll forget their brusqueness the second you dig into the juicy wet-aged New York strip or the 18-ounce filet that stands some four inches tall.

Italian, Steak. Lunch, dinner. Closed Sunday. Bar. $36-85

★★★GRAHAM ELLIOT

217 W. Huron St., River North, 312-624-9975; www.grahamelliot.com

You'll either love or loathe the kookiness at acclaimed chef Graham Elliot Bowles' River North restaurant. The "informalized" dining room features '80s pop tunes (think Flock of Seagulls and Billy Ocean), and the snack between courses is popcorn (Parmesan-dusted and truffled popcorn, but popcorn nonetheless). Clad in jeans and Chuck Taylors, servers bring Bowles' playful haute cuisine that's divided into hot and cold appetizers and land and sea entrées. Bowles seems to have a jones for cheap beer—his openers include a duck leg confit served with Maytag blue cheese and Budweiser beer foam, and an aged cheddar risotto, featuring Pabst-glazed onions and Cheez-It crackers. He tones it down a little for his entrées, as the grilled rack of pork features a massive loin tastefully infused with root-beer barbecue sauce, while the salmon BLT served with crispy bacon and fresh

NAHA

tomatoes is delicious—good enough, even, for us to endure the overly-loud Reagan-era jams.

Contemporary American. Dinner. Closed Sunday. $36-85

★★★JAPONAIS
600 W. Chicago Ave., River West, 312-822-9600;
www.japonaischicago.com

You'll need to cab it over to this gentrifying but not exactly glitzy part of town. But when you're enjoying Japanese-French fusion next to some of the city's most stylish foodies, you'll see why Japonais remains one of the hottest tables in town. Gently thumping lounge music and chic décor provide a perfect environment for the glammed-up crowd (Brad and Angelina dined here when she was filming *Wanted*) that can be found sipping on colorful

---

WHAT ARE THE TOP ROMANTIC RESTAURANTS?

Café Absinthe *(page 90)* The restaurant's dimly lit, romantic atmosphere is the perfect backdrop to the seasonal, American-oriented menu. Be sure to order the dark chocolate lava cake infused with Grand Marnier liqueur and served with a prickly-pear sauce.

Les Nomades *(page 60)* From its location in a former townhouse to the fresh flowers placed throughout the restaurant, Les Nomades is nothing but low-key elegance. The serene spot is secluded and intimate for those seeking a romantic getaway within the city.

North Pond *(page 85)* Situated in the middle of a pastoral setting in Lincoln Park, the restaurant's gorgeous Prairie-style building overlooks a small pond and provides a stunning view of the Chicago skyline. Almost as impeccable is chef Bruce Sherman's sustainable-minded fare.

WHAT ARE THE BEST PLACES FOR A CASUAL LUNCH?

When a hot dog just won't do, turn your tastebuds to fast food that's decidedly more interesting, and healthy. Big-name chefs are increasingly opening up more casual spots, so you always have access to delicious food when you're in town.

Rick Bayless—a chef, a businessman and a cookbook author—opened a few quick-service Mexican restaurants in 2007. **Frontera Fresco** (*111 N. State Street, 312-781-1000; www.fronterafresco.com*) boasts gourmet Mexican dishes comprised of the freshest ingredients from aromatic herbs to all-natural salsas to baked flatbreads. Striking a deal with Macy's department store, Bayless placed his fast-food restaurants in two great locations, offering both Chicago and Skokie shoppers a place to grab a bite, with plenty of space for their bags of goodies. The *Top Chef Masters* winner also opened up **XOCO** (located next door to Frontera Grill)—and people have been lined up since day one for the flavorful tortas.

Charlie Trotter grew up in Chicago and opened up his first restaurant here in 1987. The meals created by this talented chef were in such high demand, he decided to open **Trotter's To Go** (*1337 W. Fullerton, 773-868-6510; www.charlietrotters.com/togo*) to make his gourmet meals available for anyone who either didn't want to spend over $50 on a three-course dinner, or didn't feel like dressing up in a spiffy outfit to go out to eat. Chef Trotter gets you into the act of being a gourmet chef by selling prepared foods in his "chef's case", which are already marinated and seasoned; all you have to do is pop them in the oven. He also offers ready-made salads, sandwiches, soups and desserts if you're really hungry and want to eat right away.

Chef **Marcus Samuelsson** had long been earning raves at Aquavit in New York City before opening up C-House at the Affinia Hotel in Chicago a few years ago. Recently, he also unveiled **Marc Burger** at the new food court at Macy's, where the signature burger is a juicy 10-ouncer topped with homemade steak sauce and a fried egg.

If it's Asian food you're craving, you have **Bill Kim** to thank for creating the affordable cuisine available at **Urban Belly** (*3053 N. California Avenue, 773-583-0500; www.urbanbellychicago.com*). Kim makes a pork belly, shitake and pho ramen that's better than any cup of noodles you've ever tasted. He is, after all, a veteran chef who has worked all over the United States. Urban Belly offers a communal dining concept, where you are seated next to complete strangers while you enjoy an affordable meal.

WHAT ARE THE BEST RESTAURANTS FOR AN UPSCALE LUNCH?

Blackbird *(page 76)* Lunch is the perfect time to enjoy chef Mike Sheerin's artisanal cooking. The three-course prix fixe includes a choice of appetizer, entrée and a dessert, with options like the pork belly sandwich with cabbage slaw and garlic frites.

NAHA *(page 72)* The excellent contemporary cuisine with a Mediterranean flair served at this elegant and tranquil restaurant is always wonderful. The Angus hamburger served on a sea-salt crusted ciabatta bun with cured tomatoes wins is one of the best in the city—and is only available at lunch.

drinks in the downstairs lounge and outdoor patio. If you're all about the food, you'll be just as pleased. The menu leans toward sushi but also includes a seven-spice Kobe rib eye and Le Quack Japonais, a smoked duck served with hoisin sauce and chutney (yes, that's neither Japanese nor French, but trust us, it's delicious). If you like to play with your food, order The Rock, in which thinly sliced New York strip steak is cooked on a hot rock at your table. Whatever you order, be sure to add a side of fries, which come with a spicy sauce that's always a crowd pleaser. Cap off the night with an after-dinner drink in the downstairs lounge, where in summer months, you can sip on a patio overlooking the river.

Japanese, French. Lunch (Monday-Friday), dinner. Bar. $36-85

★★★LA MADIA

59 W. Grand Ave., River North, 312-329-0400; www.dinelamadia.com
You know a place is good when restaurant owners go there to eat. The heavenly pies served at this contemporary pizzeria have a crispy and slightly chewy crust and come in such interesting combinations as triple pepperoni with truffle oil and taleggio with three-hour roasted grapes. Unfortunately, everything else on the menu here is equally delicious, making ordering tough. Chef Jonathan Fox often uses ingredients he picked up at the market that morning to make lovely dishes such as butternut squash tortellacci with brown butter and whipped Greek yogurt (paired with a surprisingly effervescent Millbrandt riesling from Washington State) and pulled pork shoulder over creamy, organic polenta.

American, Italian. Lunch, dinner. $16-35

★★★MK

868 N. Franklin St., River North, 312-482-9179; www.mkchicago.com
Founder Michael Kornick is no longer preparing meals at his namesake restaurant (that falls to chef Erick Simmons), but there's still a lot of substance beneath the style of this renowned loft-like spot with the brick walls and massive skylight. The chic lounge is a popular stop for a pre-dinner drink, while the spacious bi-level dining room provides a warm atmosphere for a classic contemporary American menu. Simmons doesn't exactly reinvent the wheel, but we're not complaining: His specialties include grilled veal porterhouse with balsamic brown butter, and bison rib eye with a cabernet sauce. The dessert menu offers standbys like crème brûlée and sorbet, but you'll be glad to step outside the box for the Cake & Shake, which

---

WHAT ARE THE BEST CELEBRITY CHEF RESTAURANTS?

Frontera Grill *(page 66)* The always-popular spot has a festive atmosphere with colorful walls and hanging papier-mâché animals, which provides a perfect environment to enjoy Rick Bayless's housemade moles and freshly ground corn tortillas.

Table Fifty-Two *(page 62)* Art Smith will likely forever be known as Oprah's chef, although that's probably not such a bad thing. The menu boasts Smith's upgraded take on Southern classics.

Charlie Trotter's *(page 84)* The master chef's eponymous Lincoln Park restaurant is a fixture in Chicago, consistently great year after year.

OTOM

features layers of buttermilk chocolate cake, chocolate mousse, bittersweet chocolate pavé and a vanilla malted milkshake. The buzz isn't as deafening as it was a few years ago, but scoring a table is ten times easier.
Contemporary American. Dinner. $36-85

★★★NACIONAL 27
325 W. Huron St., River North, 312-664-2727; www.nacional27.net
The "27" in the name refers to the number of Latin American countries, but it also reflects this stylish restaurant's culinary diversity. In a large, dramatic space, Nacional 27 offers Nuevo Latino dishes that blend flavors and influences from throughout Central and South America. Starters include ceviche sampling platters with shrimp, scallops, ahi tuna and cold-smoked Tasmanian salmon. The menu also offers tapas (such as miniature lamb tacos with avocado salsa and smoked chicken empanadas), a five-course tasting menu, and à la carte dishes including a delicious grilled marinated skirt steak. If the food itself doesn't get you dancing, the restaurant's resident DJ will get you on the floor with weekend salsa and merengue music. (Have a spiked apple cider to best bring out your dance moves.)
Latin American. Dinner. Closed Sunday. Bar. $36-85

★★★NAHA
500 N. Clark St., River North, 312-321-6242; www.naha-chicago.com
In-the-know Chicagoans didn't need proof that NAHA, the creation of cousins Carrie and Michael Nahabedian, offers excellent contemporary cuisine with a Mediterranean flair. But that validation came anyway in the form of a 2008 James Beard award. Carrie's meals are served in an elegant, tranquil setting and emphasize locally grown, organic fare such as wood-grilled rib eye with braised red shallots in an oxtail red-wine sauce, and honey-lacquered aged moulard duck breast with apricots and turnips. Not everything is such highbrow fare: The Angus hamburger served on a sea-salt crusted ciabatta bun with cured tomatoes wins raves as well, elevating the simple hamburger above its typical reputation. You have to get it for lunch, though. Otherwise, you're stuck ordering from the fantastic dinner menu.
Contemporary American. Lunch (Monday-Friday), dinner. Closed Sunday. Reservations recommended. Bar. $36-85

★PIZZERIA UNO
29 E. Ohio St., River North, 312-321-5125; www.unos.com
Despite the trendy thin-crust-pizza spots that have been popping up across Chicago lately, many still come to the city for chewy, gooey deep-dish pizza.

WHAT ARE THE BEST STEAKHOUSES?
Gene & Georgetti *(page 67)* This timeless Italian steakhouse has resided in the shadow of the El since 1941. The atmosphere isn't much (apart from old photos on the wall) and the waiters aren't known for their geniality, but you'll forget all that the second you dig into the juicy wet-aged New York strip or the 18-ounce filet that stands some four inches tall.

Gibsons *(page 60)* It may be a scene but the steaks at Gibsons are some of the best in town: thick, juicy and cooked to perfection.

SIXTEEN

There are many arguments about whose stuffed pizza is the best, but no matter who's doing the rating, Pizzeria Uno is almost always near the top. This standby—which actually served the world's first stuffed pizza, back in the 1940s—draws huge crowds, and it's not exactly spacious, so either arrive early (the restaurant doesn't take reservations) or be prepared for a long wait for a table (which will likely be cramped). But oh, how it's worth the wait: The cheese is melty, the tomato sauce is sweet but has a nice zip of garlic, and the crust is slightly crunchy. You'll quickly tune out the tourists that surround you as you dig in.

Pizza. Lunch, dinner. $16-35

★★★★SIXTEEN

401 N. Wabash Ave., River North, 312-924-7600;
www.trumpchicagohotel.com

As you might expect, everything at Sixteen (on the 16th floor of Donald Trump's hotel) is larger-than-life. The hostesses dress like they're about to walk down a Paris runway. The views of the city through the floor-to-ceiling windows are dazzling (and the ceiling in one of the three dining rooms is 30 feet high). Then there's the food. Chef Frank Brunacci meticulously crafts entrées like Duck Percik with two duck breasts in a date-and-kumquat chutney with black cumin, and prime tenderloin with snail ravioli and horseradish risotto. The desserts, which include Pierce Neige (a chestnut meringue accompanied by port-wine ice cream and port reduction), take so much effort that it's recommended you order them at the start of your meal. All of this is almost enough to take your eyes off the gargantuan chandelier, which comprises more than 19,000 Swarovski crystals, or the views, which, from the 16th floor in the city's best location, are larger than life.

Contemporary American. Breakfast (Sunday-Friday), lunch (Monday-Saturday), dinner, Sunday brunch. Reservations recommended. Bar. $86 and up

---

WHICH RESTAURANTS HAVE THE BEST VIEWS?

Everest *(page 78)* Appropriately located on the 40th floor of the Chicago Stock Exchange, its magnificent city views (framed by floor-to-ceiling drapes) are a perfect companion for the highbrow Alsatian cuisine.

NoMI *(page 61)* The beautiful space, which offers stunning views of Michigan Avenue and the Water Tower across the street, is particular festive during the holidays when the lights on Michigan Avenue make everything twinkle.

Sixteen *(page 73)* Located on the 16th floor of Donald Trump's hotel, the views of the city through the floor-to-ceiling windows are dazzling (and the ceiling in one of the three dining rooms is 30 feet high).

★★★SHANGHAI TERRACE
The Peninsula Chicago, 108 E. Superior St., River North, 312-573-6695; www.chicago.peninsula.com

The main draw at the intimate Shanghai Terrace isn't the generous menu, with its emphasis on meticulous dim sum creations, or the elegantly appointed dining room with black lacquer chairs and daring red trim. The best reason to come here is the outdoor deck, with its stunning view of the soaring buildings that surround The Peninsula hotel. The alfresco area provides the perfect place to enjoy chef Thi Ting's delicious fare, which features a dim sum sampler that includes spicy beef gyoza and foie gras and lobster dumplings. For a more complete meal, you can't go wrong with the traditional Peking duck, which includes five courses.
Asian. Lunch, dinner. Closed Sunday. Bar. $36-85

★★★TOPOLOBAMPO
445 N. Clark St., River North, 312-661-1434; www.rickbayless.com

You can't turn on a TV today without seeing chef Rick Bayless work his culinary magic with Mexican food—the ubiquitous chef from Chicago even won *Top Chef Masters*. But you don't have to just stare in awe if you make the trip to Topolobampo, the sleek, multicolored restaurant that serves Bayless' inventive cuisine with a monthly changing menu. Bayless isn't always in the kitchen (chef Brian Enyart is the man in the toque here), but Bayless' influence is all over the menu that uses sustainably raised veggies, meat and fish to craft stunningly imaginative Oaxacan cuisine. Favorites include Puerco Pibil, achiote-marinated Maple Creek Farm pork served as a grill-roasted loin and a slow-cooked shoulder in banana leaves, and langosto al mojo de ajo, pan-roasted Maine lobster served with olive oil-poached garlic, giant butter beans and roasted fresh favas. It's the furthest thing from a taquería, but it's a lot more memorable.
Mexican, Southwestern. Lunch (Tuesday-Friday), dinner. Closed Sunday-Monday. Reservations recommended. $36-85

LOOP/WEST LOOP
★★★ARIA
The Fairmont Chicago, 200 N. Columbus Dr., Loop, 312-444-9494; www.ariachicago.com

Technically, Aria is located inside the Fairmont hotel, just east of tony Michigan Avenue. But the fact that the restaurant has its own entrance symbolizes how chef Brad Parsons wants his eclectic spot to separate itself

THE PUBLICAN

from the norm. The globally influenced restaurant boasts its own tandoori oven for naan bread, and a hip sushi bar draws a lively crowd of saketini sippers. Those who want a globe-spanning culinary experience will have a great time in the dramatic dining room, which is filled with orchids and Tibetan artwork. The menu ranges from shrimp and chicken pad thai to a perfectly prepared New York strip steak to Hong Kong barbecue duck and lobster chow mein. The menu is all over the map, but it works.
International. Breakfast, lunch, dinner. Bar. $36-85

★★★ATWOOD CAFÉ
Hotel Burnham, 1 W. Washington St., Loop,
312-368-1900; www.atwoodcafe.com
You can't get much more centrally located than the Atwood Café, which sits in the heart of the action of Chicago's Loop and provides floor-to-ceiling views of bustling State Street. And you can't get much more comfortable than the food on the Atwood Café's menu, which presents new takes on classic American standbys. Chef Heather Terhune prepares dishes like a huge Comport Family Farm pork chop served with vanilla-honey peach jam, and a tender grilled filet mignon with truffle butter and port wine sauce. She also wins plaudits for her dessert menu, which includes perfectly made classics such as scrumptious dark-chocolate soufflé cake and warm roasted banana and white chocolate bread pudding. The expansive bar serves as an ideal place for a drink before heading to the nearby Theater District (we told you it was centrally located) for a show.
Contemporary American. Breakfast, lunch, dinner, Sunday brunch. $36-85

★★★AVEC
615 W. Randolph St., West Loop, 312-377-2002;
www.avecrestaurant.com
Avec means "with" in French, which fits here because you're likely to end up dining with complete strangers at one of the communal tables. You won't mind, because the restaurant's Euro-Mediterranean fare and surprisingly

EVEREST

reasonable prices put you in such a good mood that you're happy to talk with your neighbors about the amazing food in front of you. Co-owned by chef Paul Kahan (better known for Blackbird, Avec's sister restaurant next door), Avec offers delicious fare such as the popular chorizo-stuffed madjool dates wrapped in smoked bacon and topped with a piquillo pepper-tomato sauce, and the crispy focaccia with taleggio cheese, truffle oil and fresh herbs. The menu, which is divided into large and small plates, is always changing, which means this restaurant is worth a trip every time you're in town. The small room looks almost sauna-like with its fully paneled cedar walls and ceiling, and its back display of glass wine bottles is both colorful and whimsical. Speaking of bottles, Avec offers some 125 wines from France, Italy, Spain and Portugal; we recommend buying a bottle to share with the newfound friends you'll undoubtedly meet at your table.

Contemporary American, Mediterranean. Dinner. Bar. $36-85

★★★BLACKBIRD
619 W. Randolph St., West Loop, 312-715-0708;
www.blackbirdrestaurant.com

In an almost sacrilegious move, Blackbird's main man Paul Kahan recently handed over the apron at this spot to Mike Sheerin, formerly of New York's famed WD-50. It's not just that Kahan, who was named the James Beard Foundation's Best Chef in the Midwest in 2004, surrendered control—it's also that Sheerin has brought a slight element of playfulness to Kahan's solid menu. Now, for instance, the short ribs come with sesame gnocchi and ground cherries and the "fried" chicken comes with smoked potato salad. Foodies love it just as much as they always have. As for the restaurant itself, it's sleek and minimalist—but it's not exactly roomy. Tables are packed tightly together, but you won't mind overhearing a few conversations for food of this caliber.

Contemporary American. Lunch (Monday-Friday), dinner. Closed Sunday. Reservations recommended. $36-85

WHAT ARE SOME GREAT ETHNIC RESTAURANTS?
Some of the city's most popular eateries are nothing-to-look-at places that serve the most deliciously authentic (and inexpensive) food. Here are a few to try on your next visit to Chicago.

90 Miles Cuban Café
3101 N. Clybourn Ave., Roscoe Village, 773-248-2822;
www.90milescubancafe.com
Named after the number of miles between Miami and Cuba, this place is the closest you'll get to Little Havana from Chicago. The tiny spot, located west of Lakeview, specializes in classics like Cubanos (panini-style traditional Cuban sandwiches made of ham, roasted pork, Swiss cheese, mustard and pickles) and heavenly guava and cheese pastries. Throw down the house café con leche, and you'll be wired for days.

Borinquen
1720 N. California Ave., Humboldt Park, 773-227-6038;
www.borinquenjibaro.com
This Puerto Rican eatery—which sits in a predominantly Puerto Rican neighborhood west of Wicker Park—is so hot, it has opened two other locations. But this, the original, is still the most popular, for it's here that the café's famed jibarito—a steak sandwich in which crunchy pounded plantains stand in for bread slices—was born.

Irazú
1865 N. Milwaukee Ave., Bucktown, 773-252-5687;
www.irazuchicago.com
This Costa Rican gem has been a Bucktown fave since before the boutiques moved in, and it's easy to see—rather, taste—how the tiny restaurant stays in business. Don't leave without trying the thick, cinnamon-sprinkled oatmeal shake, the refreshing and hearty heart of palm salad, and the perfectly fried sweet plantains.

Lao Szechuan
2172 S. Archer Ave., Chinatown, 312-326-5040;
www.tonygourmetgroup.com
Local foodies head to this no-frills Szechuan in droves for the crispy eggplant with pork, ma po tofu and signature "chef's special" dry chili chicken (an addictive blend of wok-fried chicken, hot chili peppers, garlic and ginger). Chow down on the latter with plenty of cooling, complimentary tea, and you'll feel just like a regular.

Nuevo León
1515 W. 18th St., Pilsen, 312-421-1517; www.nuevoleonrestaurant.com
The neighborhood of Pilsen is home to a sizable Mexican-American population and a growing art community. Both collide at this 47-year-old Mexican eatery. The harried waitstaff brings out a savory amuse-bouche while you peruse a menu teeming with classics, such as tamales and chorizo tacos. On Sundays, neighborhood regulars fill the seats for restorative menudo, a traditional Mexican tripe soup said to help with hangovers.

Pho Xe Tang
4953 N. Broadway, Uptown, 773-878-2253
Most locals refer to this low-key but always-packed Vietnamese noodle house as Tank. We call it heaven in winter, thanks to the hearty, warming house specialty: pho, a Vietnamese soup that comes with meat (if you so desire), plus plates of add-ons like fresh lime, basil, chilies and sprouts.

CHARLIE TROTTER'S

★★★CUSTOM HOUSE
500 S. Dearborn St., Loop, 312-523-0200; www.customhouse.cc
This elegantly low-key Printers Row spot has a Zen-like feel with its decorations of pebbles, twigs and rocks, but the menu is all meat, all the time (save for some seafood). Appetizers include Wagyu beef tartare with potato chips and farm fresh egg, and rich veal sweetbreads with glazed bacon and mushrooms. Be sure to save room for the entrées, which feature such perfectly crafted steaks as a tender flatiron cut with onion rings, and a tender bone in short rib with horseradish cream puffs. If you have a finicky vegetarian in your group, don't despair; the chef will indeed make a special meal for him or her, proving that the restaurant is indeed aptly named. (At press time, there was talk of this restaurant being recast as a tavern.)
Steak. Lunch, dinner. Reservations recommended. Bar. $36-85

★★★★EVEREST
440 S. LaSalle St., Loop, 312-663-8920; www.everestrestaurant.com
It takes a certain bravado to name a restaurant after the tallest mountain in the world—the damning reviews practically write themselves. Thankfully, chef Jean Joho's Everest has scaled the culinary heights and remains perched at the top of Chicago's fine-dining realm. Appropriately located on the 40th floor of the Chicago Stock Exchange, its magnificent city views (framed by floor-to-ceiling drapes) are a perfect companion for Joho's highbrow Alsatian cuisine. Served by an exceedingly polite waitstaff clad in suits, the menu includes a filet of wild sturgeon wrapped and roasted in cured ham, and venison served with wild huckleberries and braised pear. It's safe to say that a night at Everest will leave you feeling, well, on top of the world.
French. Dinner. Closed Sunday-Monday. $86 and up

WHICH RESTAURANTS ARE BEST FOR A LIVELY SCENE?

Avec *(page 75)* This tiny restaurant fills up every night with locals and in-the-know visitors who talk about what to order at the communal tables. Servers are dressed in jeans, wine is served in stemless glassware and some of the seats are really just stools—but it's all part of the casual charm.

Gibsons *(page 60)* Gibsons fills up every night of the week with people looking for a fishbowl-sized martini and a giant steaks.

Japonais *(page 68)* When you're enjoying Japanese-French fusion next to some of the city's most stylish foodies, you'll see why Japonais remains one of the hottest tables in town. Gently thumping lounge music and chic décor provide a perfect environment for the glammed-up crowd that can be found sipping colorful drinks in the downstairs lounge and outdoor patio.

Landmark *(page 84)* With its striking décor and boisterous crowd, you'd forgive the owners of Landmark if they concentrated a little less on the food. But it's equally worth going here for the barbecue glazed pork chop and braised short ribs, so go early.

Nacional 27 *(page 72)* In a large, dramatic space, Nacional 27 offers Nuevo Latino fare along with cocktails such as spiked apple cider. The restaurant's resident DJ will get you on the floor with weekend salsa and merengue music.

★★THE GAGE
24 S. Michigan Ave., Loop, 312-372-4243; www.thegagechicago.com
From the elk ragout poutine to the Bison tartare to the roast elk with butter poached apples and ricotta, the Gage's pub grub is anything but common. Even the good ol' fish and chips get dressed up—in newspaper. The fringe-hugging menu combined with the hopping happy hour singles scene drew Christian Bale in while he was on location in the Windy City shooting *The Dark Knight*. Lunchtime service can get bogged down with larger groups meeting for business. Go elsewhere for a quick bite.
Gastropub. Lunch, dinner, Saturday-Sunday brunch. Bar. $36-85

★★★MARCHÉ
833 W. Randolph St., West Loop, 312-226-8399;
www.marche-chicago.com
Marché is hardly what you call subtle: Its light-filled dining room is packed with flamboyant touches, from gargantuan red lampshades hanging from the high ceilings to large metal bookshelves teeming with antique cameras and globes. But there's some serious culinary work going on behind the Moulin Rouge décor—the open kitchen gives you the opportunity to see chef Matt Tobin prepare dishes like his adored duck à la Montmorency, which is grilled over apple and cherry wood. The classic French menu also features standbys like moules mariniere and a lamb shank with sour cream whipped potatoes, while the dessert options include a decadent plat à trois chocolats and a sumptuous classic crème brûlée. Come hungry, and come early unless you enjoy a little rowdiness with your frites—this place gets boisterous as the night goes on.
French. Lunch (Monday-Friday), dinner. Bar. $36-85

SCOTCH QUAIL EGG AT BLACKBIRD

★★★MOTO

945 W. Fulton Market, West Loop, 312-491-0058;
www.motorestaurant.com

Moto's brilliant chef Homaro Cantu has repeatedly said he wants his customers to play with their food. But sometimes, when facing the concoction the renowned chef has created, the desire is to stare in awe rather than disrupt such a lavish creation. Cantu's whimsical dinners begin with an edible menu (vegetable inks on modified food starch) and go on to include 10 to 20 courses, which may include inverted pumpkin pie or instant risotto. Some of Cantu's more celebrated dishes have included veal breast served with rice and runner beans, and fish cooked in an insulated box at the table. As you might expect, the presentation is both outrageous and practical. The "toro, sturgeon caviar, and utensil study," for instance, features a piece of tuna dabbed with caviar, served on a custom-made utensil for which the stem has been hollowed out and filled with fresh thyme. Playful? Certainly. Sublime? Absolutely.

International. Dinner. Closed Sunday-Monday. Reservations recommended. Bar. $86 and up

★★★N9NE

440 W. Randolph St., West Loop, 312-575-9900;
www.n9negroup.com

With its subtly changing light scheme and cosmo-sipping, air-kissing crowd, the slick N9NE occasionally gets criticized for being more of a scene than a restaurant (albeit one with a hip club, Ghostbar, on the second floor). Whoever says that likely hasn't delved into the menu, which features huge, prime-aged steaks and chops, augmented with a Maine lobster tail or Alaskan crab legs for a reasonable $23. There's also a wide array of seafood options, including a miso-marinated cod with scallions and shiitake mushrooms. Bolstering the restaurant's argument is a caviar service, offering Russian caviar by the ounce. But would a steakhouse dedicated only to the see-and-be-seen crowd offer a $26 hamburger? They must be doing something right, as this spot begat the N9NE/Ghost Bar in Las Vegas and Dallas.

Steak. Lunch (Monday-Friday), dinner. Closed Sunday. $36-85

★★★ONE SIXTYBLUE
1400 W. Randolph St., West Loop, 312-850-0303;
www.onesixtyblue.com

For many Chicagoans, One Sixtyblue is known only as the restaurant that features Michael Jordan as one of the owners. He's still known to occasionally drop in, which is enough to bring in a crowd hoping to shake hands with His Royal Airness. For everyone else, the French-Mediterranean cuisine—which perfectly matches the quiet, romantic atmosphere of this converted former pickle factory—is the reason to eat here. Starters include a pork belly carbonara, and entrées feature show-stoppers like pork loin with picked peach purée, and the flat iron steak with black-eyed peas and pickled okra. Even if you don't spot MJ, you'll be glad you stopped by—especially if you happen to catch one of the restaurant's many specials (at press time, Wednesday nights were all about fried chicken and champagne).

Contemporary American. Dinner. Closed Sunday. Bar. $36-85

★★★OTOM
951 W. Fulton Market, West Loop, 312-491-5804;
www.otomrestaurant.com

The lower-priced, less-formal sister of haute cuisine standby Moto, Otom is a lively mix of minimalist elegance and playful mod, with orange plastic chairs and orange tableside flowers contrasting with the exposed brick walls. Décor aside, Otom stands out for its cuisine: Salmon ceviche on crispy wontons makes a perfect light start to the meal, and chef Thomas Elliot Bowman crafts clever fare for his entrées. There's the "TV Dinner," which comprises chicken-fried duck confit, carrot and edamame pie, and the wildly popular fried beef cheek ravioli with saffron-parsnip purée. Despite its proximity to its more-famous sibling, Otom's moderate prices, unique atmosphere and excellent food make it a spot worthy of standing on its own.

Contemporary American. Dinner. Closed Sunday. $36-85

★★★THE PUBLICAN
837 W. Fulton Market, West Loop, 312-733-9555;
www.thepublicanrestaurant.com

At the Publican, the tastemakers behind Blackbird and Avec have turned their focus to pork, oysters and beer. The space resembles a swank German beer hall. If you want privacy, ask for one of the walnut booths, which have small salon doors. Dishes are served as soon as they are ready, so be prepared to share or steal as your boudin blanc may arrive prior to your date's massive porchetta or pork rinds. The frites with the sunny side egg may be tempting, but go for the addictive aioli instead. The family-style Sunday dinners are a great way to try the restaurant. One recent menu featured a salad with a pancetta, basil and a poached farm egg, mussels with pork confit, whole roasted pig, and butterscotch pudding for dessert.

Gastropub. Lunch, dinner, Sunday brunch. $36-85

PERENNIAL

★★SANTORINI

800 W. Adams St., West Loop, 312-829-8820;
www.santorinichicago.com

Chicago's Greektown is packed with restaurants that make a solid spana-
kopita and serve a decent flaming saganaki. But the rustic Santorini stands
apart from the crowd with its fresh seafood, white walls with dark wood trim,
and bi-level dining room featuring a large fireplace. The spot serves excellent
versions of Greek standards, like melt-in-your-mouth center-cut lamb chops
and juicy chicken baked with vegetables and zesty feta cheese in phyllo
dough. The true don't-miss entrées here are the grilled octopus (a house
specialty) and whole fish such as tender red snapper, which can be fileted
tableside and served in a tangy simple sauce of olive oil and lemon juice.
Greek. Lunch, dinner. $36-85

★★★SEPIA

123 N. Jefferson St., West Loop, 312-441-1920;
www.sepiachicago.com

A relative newcomer to the Chicago dining scene, Sepia wasted no time
creating a deafening buzz in its already-happening West Loop neighborhood. Situated inside an 1890s print shop, Sepia's décor craftily mixes the
old and new, much like contemporary American dishes rooted in tradition,
including the pork porterhouse with bourbon, peaches and grits and the
chicken with panzanella salad. Liquor aficionados flock here for the creative
cocktails, which feature handmade syrups and bitters.
Contemporary American. Lunch (Monday-Friday), dinner. $36-85

★★SUSHI WABI

842 W. Randolph St., West Loop, 312-563-1224; www.sushiwabi.com

From the industrial-chic exposed ductwork to the DJ spinning tunes
above the dimly lit dining room, Sushi Wabi feels as much like a club
as it does one of Chicago's most popular sushi restaurants. For every
hipster reveling in the loft atmosphere and cool tunes, there's a sushi

aficionado delving into the restaurant's fresh fish and unique creations. The maki rolls include the tried-and-true, from an expertly crafted dragon roll brushed with eel sauce to decadent specialties like the Tarantula, which bursts with soft-shell crab, avocado, chili sauce and masago mayo. Leave room for the green-tea cheesecake, which may be the world's most delicious way to enjoy antioxidants.

Japanese. Lunch (Monday-Friday), dinner. Bar. $16-35

★★TRATTORIA NO. 10
10 N. Dearborn St., Loop, 312-984-1718; www.trattoriaten.com

Given its Loop location and subterranean, Old World feel, it's surprising to learn that Trattoria No. 10 chef Douglas D'Avico is fairly progressive with his menu: He features organic and locally grown ingredients in items like handcrafted ravioli filled with asparagus tips and aged provolone topped with sun-dried tomato sauce, and butternut and acorn squash in a sweet walnut-butter sauce. Although it's big with the lunch crowd, Trattoria No. 10's low ceilings, alfresco-style murals and textured walls help the restaurant overcome its substreet-level locale and create romantic, cozy environs for dinner in a decidedly non-cozy neighborhood.

Italian. Lunch (Monday-Friday), dinner. Closed Sunday. $36-85

LINCOLN PARK
★★★★★ALINEA
1723 N. Halsted St., Lincoln Park, 312-867-0110;
www.alinea-restaurant.com

Not only did Alinea's internationally respected chef Grant Achatz win the 2008 James Beard Outstanding Chef Award, he's also got a hell of a story to tell. In 2007, Achatz was diagnosed with tongue cancer, and doctors said he might lose his sense of taste forever. Thankfully, an aggressive treatment looks to have beaten the cancer, and Achatz's sense of taste was saved. So now he's back in the kitchen, creating some of the most wildly creative dishes in the country. Alinea, the Latin word for that funny little symbol (¶) indicating the need for a new paragraph—or a new train of thought—is at the forefront of the molecular gastronomy movement, which re-imagines

---

WHICH RESTAURANTS SERVE THE BEST PIZZA?

Coalfire *(page 88)* Will thin-crust replace deep-dish as the quintessential Chicago pizza? This acclaimed pizza restaurant aims to claim its place as the city's preferred pie.

Crust *(page 91)* Using organic flour and ingredients including fresh-pulled water buffalo mozzarella, Altenberg coaxes delicious pizzas from the tile-encrusted wood-burning oven.

La Madia *(page 70)* The heavenly pies served at this contemporary pizzeria have a crispy and slightly chewy crust and come in such interesting combinations as triple pepperoni with truffle oil.

Piece *(page 92)* Piece serves huge rectangular pizzas featuring toppings that are both standard (pepperoni, onions) and not-so-standard (mashed potatoes, clams). Some of the combinations might sound strange but they somehow meld perfectly with the pizza's crunchy thin crust and tangy tomato sauce.

familiar foods in stunningly innovative ways. Behind the restaurant's purposefully hidden entrance and up a floating glass-and-metal staircase, you'll be treated to breathtaking creations such as the black truffle explosion, featuring truffle-topped ravioli filled with truffle broth which "explodes" in your mouth. Another dish is duck served with mango and yogurt on a pillow of juniper air. The complex meals often require equally complicated instructions from the patient waitstaff, but trust us—you won't complain.
Contemporary American. Dinner. Closed Monday-Tuesday. $86 and up

★★★★★CHARLIE TROTTER'S
816 W. Armitage Ave., Lincoln Park, 773-248-6228;
www.charlietrotters.com
There's not much about internationally renowned chef Charlie Trotter that hasn't already been said. Awards? He has them in spades. Books? He's written them. TV shows? He stars in a cooking series. Which brings us back to Trotter's food, and for that he uses only naturally raised meats, line-caught fish and organic produce to craft his world-famous fare. The formal waitstaff speak in hushed tones when talking about Trotter's exactingly prepared menu, which includes dishes such as chilled trout with watercress and crayfish, and Crawford Farm lamb rack with chanterelle mushrooms and fermented black garlic. Housed in an unassuming brick building in the tony Lincoln Park neighborhood, the understated restaurant—there is no art on the walls, as Trotter believes any art should be on the plate—provides a tasteful environment for what is always a remarkable evening. For those who want to see the restaurant's inner workings firsthand, Trotter's offers a table in the kitchen that comes with its own custom-prepared menu.
Contemporary American. Dinner. Closed Sunday-Monday. $86 and up

★★★★L2O
2300 N. Lincoln Park West, Lincoln Park, 773-868-0002;
www.l2orestaurant.com
L2O has big shoes to fill: The restaurant resides in the space formerly taken up by Ambria, a longtime Chicago favorite. But award-winning chef Laurent Gras is up to the challenge, offering a French-oriented seafood menu that's as sophisticated as the restaurant's beautiful décor, with the dining room separated by partitions of stainless-steel cables. The menu is divided into Raw, Warm and Main sections, with the four-course tasting option offering one of each, plus a dessert. The generous selections range from fluke with lemon vinegar, caviar and basil seeds to black bass in shellfish bouillon with saffron and Rhode Island mussels. Even the bread service is memorable, with offerings of bacon croissants, anchovy twists and demi-baguettes served with housemade butter. To get an idea of Gras's meticulous nature, seize the opportunity to take the optional tour of the painstakingly clean kitchen—and keep an eye out for his astounding array of spices.
French, Contemporary American. Dinner. Closed Tuesday. $86 and up

★★★LANDMARK
1633 N. Halsted St., Lincoln Park, 312-587-1600;
www.landmarkgrill.net
With its striking décor and boisterous crowd, you'd forgive the owners of Landmark (who also run nearby Perennial and Boka) if they concentrated a little less on the food. But chef Kurt Guzowski ensures the fare remains a priority at this massive Lincoln Park favorite, committing to the details on his

ALINEA

wide-ranging menu. Appetizer options include smoked ravioli with braised pork belly, and Kobe beef sliders with truffles, foie gras and Moroccan ketchup. Entrées including a lobster club sandwich and grilled black pepper ribeye with blue cheese potato gratin. We recommend going earlier in the evening, because the place gets packed at night with a throng that's clearly not there for the food.

Contemporary American. Dinner. Closed Monday. Bar. $16-35

★★★NORTH POND

2610 N. Cannon Drive, Lincoln Park, 773-477-5845;
www.northpondrestaurant.com

Talk about off the beaten path: North Pond is situated in the middle of a pastoral setting in Lincoln Park, surrounded by trees and blocks away from the neighborhood's occasionally lunkheaded bar scene. The restaurant's gorgeous Prairie-style building—originally built in 1912 as a lodge for ice-skaters—overlooks a small pond and provides a stunning view of the Chicago skyline. Almost as impeccable is chef Bruce Sherman's sustainable-minded fare, which emphasizes seasonal local items in specialties such as oil-poached Alaskan halibut with smoked caviar, and Dijon-crusted rib eye with roasted farro. Sherman puts the Web sites of local nonprofits on his menu, but with a meal this delicious—capped by the chocolate-cherry dessert that boasts a decadent chocolate panna cotta with bing cherries and red beet sorbet—you'll put up with a little political grandstanding.

Contemporary American. Lunch (June-September, Wednesday-Friday), dinner (closed Monday-Tuesday from January-April), Sunday brunch. $36-85

★★★PERENNIAL

1800 N. Lincoln Ave., Lincoln Park, 312-981-7070;
www.perennialchicago.com

One thing has become clear with the recent opening of Perennial: Lincoln Park has a new hot spot. The masterminds behind Chicago fixtures Boka and Landmark have transformed this space—formerly an unimaginative chain bar/restaurant—into a must-visit scene. With its canvas ceiling, birch trees in the center of the room, and floor-to-ceiling windows, Perennial's décor is as inviting as the perpetually smiling staff and the thoughtful cuisine prepared by chef Ryan Poli. The menu features crispy duck breast with herb bread pudding, braised red cabbage, chestnuts and foie gras emulsion, and housemade linguini carbornara that's worth every fat gram. The adjacent lounge provides an elegant spot for a post-dinner drink—provided you can get a seat, that is.

Contemporary American. Dinner. Bar. $36-85

★★SAI CAFÉ

2010 N. Sheffield Ave., Lincoln Park, 773-472-8080; www.saicafe.com

There are plenty of neighborhood sushi restaurants in Chicago, but few offer fish that's as fresh—and generously portioned—as this Lincoln Park standby. The menu offers several different entrées, but it's the sushi that packs people into the restaurant's three laid-back rooms. Any of the sushi creations will delight you, but the rainbow maki with tuna, yellowtail, salmon and avocado delicately wrapped around rice and a crab stick is particularly fresh and delicious.

Japanese. Dinner. $36-85

WHICH RESTAURANTS HAVE THE MOST CUTTING-EDGE FOOD?

Alinea *(page 83)* Some people call it sci-fi food. Chef Grant Achatz's food is indeed high-tech. The chef endlessly plays with food—the textures, the aromas, the flavors—as if he were in a chem lab, and yet it somehow manages to all feel familiar at the same time.

Avenues *(page 64)* Chef Curtis Duffy offers cuisine that manages to be both simple and extravagant. He favors unusual pairings that work despite seeming contradictory, such as the grilled Wagyu steak with smoked coconut and African blue basil.

L20 *(page 84)* Chef Laurent Gras offers a French-oriented seafood menu in which hard-to-find varieties are prepared in interesting ways, say, lobster that has been vacuum-cooked or snapper smoked over cherry wood.

Moto *(page 80)* Chef Homaro Cantu of Moto keeps liquid nitrogen, helium and organic food-based inks sitting alongside pots, pans and spoons. After you order, the rice-paper menu itself is the first course (it tastes like risotto).

Scwha *(page 93)* Maverick chef Michael Carlson is bare bones—tiny room, no liquor license, the cooks also serve as the waitstaff—but the food is remarkably innovative. Carlson offers three- and nine-course menus that feature knockout dishes such as a savory beer cheese soup with a pretzel roll, and a gently-seared kona kampachi with galangal, lime and a tiny splash of maple syrup.

SEPIA

LINCOLN SQUARE/ANDERSONVILLE/NORTHWEST SIDE

★★★ARUN'S
4156 N. Kedzie Ave., Northwest Side, 773-539-1909;
www.arunsthai.com

Thai cuisine in Chicago was once consigned to BYOB storefronts, but owner Arun Sampanthavivat's gorgeous restaurant, which he opened in 1985, brought his native land's food to the level of haute cuisine. The 2,500-square-foot, bi-level dining room—its every nook and cranny filled with gorgeous Thai art (much of it painted by the owner's brother)—is located in far-flung Albany Park. The almost museum-like surroundings complement a dining experience that brilliantly combines heat and sweetness. The constantly changing offerings are part of a 12-course tasting menu consisting of six appetizers, four entrées and two desserts, and preparations range from a beef curry in a spicy sauce to whole tamarind snapper. The personable service is always ready to accommodate any preferences or tolerance for spiciness, and a meticulous wine-pairing is available for the asking.
Thai. Dinner. Closed Monday. $86 and up

★★★BISTRO CAMPAGNE
4518 N. Lincoln Ave., Lincoln Square, 773-271-6100;
www.bistrocampagne.com

We know this Lincoln Square bistro isn't exactly centrally situated, but the classic French fare and immaculate wine list make the cozy neighborhood spot well worth the trip to the North Side. Acclaimed chef Michael Altenberg is a vocal sustainable-food advocate, so he uses local, organic ingredients to create dishes like his flawless pan-seared salmon with braised lentils and succulent steak piled high with delicious fries. We can't talk about Bistro Campagne—let alone visit here—without mentioning Altenberg's steamed mussels, served in a tasty Belgian ale. The restaurant itself has a rustic feel with Prairie-style design touches and dark wood trim, while the outdoor space provides a beautiful mosaic fountain and a quaint cottage for a

secluded retreat.
French. Dinner, Sunday brunch. Bar. $36-85

★★★SOLA
3868 N. Lincoln Ave., Northwest Side, 773-327-3868;
www.sola-restaurant.com

Drawing inspiration from the sun (sol), her own independence (solo) and her roots (she's so L.A., as her friends joke), chef/owner and former surfer Carol Wallack dove headfirst into Chicago's dining scene when she opened Sola in January 2006. Wallack's focus is on freshness, so she sources all her produce from local farmers and all her seafood from Hawaii. Perhaps you'll find the culmination of these ingredients brought to your table in the form of a salad of Asian greens, housemade bacon, pineapple, rosemary and black vinegar; or halibut atop a bed of soy beluga lentils and wilted watercress, dressed with a lobster butter sauce. If these inventive takes on island-style dishes aren't enough to make you feel like wearing a grass skirt in Chicago, nothing will be.

Contemporary American, Hawaiian. Lunch (Thursday-Friday), dinner, Saturday-Sunday brunch. $36-85

UKRAINIAN VILLAGE/WEST TOWN
★COALFIRE
1321 W. Grand Ave., West Town, 312-226-2625;
www.coalfirechicago.com

Chicago's reputation is changing dramatically these days: No one talks about Al Capone anymore, the Cubs are actually a good team and the city's pizza fans aren't all heading out for deep dish. The unassuming, relatively new Coalfire is a big reason for this last shift. This restaurant bakes its pies in a coal-heated oven, which produces an eyebrow-singeing temperature of 800 degrees. This high heat produces a smoky, slightly charred crust that's both crispy and chewy, while the housemade tomato sauce has the perfect amount of sweetness. The surprisingly spartan list of toppings includes prosciutto, red peppers and anchovies, but regulars swear by the simple margherita, which is made up of sauce, fresh buffalo mozzarella, ricotta and freshly cut basil leaves.

Pizza. Lunch (Saturday-Sunday), dinner. Closed Monday. $16-35

WHAT ARE THE BEST NEIGHBORHOOD RESTAURANTS?

Bistro Campagne *(page 87)* We know this Lincoln Square bistro isn't exactly centrally situated, but the classic French fare and immaculate wine list make the cozy neighborhood spot well worth the trip to the North Side.

Le Bouchon *(page 91)* There's a reason this tiny storefront bistro has been packing in a crowd of regulars for more than 15 years: The food is delicious, the prices are reasonable, the mood is convivial, and the feeling is somehow unmistakably Parisian.

West Town Tavern *(page 89)* The contemporary American cuisine with a comfort-food touch is wonderful, and the specials—especially the fried chicken on Monday nights—can't be beat.

★★★GREEN ZEBRA

1460 W. Chicago Ave., Ukrainian Village, 312-243-7100;
www.greenzebrachicago.com

Vegetarians often feel like they get a raw deal at restaurants, with maybe a token eggplant dish tossed their way at the corner of the menu. Not so at Green Zebra, chef Shawn McClain's small-plates ode to non-carnivores. After all, even a filet fanatic would get hooked on slow-roasted shiitake mushrooms in a crispy potato with savoy cabbage, or grilled asparagus with Camembert beignets. The elegant, earth-toned décor is more upscale than granola; you're more likely to hear Joy Division than the Grateful Dead, and the service is efficient and refined. If you simply must eat meat, there are one or two non-vegetarian items on the menu—though considering the diverse and delicious plant-based options, why settle for chicken?

Contemporary vegetarian. Dinner, Sunday brunch. $16-35

★★★WEST TOWN TAVERN

1329 W. Chicago Ave., West Town, 312-666-6175;
www.westtowntavern.com

You can get fried chicken just about anywhere, but for Susan Goss' great-grandmother's tried-and-true recipe, you have to come to the West Town Tavern. Co-owner Goss breaks out the recipe every week for the popular Fried Chicken (and Biscuit) Mondays, while serious carnivores make weekly pilgrimages here for the juicy, 10-ounce Wagyu beef creations (served on grilled focaccia with herbed mayo and grilled onions) on Burger Tuesdays. The restaurant's blond wood floors, exposed brick and warm lighting also provide a welcoming environment for the tavern's delicious contemporary American cuisine with a comfort-food touch, such as the pot roast that's braised in zinfandel, and the gently seared diver scallops served with a delicate mushroom-leek risotto.

Contemporary American. Dinner. Closed Sunday. Bar. $36-85

BUCKTOWN/WICKER PARK

★★★BOB SAN
1805-07 W. Division St., Wicker Park, 773-235-8888;
www.bob-san.com

Bob San's owner Bob Bee has created a veritable sushi empire throughout Chicago, giving the city fixtures like Sai Café, Sushi Naniwa and Hachi's Kitchen. But it's Wicker Park's bustling Bob San that's earned Bee his biggest buzz. The restaurant features lively lounge music, an open wooden-beam ceiling and playful fish-shaped lighting fixtures. But the focus here is the expansive menu, which features some 45 handcrafted rolls that include classics like the spider roll with soft-shell crab, avocado and cucumber. There are also a dozen entrées for non-sushi eaters, including a teriyaki New York strip steak. The tables are packed closely together, so if you're hoping for a romantic meal, try to get one of the tables by the window, close to the bar.
Japanese. Dinner. Bar. $36-85

★★BONGO ROOM
1470 N. Milwaukee Ave., Wicker Park, 773-489-0690; 1152 S. Wabash Ave., South Loop, 312-291-0100

If you're looking for an imaginative breakfast in a playful environment, you'd better head to the Bongo Room early. Even 30 minutes before the doors open, the sidewalk outside this Wicker Park standby is packed with hungover urbanites anxiously awaiting a table. The breakfast burrito filled with guacamole and fluffy scrambled eggs is a favorite, but most come here for the outrageously sweet concoctions that mix breakfast with dessert, such as Oreo cookie pancakes or chocolate tower French toast. The spot is a little less crowded when lunchtime rolls around, when the kitchen offers inventive fare like a tasty maple-and-mustard-roasted pork loin sandwich and a delectable baby spinach, golden beet and duck confit salad. If you can't stomach the interminable brunch wait, try the South Loop location, where it's slightly—note, we said slightly—less crowded.
Contemporary American. Breakfast, lunch, Saturday-Sunday brunch. $16-35

★★CAFÉ ABSINTHE
1958 W. North Ave., Wicker Park, 773-278-4488;
www.cafeabsinthechicago.com

It's telling that the entrance to this Wicker Park fave is not on teeming North Avenue but in an alley around the corner. The off-the-beaten-path entry likely keeps the tippling masses from stumbling in and disrupting the restaurant's dimly lit, romantic atmosphere. Chef Jose Garcia's seasonal, American-oriented menu changes daily, but a recent incarnation featured Australian herb-marinated lamb with sautéed watercress and rosemary jus, and horseradish-encrusted salmon with garlic mashed potatoes and cabernet butter sauce. The signature dessert is a dark chocolate lava cake infused with Grand Marnier liqueur in a prickly-pear sauce—a treat that's well worth a trip down any alley.
Contemporary American. Dinner. $36-85

NORTH POND

★★CRUST
2056 W. Division St., Wicker Park, 773-235-5511;
www.crustchicago.com

With its stark white-brick walls and orange plastic chairs, Crust sure doesn't seem like it's at the forefront of a revolution. Yet the spot, helmed by Bistro Campagne's Michael Altenberg, has created the Midwest's first certified organic restaurant. Using organic flour and ingredients including fresh-pulled water buffalo mozzarella, Altenberg coaxes delicious pizzas (inexplicably called "wood-oven flatbreads" on the menu) from the tile-encrusted wood-burning oven. The surprisingly small menu features only 12 options, but the possibilities include such gourmet combinations as the Carbonara—topped with roasted slab bacon, peas and an egg sunny-side up—and the Mexicali blues—with provolone, mozzarella, roasted shrimp, cilantro and pico de gallo. Even some of the beer offerings are organic, letting you get soused as sustainably as possible.

Pizza. Lunch, dinner. $16-35

★★LE BOUCHON
1958 N. Damen Ave., Bucktown, 773-862-6600;
www.lebouchonofchicago.com

There's a reason this tiny storefront bistro has been packing in a crowd of regulars for more than 15 years. The food is delicious, the prices are reasonable, the mood is convivial, and the feeling is somehow unmistakably Parisian. The menu reflects owner Jean-Claude Poilevey's French roots (he's a native of Burgundy); Le Bouchon features standbys such as a creamy housemade pâté, beef Bourguignon over mashed potatoes, and white-wine poached salmon with cucumber and tomato beurre blanc. The onion tart—a classic intermingling of crispy pastry and tangy caramelized onions—is a signature dish. The closely packed tables and noisy room aren't for everyone, but those who seek out Le Bouchon's authentic environs will likely be glad they made the effort.

French. Lunch, dinner. Closed Sunday. $16-35

SPRING

★★★MIRAI SUSHI

2020 W. Division St., Wicker Park, 773-862-8500; www.miraisushi.com

Need to impress a sashimi aficionado? Head to Mirai, where the emphasis is solely on the fish. In-the-know sushi lovers flock here for the unagi trio, a roll with unagi, avocado and an unagi sauce. Chef/partner Jun Ichikawa also specializes in elegantly simple rolls, such as the tuna tuna salmon, which features poached salmon topped with tuna and drizzled with a light wasabi mayonnaise. Those who want something other than sushi won't be disappointed with offerings like the perfectly made teriyaki salmon or kani ebi korekke (shrimp and snow crab cakes). For a pre- (or post-) dinner cocktail, Mirai has a funky lounge upstairs.

Japanese. Dinner. Closed Sunday. Bar. $36-85

★PIECE

1927 W. North Ave., Wicker Park, 773-772-4422;
www.piecechicago.com

Housed in a 5,800-square-foot former garage, Piece eschews classic deep-dish Chicago pizza in favor of a delicious thin-crust variety that was invented at the famed Sally's Apizza in New Haven, Connecticut. Piece (which is co-owned by Cheap Trick guitarist Rick Nielsen, who lent one of his five-necked guitars to the restaurant) serves huge rectangular pizzas featuring toppings that are both standard (pepperoni, onions) and not-so-standard (mashed potatoes, clams). Some of the combinations might sound strange but they somehow meld perfectly with the pizza's crunchy thin crust and tangy tomato sauce. The pizzas aren't the only reason that the massive space is always packed with a randy crowd checking out the game (and each other): Piece's onsite, handcrafted brews won the World Beer Cup's Small Brewpub Award in 2006.

Pizza. Lunch, dinner. Bar. $16-35

★★★RESTAURANT TAKASHI
1952 N. Damen Ave., Bucktown, 773-772-6170;
www.takashichicago.com

It seemed like the pinnacle of chef Takashi Yagihashi's career: After putting together an award-winning résumé in Chicago and Detroit, he headed to Las Vegas to lead a restaurant in the Wynn Resort. Thankfully for Chicagoans, Yagihashi returned after 18 months to helm his namesake restaurant, a minimalist spot in Bucktown that expertly blends high-end American influences and French technique with the simplicity of Japanese fare. In a small, low-key room of gray walls accented with cherry wood, the menu offers hot and cold small plates that feature fresh hamachi, salmon, tuna and other seafood. The more substantial large plates menu offers dishes such as roasted potato/prosciutto-crusted Atlantic salmon and a roasted New York strip with fresh wasabi and miso-glazed fingerling potatoes. In a neighborhood with more than a few so-so sushi spots, Takashi simultaneously expands the palate while refining the details of Japanese cuisine.
Contemporary American, Japanese. Dinner. Closed Monday. $36-85

★★★SCHWA
1466 N. Ashland Ave., Wicker Park, 773-252-1466;
www.schwarestaurant.com

Maverick chef Michael Carlson is viewed as the enfant terrible of the Chicago dining world. His eccentric Schwa became the apple of Chicago foodies' eyes, but then he abruptly closed for four months and was vague about what he did in the meantime. Thankfully, the restaurant has reopened and while its quixotic charms are still evident—tiny room, no liquor license, the cooks also serve as the waitstaff—the food is still remarkably innovative. The charismatic Carlson—who's likely to sprinkle a few uses of "dude" during your meal—offers three- and nine-course menus that feature organic ingredients and locally grown produce. The latter option includes such knockout dishes as a savory beer cheese soup with a pretzel roll, and a gently seared kona kampachi with galangal, lime and a tiny splash of maple syrup. It's a little pricey for what it is, but the cost of the meal is offset by the restaurant's BYOB policy, which allows you to carry in your own wine for a mere $2.50-per-person corkage fee. Just be sure to call ahead to snag a table; though Carlson may be unpredictable, the restaurant's popularity is not.
Contemporary American. Dinner. Closed Sunday-Monday. $36-85

★★★SPRING
2039 W. North Ave., 773-395-7100, Wicker Park;
www.springrestaurant.net

Spring is Chicago restaurant star Shawn McClain's first local outpost, and some still say it's his best. The spartan dining room—the building was once a Russian bathhouse, and some of the original white tiles are still on the walls—provides a relaxing environ for McClain's celebrated seafood-oriented, Asian-inflected fare. The most renowned appetizer is the seared Maine scallop and potato ravioli in a heavenly mushroom black-truffle reduction. That's just a prelude to the sophisticated entrées, which include grilled Hawaiian prawns and pork belly dumplings, and the Arctic char with toasted sesame risotto and peekytoe crab. The honeydew sorbet in a plum soup makes the perfect light capper for a remarkable meal.
Contemporary American. Dinner. Closed Monday. $36-85

WHERE TO STAY

TRUMP INTERNATIONAL HOTEL AND TOWER

SLEEP ON IT

It doesn't matter whether you're in town for a convention or for the latest outdoor music festival, you can rest easy knowing there's a hotel for you somewhere in this city. Chicago's lodging options are as diverse as they are vast. So decide what you're looking for—location? fabulous spa? boutique hotel?—and then pick the perfect one for your stay.

GOLD COAST/STREETERVILLE

★★★THE ALLERTON HOTEL – MICHIGAN AVENUE

701 N. Michigan Ave., Streeterville, 312-440-1500, 877-701-8111; www.theallertonhotel.com

During the Roaring Twenties, the Allerton was one of the first high rises to pop up on the Chicago skyline. Now a designated landmark, the Michigan Avenue hotel retains some classic elements (such as its exterior sign that reads "Tip Top Tap"—the name of the popular cocktail lounge that closed in 1961) while adding some contemporary accents. The hotel had a makeover in May 2008 and the rooms are now in tip-top shape. The sophisticated spaces are done up in traditional navy blue and white, while modern touches, such as trendy patterned throw pillows, white upholstered head-boards and iPod docking stations, are sprinkled throughout. Beware of the rooms labeled "Classic"—that's code for "tiny."

443 rooms. Restaurant, bar. Fitness center. Business center. $151-250

★★★THE AMBASSADOR EAST HOTEL

1301 N. State Parkway, Gold Coast, 312-787-7200, 888-506-3471; www.theambassadoreasthotel.com

Many celebs have checked into this Gold Coast hotel, including Vince Vaughn, Richard Gere and Frank Sinatra (who has a celebrity suite named after him). One reason for its popularity is its location. The hotel sits among residential buildings in a tony neighborhood, plus it's near the jogging trail and volley-ball courts of Oak Street Beach. Another reason may be the famed Pump Room restaurant, where Old Hollywood stars flocked to its fabled Booth One, a table that only the most exclusive diners could snag. Robert Wagner and Natalie Wood toasted their wedding in that booth, as did Lauren Bacall and Humphrey Bogart when they got hitched. Frequent guest Judy Garland even paid tribute to the hot spot in her song *Chicago*: "Chicago, we'll meet at the Pump Room, Ambassador East." If you meet at the Pump Room today, you'll feast on contemporary American cuisine from executive chef Nick Sutton.

285 rooms. Restaurant, bar. Fitness center. Business center. $151-250

★★★THE DRAKE HOTEL CHICAGO

140 E. Walton Place, Gold Coast, 312-787-2200, 800-774-1500; www.thedrakehotel.com

The Drake is the hotel of choice for visiting politicians and dignitaries. Winston Churchill, Pope John Paul II and Princess Diana all roomed at the 1920 landmark hotel, ideally located at the beginning of North Michigan Avenue. But this old star could use some polish to regain its luster. While the public spaces still preserve the splendor of the past and some rooms got updated in early 2008, other guest rooms haven't yet gotten their makeovers. Avoid disappointment by asking for a newly renovated room

FOUR SEASONS HOTEL CHICAGO

(with gold and white linens and a flat-screen TV).
535 rooms. Restaurant, bar. Fitness center. Business center. $251-350

★★★EMBASSY SUITES CHICAGO - DOWNTOWN/LAKEFRONT
511 N. Columbus Drive, Streeterville, 312-836-5900, 888-903-8884;
www.chicagoembassy.com
Traveling families can spread out here and make it a home away from home.
The two-room suites have a separate living room with a sofa bed and dining
table, a microwave, a coffeemaker and a fridge. After a March 2008 renovation, the bland beige-hued suites got an upgrade with two flat-panel TVs
per room and local artwork on the walls to add some Chicago flavor. If
sticking close to your new home makes you stir-crazy, head to the atrium
lounge, order a cocktail from the nearby bar and enjoy the soothing sound
of the 70-foot cascading water wall. Or you can just wait until the free daily
manager's reception to tipple and munch on some appetizers. Also be sure
to take advantage of the complimentary made-to-order breakfast before
rounding up the kids and trekking over to nearby Navy Pier—you'll need
the energy.
455 rooms. Restaurant, bar. Complimentary breakfast. Fitness center. Pool.
Business center. $151-250

★FAIRFIELD INN AND SUITES CHICAGO DOWNTOWN
216 E. Ontario St., Streeterville, 312-787-3777, 800-228-2800;
www.fairfieldsuites.com
The Fairfield, just steps from Michigan Avenue and a half mile from Oak
Street Beach, is simply decorated and modestly sized, which suits us just
fine—the proximity to the Mag Mile is all we need to convince us to stay
here. If you are looking for incentives, check out the packages: One for
anyone who loves to shop includes a $50 gift card, plus a free breakfast
and valet parking.
159 rooms. Complimentary breakfast. Fitness center. Business center.
$61-150

★★★★★FOUR SEASONS HOTEL CHICAGO

120 E. Delaware Place, Gold Coast, 312-280-8800;
www.fourseasons.com/chicagofs

With its prime Mag Mile location and attractive, contemporary rooms, this luxe hotel is a top choice for visiting celebrities and those who appreciate the peace and quiet the polished staff practically guarantees. A recent renovation took the formerly traditional English country décor and transformed it by adding French deco style, with flowery prints replaced with rich chocolate, deep blue and shimmery silver hues, and new leather window seats in many rooms overlooking Lake Michigan and the Gold Coast. The lobby, grand ballroom, restaurants and the larger suites and apartments received updates in early 2009. Two things that haven't changed: the wonderful, personal service, and the location. It's situated just above Bloomingdale's and other stores such as Gucci, Williams-Sonoma and Michael Kors in the 900 North Michigan building.

343 rooms. Restaurant, bar. Fitness center. Spa. Pool. Business center. $351 and up

★★★HILTON SUITES CHICAGO/MAGNIFICENT MILE

198 E. Delaware Place, Gold Coast, 312-664-1100; www.hilton.com

This all-suite hotel is in the heart of downtown, making it a convenient choice for business travelers and families alike. The classic navy and maroon suites come with a separate living room complete with a flat-screen TV, mini-fridge and pullout sofa. But who would want to veg on the couch when you can head to the nearby Hancock Tower and peer out from the 94th-floor observatory or—even better—zip up to the 95th-floor Signature Lounge to relax with a sidecar and a vista of downtown? Go ahead and order another round or two; your hotel is within stumbling distance anyway.

345 rooms. Restaurant. Fitness center. Pool. Business center. Pets accepted. $151-250

★★★HOTEL INDIGO

1244 N. Dearborn St., Gold Coast, 312-787-4980, 866-521-6950;
www.goldcoastchicagohotel.com

If you want something beyond a cookie-cutter hotel room bathed in banal beige, retreat to Hotel Indigo. The guest rooms are more like calming beach

---

WHAT ARE THE MOST LUXURIOUS HOTELS?

Four Seasons Hotel Chicago *(page 97)* Recent renovations gave the comfortable guest rooms a contemporary spin on 1940s French design. What hasn't changed is the wonderful, personal service, and the location right on the Magnificent Mile.

The Peninsula Chicago *(page 98)* The rooms are beyond comfortable, with pillowy soft beds and panel-controlled everything (shades, music, lighting), while the restaurants are top-notch and the spa one of the city's best. But it's the warm, gracious service that makes a stay here special.

Trump International Hotel and Tower *(page 106)* This stainless-steel and glass hotel, which towers over the city at 92 stories, is absolutely gorgeous. Inside you'll find a lavish spa, excellent restaurant and a swank cocktail lounge, plus rooms that feel residential with fully stocked kitchens.

houses than typical hotel spaces. Hardwood floors, whitewashed furniture, teak benches, and navy and indigo blue dominate the rooms along with lime green accents, and vibrant wall-size photo murals of blueberries, irises and sky-blue cable-knit sweaters transform the space. Certain touches make it clear that it's not just another day at the beach: spa-style showerheads, sleek Melitta coffeemakers, Aveda toiletries and personal trainers at the fitness center.

165 rooms. Restaurant, bar. Fitness center. Spa. Business center. Pets accepted. $251-350

★★★HOTEL INTERCONTINENTAL
505 N. Michigan Ave., Streeterville, 312-944-4100, 866-210-8811; www.chicago.intercontinental.com

Originally the 1929 Medinah Athletic Club, Hotel InterContinental still maintains some of its old-time glory. Its 12th floor Art Deco Junior Olympic pool is where Olympic swimmer and *Tarzan* actor Johnny Weissmuller frequently escaped from the jungle to do some laps. The hotel now has a state-of-the-art three-story fitness center, one of the largest hotel gyms in the city. If you don't want to be quite that healthy, swing by ENO, where you can order wine flights accompanied by artisanal cheese or luscious chocolate. The rooms in the Main Building are plain-Jane with cream duvets, maroon throw pillows, and maroon-and-gold striped curtains. If you like Old World décor, you'll appreciate the historic tower's rooms, which use the same color palette, but replace mahogany headboards with carved ones and basic bedding with fancy patterned covers.

790 rooms. Restaurant, bar. Fitness center. Pool. Business center. Pets accepted. $251-350

★★★PARK HYATT CHICAGO
800 N. Michigan Ave., Gold Coast, 312-335-1234, 800-233-1234; www.parkchicago.hyatt.com

The luxe Park Hyatt showers guests with butlers, personal safes with laptop rechargers and storage for wardrobes (who can travel without that?). The chic décor is simple and understated with cherry wood-filled guest rooms, gold and mocha accents and leather chairs. Make sure to bathe in the oversized tub; as you soak you can slide open the wall to reveal the bedroom and views of the skyline or Lake Michigan. For more relaxation, pamper yourself at the onsite medispa Tiffani Kim Institute with a custom-ized facial. If you're the sporty type, borrow one of the hotel's free bicycles and do some sightseeing while pedaling along Chicago's many bike paths. Afterward, complete the experience with dinner at NoMI, an excellent contemporary French-Asian restaurant overlooking Michigan Avenue.

198 rooms. Restaurant, bar. Fitness center. Spa. Pool. Business center. Pets accepted. $351 and up

★★★★★THE PENINSULA CHICAGO
108 E. Superior St., Gold Coast, 312-337-2888, 866-288-8889; www.chicago.peninsula.com

Stars like Ellen DeGeneres, Chris Rock and Brad Pitt and Angelina Jolie visit The Peninsula for its luxurious rooms and spa, but don't overlook it as a dining destination. The hotel is known for its highly acclaimed Shanghai Terrace and Avenues restaurants. There are also the afternoon teas, which offer exotic blends, including those made especially for The Peninsula, as

THE PENINSULA CHICAGO

well as a lavish chocolate buffet on Fridays and Saturdays. Even without the food options, The Peninsula stands out. The Peninsula Spa by ESPA offers a full menu of services and a relaxation lounge where you can lounge under a comforter in a sectioned-off area and relax uninterrupted after your treatment. Luxurious guest rooms are bright with light wood and muted earth tones, and the marble bathrooms have roomy tubs where you can watch TV while you soak. A bedside control panel allows you to shut off the light and signal that you don't want to be disturbed, all without having to leave the comfort of your 300-thread-count sheets.

339 rooms. Restaurant, bar. Fitness center. Spa. Pool. Business center. Pets accepted. $351 and up

★★★★THE RITZ-CARLTON CHICAGO, A FOUR SEASONS HOTEL
160 E. Pearson St., Gold Coast, 312-266-1000, 800-621-6906;
www.fourseasons.com/chicagorc

When you're at the Ritz, which rests atop shopping mecca Water Tower Place, the city view from the large-windowed rooms is hard to beat. The spacious accommodations were just given a makeover, and floral-patterned duvets and dark wood furniture were replaced with crisp white linens and a soothing grey color palette. If you don't want to leave, send up for the spa's in-room signature aromatherapy massage or have a customized fragranced bath drawn for you in your marble bathroom. After your treatment and soothing bath, you might want to rest your heavy head on the down pillow and bury yourself underneath the down blanket. But force yourself to grab a cocktail in the Greenhouse, where you won't have to sacrifice the view or being comfortable, as you can enjoy the lakefront panorama from sofas and comfortable chairs.

434 rooms. Restaurant, bar. Fitness center. Spa. Pool. Business center. Pets accepted. $351 and up

THE RITZ-CARLTON CHICAGO

★★★SOFITEL CHICAGO WATER TOWER
20 E. Chestnut St., Gold Coast, 312-324-4000; www.sofitel.com
You can't miss the stylish Sofitel—look for the triangle-shaped building near downtown. The glass and steel structure looks like it leapt out from the pages of an interior design magazine and into the Gold Coast. The rooms aren't too shabby, either. They are a tad small but airy, thanks to light wood furniture, cream walls, bedding and mirrored closet doors. The bathrooms are roomier, with separate showers and tubs. This hotel goes Francophile all the way, with Café des Architectes, a French restaurant, and Le Bar, which has floor-to-ceiling glass walls and is the perfect place for a wine flight and a cheese plate.
415 rooms. Restaurant, bar. Fitness center. Business center. Pets accepted.
$251-350

★★★THE SUTTON PLACE HOTEL – CHICAGO
21 E. Bellevue Place, Gold Coast, 312-266-2100, 866-378-8866;
www.suttonplace.com
White is the shade of choice for the linens in the rooms here, while the drapes, carpeting and wallpaper are beige, replacing the old gloomy gray that used to dominate the rooms. The only vibrant color you'll see is a smattering of purple and bold blue in a stray chair or pillow. On the bright side, you can escape to MEXX Kitchen & Bar at The Whiskey to unwind with some authentic Mexican fare; try the shrimp tacos and wash them down with a margarita or two, which will put some color in your cheeks if your room is without.
246 rooms. Restaurant, bar. Business center. Fitness center. Pets accepted.
$251-350

★★THE TREMONT CHICAGO
100 E. Chestnut St., Gold Coast, 312-751-1900, 800-625-5144;
www.tremontchicago.com
The pale hues, dark wood and floral textiles in the small rooms aim for a

---

WHICH HOTELS ARE MOST HISTORIC?

The Blackstone *(page 106)* This 1910 Beaux-Arts hotel, listed on the National Register of Historic Places, has hosted presidents, royalty, sports icons and celebrities (including Rudolph Valentino, Joan Crawford, Spencer Tracy, Katherine Hepburn, Tennessee Williams, Truman Capote and Carl Sandburg).

The Drake Hotel Chicago *(page 95)* Winston Churchill, Pope John Paul II and Princess Diana all roomed at the 1920 landmark hotel, ideally located at the beginning of North Michigan Avenue.

Palmer House Hilton *(page 110)* Named after business mogul Potter Palmer, the historic Palmer House is one of the longest continuously running hotels in the U.S., and also the first to be equipped with electric lights and telephones in each room.

---

romantic vibe, but they make this European-style hotel seem dated rather than for dating. The rooms also provide a strange juxtaposition to the hotel's restaurant, the decidedly unflowery Mike Ditka's Restaurant, owned by the legendary Bears coach. The two-floor steakhouse replaces the faux romanticism with a cigar lounge and a Sinatra-esque singer. Odd pairings aside, the Tremont's best perk is its location; it's a half block away from Michigan Avenue, right near the Hancock Center and Water Tower Place shopping paradise.
130 rooms. Restaurant, bar. $151-250

★★★W CHICAGO - LAKESHORE
644 N. Lake Shore Drive, Streeterville; 312-943-9200
www.starwoodhotels.com
Business travelers who yawn at the usual tedious hotel environs will seek refuge at the W, which has a prime spot on Lake Shore Drive. After settling into your small, dimly lit but sophisticated room, which offers a mix of taupe and deep purples, head up to the hotel's eighth floor to pamper yourself with a treatment at Bliss, a cheerful spa that lives up to its name. There you can have a pedicure while you catch an episode of *Entourage* on your own personal TV. Afterward, return to your room, crawl under the goose-down duvet and watch a DVD from the lending library. Or go to the penthouse lounge, Whiskey Sky, where you sip a cocktail and admire the Lake Michigan views. Adjacent to Whiskey Sky is Altitude, a revolving banquet room that would be an impressive spot for a business meeting.
520 rooms. Restaurant, bar. Business center. Fitness center. Pool. Spa. Pets accepted. $251-350

★★★THE WESTIN MICHIGAN AVENUE
909 N. Michigan Ave., Gold Coast, 312-943-7200, 800-937-8461;
www.westin.com/michiganave
The Westin tries to offer a little something for everyone. Shopaholics will love the hotel for its location across from Water Tower Place. Kids will enjoy the Kids Club, whose membership comes with a drawstring bag with a world map and make-your-own postcard kit upon check-in. Parents of newborns will appreciate getting their own drawstring bag filled with first-aid items, socket covers and a nightlight. Pets sleep soundly on their own beds. Joggers will lap up the Runner's World-approved maps of local running routes. And everyone

will have a restful sleep on the hotel's legendary plush mattresses.
*752 rooms. Restaurant, bar. Business center. Fitness center. Pets accepted.
$251-350*

OLD TOWN/RIVER NORTH/RIVER WEST
★★★AMALFI HOTEL CHICAGO
20 W. Kinzie St., River North, 312-395-9000, 877-262-5341;
www.amalfihotelchicago.com

When you check into the Amalfi, you first sit for a consultation with your "Experience Designer" (or concierge) to discuss your stay. Then an "Impressionist" (doorman) brings your luggage up to your contemporary "Space" (room). This River North boutique hotel may be a bit pretentious, but it has the goods to back it up. You'll sleep well on the pillow-top mattresses and Egyptian cotton linens, and enjoy the multi-head showers and Aveda bath products. An in-room CD collection, the hotel's DVD library and the gratis breakfast on every floor make it feel like home. (Then the "Comfort Stylist" (housekeeper) knocks on the door and reminds you where you are.)
215 rooms. Restaurant, bar. Complimentary breakfast. Business center. Fitness center. Pets accepted. $251-350

★★★CONRAD CHICAGO
521 N. Rush St., River North, 312-645-1500; www.conradhotels.com

Architecture buffs will want to check into the Conrad, located in the landmark McGraw-Hill Building. Be sure to take a look at the façade's sculpted zodiac panels, which make the Art Deco structure stand out. Although it's situated above shops such as A|X Armani Exchange and Nordstrom, this Magnificent Mile hotel can help you find some quiet. You'll discover tranquility in your room by lounging on 500 thread-count Pratesi linens while watching the 42-inch plasma TV, playing the Bose entertainment system or listening to your iPod on the room's docking station. A better escape is the rooftop Terrace at Conrad. It may only be five stories up, but it's still a swanky place where you can enjoy a cocktail and tapas underneath the Chicago sky while gazing at the skyscrapers.
311 rooms. Restaurant, bar. Business center. Fitness center. Pets accepted. $251-350

★★COURTYARD CHICAGO DOWNTOWN/RIVER NORTH
30 E. Hubbard St., River North, 312-329-2500, 800-321-2211;
www.marriott.com

The hotel's environs are typical of the steady Marriott brand with neutral rooms and snug beds. The no-frills room won't break the bank and, since it's just outside the flurry of the Magnificent Mile, it's close enough to the action. Bliss-seekers can relax in nearby spas such as Kiva or the Tiffani Kim Institute and shoppers are only three blocks away from ritzy boutiques. Caffeine fiends don't have to look any further than the hotel lobby for their Starbucks fix.
337 rooms. Restaurant, bar. Business center. Fitness center. Pool. $151-250

JAMES HOTEL

★★★DANA HOTEL

660 N. State St., River North, 888-301-3262;
www.danahotelandspa.com

Dana is new to Chicago's boutique hotel scene, having opened in June 2008. To compete with the bigwigs, Dana offers guests some extras, including luxurious all-natural treatments at the Spa (try the hydramemory facial to treat jet-lagged skin) and tasty bites from a floating sushi bar. The rooms are filled with light wood and natural tones for a Zen vibe, and the luxe bathrooms feature Italian rain showers roomy enough for two. To unwind, dip into the stocked wine chiller in your room. Or if you want some scenery, visit the rooftop Vertigo Sky Lounge, which features a fire pit to keep you warm on those chilly Chicago nights.

216 rooms. Restaurant, bar. Fitness center. Spa. Pets accepted. $251-350

★★★EMBASSY SUITES CHICAGO – DOWNTOWN

600 N. State St., River North, 312-943-3800, 800-362-2779;
www.embassysuiteschicago.com

A less sophisticated alternative to its nearby sister inn in Streeterville, this outpost screams "hotel chain" with old-style comforters in mauves and blues and the obligatory generic framed landscapes in the bedrooms. What this place lacks in style, it makes up for in roominess. The spacious suites include a separate living room with a sofa, not to mention microwave, coffeemaker and fridge. If you don't feel like chowing down on a frozen dinner, stop off for a complimentary aperitif at the daily manager's reception (5:30-7:30 p.m.) before heading to the hotel's Osteria Via Stato & Enoteca for some Italian eats.

367 rooms. Restaurant, bar. Complimentary breakfast. Business center. Fitness center. Pool. $151-250

★★HAMPTON INN CHICAGO AND SUITES

33 W. Illinois St., River North, 312-832-0330, 800-426-7866;
www.hamptoninnchicago.com

Business travelers and Internet junkies will be at home at Hampton Inn.

PARK HYATT

Each room comes with a portable wooden laptop desk, so you can work or surf the Web from the comfort of your bed. If you have to burn the midnight oil to get that big report done, the hotel offers free coffee 24 hours a day at a beverage station and you'll have a gratis hot breakfast waiting for you in the morning. Traveling for pleasure? Go for a meal at Ruth's Chris Steak House, lounge at nightspot Ballo, laze on the sundeck or check out the Frank Lloyd Wright-inspired lobby. The hotel brags that the rooms also are influenced by the architect's signature style, but really, Wright probably would have shrugged at the standard tan-and-cream-hued suites.

230 rooms. Restaurant, bar. Complimentary breakfast. Business center. Fitness center. Pool. $61-150

★★HOMEWOOD SUITES CHICAGO DOWNTOWN
40 E. Grand Ave., River North, 312-644-2222;
www.homewoodsuiteschicago.com
Families will appreciate the roomy suites here, but the bedrooms have a cookie-cutter feel thanks to unimaginative tan décor, and although the living rooms are somewhat brighter with a red and gold sleeper sofa and chair, they're still generic. Yet the reason to come here is the full kitchen. It offers plenty of cupboard space, plates and accessories, a microwave, a fridge, a dishwasher and more. If you're not in the mood to cook, there's a free daily breakfast buffet and complimentary receptions Monday through Thursday from 5 to 7 p.m. featuring a light meal and drinks.

233 rooms. Business center. Fitness center. Pool. $61-150

★★★HOTEL SAX
333 N. Dearborn St., River North, 312-245-0333;
www.hotelsaxchicago.com
Techies will blog about the high-end game room here, which is open to all guests and includes five Xbox 360 stations with wireless controllers, five Zune MP3 players preloaded with music and movies, and two laptops with Internet access. But gossip bloggers will write about the hotel's visiting

celebs, such as Lindsay Lohan, who accompanies Samantha Ronson when she DJs at the red-hued Crimson Lounge before retiring upstairs into a suite at the mid-century cool Marina City complex. It's no wonder the hotel, which sits next to the House of Blues, draws such high-profile guests. The too-hip-to-handle slate-gray guest rooms are wallpapered with damask prints superimposed with fake shadows of candelabras, and textures abound with leather paisley headboards, suede throw pillows and chestnut furniture.
353 rooms. Bar. Business center. Fitness center. $251-350

★★★JAMES HOTEL
55 E. Ontario St., River North, 312-337-1000, 877-526-3755;
www.jameshotels.com

The James attracts more stars than an awards show swag-bag giveaway: Jessica Simpson, Jennifer Hudson, Jeremy Piven and Jack Johnson have all checked into the hotel. The draw could be David Burke's Primehouse *(page 58)*, which is known for its dry-aged steaks and whimsical desserts such as cheesecake lollipops. Or it could be popular nightspot J Bar *(page 126)*. You also can't discount the attractive rooms: Dashes of brown, red or black give the all-white, contemporary design a mod slant, and features like vinyl headboards make this one chic spot. Forget your standard mini-bar. Each room here comes outfitted with a large bar of high-end liquors.
297 rooms. Restaurant, bar. Fitness center. Business center. Pets accepted. $151-250

★★★MARRIOTT CHICAGO DOWNTOWN MAGNIFICENT MILE
540 N. Michigan Ave., River North, 312-836-0100, 800-228-9290;
www.marriott.com

As its name implies, this Marriott is conveniently situated on the Magnificent Mile. But the harried shoppers below won't faze you when you've melted underneath the plush down comforter in your bold blue- and gold-colored room (courtesy of upgrades in spring 2006) for a nap. If you can't get any Z's, take a dip in the hotel pool, or give in and join the crowds at nearby Oak Street Beach. Those who are all work-and-no-play should head to the onsite Starbucks to get some java and free WiFi. Self-check out kiosks also will help business travelers on tight schedules.
1,198 rooms. Restaurant, bar. Business center. Fitness center. Pool. $151-250

★★★OMNI CHICAGO HOTEL
676 N. Michigan Ave., River North, 312-944-6664, 888-444-6664;
www.omnihotels.com

If the name sounds familiar, it's because Oprah puts up many of her show's guests at this all-suite hotel. The beige and cream suites offer roomy digs and plasma TVs. Kids get milk and cookies every night. Ask for a free Get Fit Kit ($50 deposit is required), which includes a mat and weights so that you can work out in your hotel room while the little ones play. Afterward, head up to one of the two rooftop decks where you can catch some sun in warm weather.
347 rooms. Restaurant, bar. Business center. Fitness center. Spa. Pool. Pets accepted. $251-350

★★★★TRUMP INTERNATIONAL HOTEL AND TOWER

401 N. Wabash Ave., River North, 312-588-8000, 877-458-7867;
www.trumpchicagohotel.com

The Donald put his stamp on the Chicago skyline with his stainless-steel and iridescent glass hotel, which towers over the city at 92 stories. And he continues the splendor inside the tower. The modern, slate-gray rooms have floor-to-ceiling windows that give a gorgeous vista of the city, custom-designed furniture warms up the spaces, and chefs will come to your room to cook up a meal in your state-of-the-art kitchen. The lap-of-luxury treatment doesn't end there. You can get purifying massages using ruby and diamond-infused oils at the spa. If you don't opt for the in-room chef, go to the restaurant Sixteen, which has a seasonally driven menu. Afterward, have a drink at the inviting Rebar, which offers a lovely view of the adjacent Chicago River.

339 rooms. Restaurant, bar. Business center. Fitness center. Spa. Pool. $351 and up

LOOP/WEST LOOP

★★★THE BLACKSTONE, A CHICAGO RENAISSANCE HOTEL

636 S. Michigan Ave., Loop, 312-447-0955, 800-468-3571;
www.blackstonerenaissance.com

If there's anything to that whole law of attraction business, that's reason enough to stay at The Blackstone. This 1910 Beaux-Arts hotel, listed on the National Register of Historic Places, has hosted presidents, royalty, sports icons and celebrities (including Rudolph Valentino, Joan Crawford, Spencer Tracy, Katharine Hepburn, Tennessee Williams, Truman Capote and Carl Sandburg). If you are not one to name names, though, the handsome renovation completed in the spring of 2008 will still convince you. Preserving the old-fashioned elegance and architectural integrity, Sage Hospitality Resources bought the long-dormant property, stripped it, then gave it a modern edge. The finished product features a grand gilded lobby with opulent designer details and extravagant extras like a video-generated computer art piece or the constantly changing lakefront landscape; a curated collection of more than 1,400 pieces of original art by Chicago artists is displayed on the walls. The guest rooms weren't forgotten either, tastefully adorned with black, white and red décor, rainshowers, Aveda bath amenities, Eames furniture, flat-screen TVs (and TVs integrated into the bathroom mirrors in upgraded rooms). Locals crowd the restaurant, Mercat a la Planxa, for delicious Catalan-inspired food and drinks.

332 rooms. Restaurant, bar. Business center. Fitness center. $251-350

★★★THE FAIRMONT CHICAGO, MILLENNIUM PARK

200 N. Columbus Drive, Loop, 312-565-8000, 866-540-4408;
www.fairmont.com

The Fairmont wrapped up renovations in June 2008, and with them came a change from traditional chintzes and furniture to Mid-Century modern neutrals and striped wallpaper. While the hotel is still in transition (you may spot those classic florals in some of the hallways and common areas), rooms are an updated retreat with flat-screen TVs and remodeled bathrooms with natural stone tile and rainshowers. Locals head to the new mySpa for treatments. The spa is all about the details: It uses vegan nail polish and pipes your iPod's music into the treatment room, with nary a stripe in sight.

687 rooms. Restaurant, bar. Fitness center. Pets accepted. $151-250

TRUMP INTERNATIONAL HOTEL AND TOWER

★★★HARD ROCK HOTEL
230 N. Michigan Ave., Loop, 312-345-1000, 866-966-5166;
www.hardrockhotelchicago.com

Located in the landmark Carbide and Carbon Building, the Hard Rock gives some edge to the Art Deco skyscraper. Step into the lobby, which was recently renovated for a classic vibe. Be sure to tour the hotel's display cases, which show off noted musicians' outfits, instruments and other rock 'n' roll memorabilia. But the hotel is more sleek than kitschy. Its modern silver-gray rooms offer Aveda toiletries, pillow-top beds and laptop safes, and they keep to the music theme with bathroom murals of icons such as Bowie and the Beatles. Get the rock-star treatment by staying in the Extreme Suite, a 950-foot-space penthouse that's on its own floor with private elevator access.

381 rooms. Restaurant, bar. Business center. Fitness center. Spa. Pets accepted. $151-250

★★★HILTON CHICAGO
720 S. Michigan Ave., South Loop, 312-922-4400; www.hilton.com

Overlooking Grant Park, Lake Michigan and Millennium Park, this South Loop hotel is all about grandeur. The sumptuous Renaissance-style Great Hall is decorated in white with towering columns and gold accents to go along with intricate ceiling work. The theme tries to carry to the guest rooms with gold-trimmed wood dressers and cabinets and gold-tinged ornate duvets, but it doesn't translate as well in a smaller space. Still, the location across from Grant Park is superb, and if you're in town for St. Patrick's Day, onsite Kitty O'Shea's is the place to be.

1,544 rooms. Restaurant, bar. Business center. Fitness center. Pool. Pets accepted. $151-250

THE FAIRMONT CHICAGO, MILLENNIUM PARK

★★★HOTEL ALLEGRO

171 W. Randolph St., Loop, 312-236-0123, 800-643-1500;
www.allegrochicago.com

An early 2008 renovation has transformed Hotel Allegro into a posh retreat. The stylish blue and gray rooms have sleek geometric-patterned walls, 37-inch flat-screen TVs, animal-print bathrobes, Aveda toiletries and alarm clocks with iPod docking stations. Savor the soothing ambiance by indulging in an in-room spa treatment—go for the Calm Mind massage, which will fill the room with scents of lavender. If you can pry yourself out of your room, head to the gratis wine hour in the lobby. For sustenance, grab dinner at 312 Chicago for some delicious Italian eats, and then sip a pomegranate Mojito from Encore Liquid Lounge before catching a play at the Cadillac Palace Theatre next door.

483 rooms. Restaurant, bar. Business center. Fitness center. Spa. Pets accepted. $251-350

★★★HOTEL BLAKE

500 S. Dearborn St., Loop, 312-986-1234; www.hotelblake.com

Hotel Blake stands out from the ostentatious old-fashioned Chicago hotels, offering instead a more stylish option in Printers Row. The contemporary, spacious rooms feature floor-to-ceiling windows, earth tones with splashes of red, and black and white photos of barren tree limbs, which are a nice alternative to the forgettable landscapes that usually hang on hotel walls. For dinner, head to the hotel's equally sophisticated Custom House restaurant *(page 67)*, where you'll find delicious Mediterranean-influenced artisanal meat dishes (though at press time there was a rumor that this restaurant was going to be reconcepted).

162 rooms. Restaurant, bar. Business center. Fitness center. Spa. $151-250

★★★HOTEL BURNHAM
1 W. Washington St., Loop, 312-782-1111, 877-294-9712;
www.burnhamhotel.com

The landmark Hotel Burnham, the first precursor to modern skyscrapers, retains touches of its past life, with mosaic floors, marble ceilings and walls, and ornamental metal grills on the elevators and stairwells. The rooms, well, not so much: Decked out in navy and gold, they take on a nautical look, with the sunburst mirror and gold emblem on the deep-blue headboard mimicking a ship's wheel. Located across from the former Marshall Field's department store (now Macy's), the hotel is nestled in the middle of the Theater District. Before you catch a show, stop in the Atwood Café *(page 66)*, an upscale American restaurant with an inviting jewel-tone dining room that resembles an old Parisian brasserie. Perks for pets are as swanky as those for you: Animals get beds made of hypoallergenic fleece and cedar chips with an optional turndown service. If you left Fido at home and are feeling lonely, the hotel will lend you a goldfish to keep you company.

122 rooms. Restaurant, bar. Fitness center. Pets accepted. $151-250

★★★HOTEL MONACO
225 N. Wabash Ave., Loop, 312-960-8500, 866-610-0081;
www.monaco-chicago.com

It's om sweet om at the Hotel Monaco. Although the rooms feature whimsical Art Deco-inspired décor, with thick pistachio and butter cream striped walls, they are actually Zen dens. Each room comes with a meditation station, a large window with fluffy pillows meant for reflection. You can flip on the in-room yoga program and use the provided accessories to practice your sun salutation. If that doesn't work, take a bath with L'Occitane products. Then slip into the pillow bed and put the Relaxation Station on the TV, which will fill the room with soothing sounds and images. The height-advantaged will get restful sleep, when they stay in the Tall Rooms, which feature 9-foot-long, king-size beds. But if you don't do low-key, book the Rock and Roll Suite, which rolls out the zebra-print carpet with plush red velvet couches, a jukebox, guitar and amp.

192 rooms. Restaurant, bar. Fitness center. Business center. $151-250

WHAT ARE THE BEST BOUTIQUE HOTELS?
Dana Hotel *(page 103)* To compete with the other boutique hotels, Dana offers guests some extras, including luxurious all-natural treatments at the spa and tasty bites from a floating sushi bar, luxe bathrooms featuring Italian rain showers roomy enough for two and stocked wine chillers in the rooms.

James Hotel *(page 105)* This comfortable boutique hotel features rooms with full-size bars—not that you're likely to spend much time in your room considering that the bar and lounge are both hotspots, and David Burke's steakhouse is downstairs.

The Wit *(page 111)* The city's newest boutique hotel is located in the Loop in a stylish glass-encased tower. While rooms are contemporary and comfortable, the main draw here is the wildly popular rooftop bar.

★★★PALMER HOUSE HILTON

17 E. Monroe St., Loop, 312-726-7500; www.hilton.com

Named after business mogul Potter Palmer, the historic Palmer House is one of the longest continuously running hotels in the U.S., and also the first to be equipped with electric lights and telephones in each room. A 2008 renovation aimed to return the massive hotel to its roots, and thankfully it included more than just lights and phones; a health club and spa, standard elsewhere, are finally forthcoming. The rooms are now bathed in lavender, brown and sage, shades that mimic the lobby's original terrazzo flooring and opulent Beaux-Arts ceiling, but the décor is updated with monogrammed pillows, swirly and striped linens, and ebony headboards. Executive level rooms didn't get the modern makeover—they have a French Empire style with flowery pastels and ornate gold mirrors—but you'll get your own private concierge and a buffet of goodies such as the Palmer House brownies, which is appropriate since Bertha Palmer invented the chocolaty creation and the Palmer House debuted it at the 1893 World's Fair.

1,639 rooms. Restaurant, bar. Business center. Fitness center. Pool. Pets accepted. $151-250

★★★SHERATON CHICAGO HOTEL AND TOWERS

301 E. North Water St., Loop, 312-464-1000, 800-325-3535; www.sheratonchicago.com

Overlooking the Chicago River, the Sheraton chain's flagship branch touts itself as the "premier convention and business hotel in the Midwest." In fact, its enormous size makes it seem more like a convention center than a luxury hotel. But the simply decorated cream and beige rooms with beds resting against wood-paneled walls are inviting, especially when you add in the calming views of the water. For a change of scenery, visit the surprisingly hip Chi Bar, where you can kick back in a cocoa-colored leather chair with a Chicago Sunset martini and forget about the conventioneers flitting around the rest of the hotel.

1,209 rooms. Restaurant, bar. Business center. Fitness center. Pool. Pets accepted. $151-250

★★★SWISSÔTEL CHICAGO

323 E. Wacker Drive, Loop, 312-565-0565, 800-637-9477; www.swissotelchicago.com

After renovations in April 2008, the Swissôtel Chicago—the sole stateside outpost of the Swiss hotel chain—is more appealing to business travelers. Upgrades included larger desks, ergonomic chairs, tech docking stations to use various media devices simultaneously and 37-inch split-screen plasma TVs. And the hotel recently added more meeting space. But families will be at home here, too. Kid-friendly suites have child-sized beds, toys, a play area and books. Parents can hunker down within the heather gray and ivory striped walls and rest in a white bed with an oversized fabric headboard. Whether you're there for business or pleasure, be sure to take a dip in the 45-foot indoor pool. It's on the 42nd floor and offers a nice view of Lake Michigan, as well as a wall that features a beautiful tiled mural of the Chicago skyline.

661 rooms. Restaurant, bar. Business center. Fitness center. Pool. $251-350

HOTEL SAX

★★★W CHICAGO – CITY CENTER

172 W. Adams St., Loop, 312-332-1200, 888-625-5144;
www.whotels.com

Staying at the W is less about the rooms and amenities and more about the
scene. Socialites and Loop workers crowd the bar for happy hour in the
neo-gothic lobby, or the "Living Room," with long drapes at the entryways,
and art projected on a wall set to music. The onsite Ristorante We serves
Tuscan-inspired cuisine, and rooms are stylish and comfortable with pillow-
top beds and eggplant comforters. The downside: if you want to visit the
excellent Bliss spa, you'll have to head to the W's Lakeshore location.

369 rooms. Restaurant, bar. Business center. Fitness center. Pets accepted.
$251-350

THE WIT

201 N. State St., Loop, 312-467-0200; www.thewithotel.com

Wake-up calls from Barack Obama and Harry Caray are par for the course at
The Wit. And while they're just recordings, they give a feel for the tongue-in-
cheek nature on display at this unique Loop hotel. Rooms are cheerful and
contemporary, with pillow-top beds and down duvets, plus flat-screen TVs
and in-room snack bars. You'll have to compete for a seat with the locals
who crowd into ROOF, the 27th-floor roof-top lounge that offers incredible
city views and cozy seating arranged around indoor fireplaces. The hotel
also houses its own high-definition theater, which is available for private
screenings, as well as a spa and two onsite restaurants.

298 rooms. Restaurant, bar. Business center. Fitness center. Spa. $251-350

LAKEVIEW

★BEST WESTERN HAWTHORNE TERRACE

3434 N. Broadway, Lakeview, 773-244-3434, 888-860-3400;
www.hawthorneterrace.com

If you are more into the Cubs than Chanel, try this Lakeview hotel for a more
neighborhood experience. Located about a half-mile from Wrigley Field,

W CHICAGO - LAKESHORE

the hotel copies the Friendly Confines' ivy exterior, but the vines cover a charming brick, canopied building rather than a ballpark. The rooms aren't as quaint, but the place tries to make up for it with a free breakfast buffet as well as in-room kitchenettes. Business travelers will appreciate the free wireless Internet.

59 rooms. Complimentary breakfast. Fitness center. $61-150

SPAS

MYSPA FAIRMONT

URBAN RENEWAL

In a place where city dwellers are slapped with ice-cold winters and jungle-humid summers, it's no surprise that there are an abundance of soothing retreats. From the head-to-toe treatments at upscale spots like the Spa at Four Seasons to quick beauty rituals (such as expert acupuncture at Ruby Room Spa), there's something for everyone—because everyone needs pampering now and again.

STAR-RATED SPAS

★★★★THE PENINSULA SPA BY ESPA

The Peninsula Chicago, 108 E. Superior St., River North, 312-337-2888; www.chicago.peninsula.com

East meets Midwest at this 15,000-square-foot spa, where down-to-earth hospitality complements a full range of Asian-inspired treatments. To begin your visit, step through a giant oak door and enter the newly renovated Relaxation Lounge. The area's plush wooden beds, separated by individual curtains, set the mood for serious pampering. All treatments are exclusively designed by ESPA, an English product line focusing on high-quality, all-natural ingredients. Both mind and body get attention with the Chakra Balancing Massage ($275), which uses smooth volcanic stones to ground and balance your energy. (Sounds wacky, feels great.) Post-treatment, swim in the spa's half-Olympic size pool; its floor-to-ceiling windows provide beautiful views and a chance to find your own moment of Zen.

★★★SPA AT THE CARLTON CLUB

The Ritz-Carlton Chicago, 160 E. Pearson St., Gold Coast, 312-266-1000; www.fourseasons.com

With names like Azalea, Magnolia and Lilac, treatment rooms at this elegant spa are all about organic luxury. Start your visit with a trip to the sophisticated locker room, which features a cedar sauna and private vanity areas. From there, try the Aroma-Tonic Body Envelopment ($145), which begins with a full-body exfoliation and finishes with a clay and papaya cream mask to soothe dull, dry skin (perfect if you're here during the harsh winter). When the weather is nice, be sure to slather on the SPF before heading to the sun deck, where terrific views of the neighboring John Hancock Center make you feel like you're on top of the world. Considering the level of service you'll find here, it's more or less true.

★★★★SPA AT FOUR SEASONS

Four Seasons Hotel Chicago, 120 E. Delaware Place, Gold Coast, 312-280-8800; www.fourseasons.com

This spa's plush interior makes you feel right at home—that is, if fountains and marble floors are what you're used to. White suede wall panels and soundproofed treatment rooms add to the spa's elegant feel. Put on one of the spa's thick, silky robes and prepare for the royal treatment—literally. You can enjoy a facial massage with ruby-infused oil during the 80-minute Essence of Rubies Treatment ($225). In gemstone therapy, rubies promote passion and well-being; in this treatment, they just make our muscles feel like jelly. Or try the Champagne Paraffin Pedicure ($90), which begins with an antioxidant-rich grape seed oil exfoliation, and ends with a glass of bubbly. (The heated massage chairs make this decadent pedicure more indulgent.) The gracious staff makes you feel even more relaxed. Extend your stay as much as possible by lounging in one of the day beds after your treatment.

THE PENINSULA SPA BY ESPA

★★★★THE SPA AT TRUMP

Trump International Hotel and Tower, 401 N. Wabash Ave.,
River North, 312-588-8020; www.trumpchicagohotel.com

The Donald wants to know your intentions—your spa intentions, that is.
Whether you're looking to calm, balance, purify, heal or revitalize, you'll
find what you need in this 23,000-square-foot den of relaxation. In concert
with the property as a whole, the spa's décor is modern and sophisticated.
Smooth blond wood, dim lighting and simple orchids create a comfortable,
surprisingly unpretentious atmosphere. Still, it should come as no surprise
that all the amenities here are the best: extra-spacious treatment rooms,
deluge mood-enhancing showers (the shower lights up while water comes
at you from everywhere) and an enormous health club boasting one of
the most striking views in Chicago. As for the treatments, many of them
focus on—what else—jewels. The Black Pearl Rejuvenation Facial ($185)
combines crushed black pearls and mineral-packed oyster shell extracts
to firm and tone your skin, while the Emerald Oasis Body Treatment ($325)
uses mineral salt, mint and emerald-infused oils to exfoliate. If it's true that
diamonds are a girl's best friend, maybe you should opt for the Purifying
Diamonds Massage ($300) instead. The precious diamond and botanical
essences will have you feeling engaged in Trump-style tranquility.

OTHER SPAS

BLISS

W Chicago - Lakeshore, 644 N. Lake Shore Drive, Streeterville, 312-266-
9216; www.blissworld.com

Cheerful and cheeky, the Chicago outpost of the New York-based spa
rejects touchy-feely spa staples like piped-in new age music for a hipper,
more upbeat environment. Each of its four nail stations has its own TV,
where you can watch whatever you like while having your toes polished.
The menu here is extensive and clever: try the Youth As We Know It Facial
($185), which includes a mushroom enzyme peel. Or go for the Quadruple

THE SPA AT TRUMP

SPA AT DANA HOTEL

Thighpass Massage ($125), an anti-cellulite treatment that uses a vacuum roller to leave your thighs dimple-free (or at least, less dimply) after six sessions. Instead of choking down diet food as you would at the average spa, you can nibble on brownies and cheese at Bliss, and after your treatment, step into a eucalyptus-infused steam shower—which, true to the spa's name, is pretty blissful indeed.

SPA AT DANA HOTEL
Dana Hotel and Spa, 660 N. State St., River North, 888-301-3262; www.danahotelandspa.com
One of the newest additions to Chicago's spa scene, this spot is built to impress. Green mosaic tiles shimmer in the oval-shaped lobby, while all treatment rooms include an iPod-ready Bose stereo—so you can be buffed and polished to your own beat. Signature treatments include the Aromasoul Massage ($95), which incorporates essential oils from India, Asia, the Middle East and the Mediterranean. Or try the Nourishing Organics Manicure ($35), which wraps hands in a mask made from pumpkin, tomato, artichoke and beet. Afterward, work up a sweat in the spa's cutting-edge gym—its ultra-sleek fitness equipment, called "Technogym," will give you a great workout. After your treatment, you might want to check out the "true daylight" mirrors in the locker rooms, which are great for applying makeup.

WHICH SPAS HAVE THE BEST FACIALS?

Spa at Four Seasons *(page 114)* Facials here are ultra-luxe; ingredients include precious rubies and caviar for the ultimate in pampering.

The Peninsula Spa by ESPA *(page 114)* Facials here use high-quality ESPA products, which feel luxurious and cleansing; estheticians give you a gentle massage to give you the perfect glow.

EXHALE SPA
945 N. State St., Gold Coast, 312-753-6500; www.exhalespa.com

Pull up a yoga mat and start stretching at this New York City import, which combines fitness classes with traditional spa offerings. Choose from an extensive menu of holistic, Eastern-inspired spa treatments like cupping—a process in which heated glass cups are applied to skin to remove toxins. For something a little less exotic, try the Deep Flow Massage ($130), which uses pulsating, wave-like movements to break up "tsubos," or energy blocks. The effects are similar to a deep tissue massage, only you won't endure any pain. When you're knot-free, chill out in the spa's lounge, where herbal teas and chai-scented neck warmers await. If you're truly ambitious, you could partake in a Core Fusion class, which works the body's core muscles.

KIVA SPA
196 E. Pearson St., Gold Coast, 312-840-8120

This Southwest-inspired spa takes its cue from the Native American Anasazi tribe, who referred to their sacred relaxation spaces as "kivas." Feathers hang from doors of the spa's 11 treatment rooms, and a giant, two-story wooden ladder embodies the spa's lofty goal: to take you to a deeper, yet higher, place. Many of the spa's facials and massages use the luxury Yon-Ka Paris skincare line from France. The Yon-ka Aromatherapy Massage ($100) begins with a hot towel compression and is followed by stretching and Swedish massage strokes. Along with hand, body and foot treatments, this spa also offers salon services. We don't love the daytime crowds, so to find your own "kiva," try visiting in the evening.

KOHLER WATERS SPA
775 Village Center Drive, Burr Ridge, Suburbs, 630-323-7674; www.kohlerwatersspa.com

Who knew that faucet manufacturers would turn out to be so adept at running a spa. The centerpiece of this recently opened space, located 20 miles from Chicago, is the Circle of Tranquility relaxation area. Inspired by Roman-style baths, the facility includes three showers, a 25-foot whirlpool, and even more ways to splash and soak. Let a thundering eight-foot waterfall massage your shoulders or, for a more comprehensive experience, try the 50-minute Go With The Flow Treatment ($115). It begins with a Vichy shower, a French technique in which your therapist guides a five-headed

---

WHAT ARE THE BEST HOTEL SPAS?

The Peninsula Spa by ESPA *(page 114)* This spa is one of the best for its down-to-earth hospitality, exquisite Asian-inspired treatments and sumptuous relaxation lounge. What's more, the pool with its floor-to-ceiling windows overlooking the city, is worth the price of admission.

Spa at Four Seasons *(page 114)* Everything about this spa is heavenly, from the fountains to the thick robes to the white suede walls in the treatment rooms to the heated massage chairs used for pedicures.

The Spa at Trump *(page 115)* The spa's décor is modern and sophisticated (and surprisingly unpretentious) and the amenities are the best: extra-spacious treatment rooms, deluge mood-enhancing showers and an enormous health club boasting one of the most striking views in Chicago.

SPA AT THE CARLTON CLUB

shower bar over your body. After you're thoroughly soaked, the treatment finishes up with a full-body exfoliation and massage. This spa isn't too far from the city, but you'll feel like you're a world away.

RED DOOR SALON AND SPA
919 N. Michigan Ave., Gold Coast, 312-988-9191;
www.reddoorspas.com
Elizabeth Arden's famous red door welcomes you to 15,000 square feet of pampering. With a staff of more than 100, this busy space includes 26 hairdressing stations, 16 treatment rooms and a café that accommodates up to 20 people. We love the new Abhyanga Massage ($125), an Indian-inspired treatment that aligns your three "subtle energies," called "Doshas." Honeymooners and lovebirds won't have to be separated for their pampering; the spa added a couples' room in the fall of 2008. Bonus: This is Elizabeth Arden's spa, after all, so facials include a complimentary make-up application; just be sure to ask your esthetician to use a light hand, as they seem to practice the "more is more" philosophy when it comes to cosmetics.

RUBY ROOM SPA
1743-45 W. Division St., Wicker Park, 773-235-2323;
www.rubyroom.com
This Wicker Park spa, yoga studio and salon focuses as much on inner healing as it does on outer beauty, incorporating new age philosophies into its offerings. In the Intuitive Exploration Treatment ($60-$150), for example, you'll verbally work with an energy healer to balance your aura. Using a computer-generated photo of your aura, your healer will address possible issues in your life. Not in the mood for this kind of therapy? Go for a range of facials and massages, or choose a treatment with Chinese healing techniques like acupuncture and herb consultation. The Chakrassage Treatment ($100) is a combination of massage and energy work: therapists use both techniques to distribute blocked energy from head to toe. It all

sounds a little hippie-dippy, but the overall experience is more posh than patchouli.

SPA SOAK

1733 N. Milwaukee Ave., Bucktown, 773-395-9000;
www.spasoakchicago.com

With creaky wood floors and high-ceilinged suites, this homey spa gets rid of the frill and focuses on making you relax. Piano music sets the mood in the six treatment rooms, while pop tunes accompany manicures and pedicures. For breakfast on the go, try the Cereal Soak Pedicure ($50). It begins with a milk foot bath and finishes with a vitamin-rich oats and honey mask. Along with nail services, this spa offers facials, waxing, massages and body treatments. The most comprehensive of them all may be the Look Better Naked Body Facial ($125). After this 75-minute treatment, which uses clay and sea salt to buff your body, your skin will feel like butter.

URBAN SPA CHIC

1401 W. Hubbard St., West Town, 312-492-8050;
www.urbanspachic.com

This bright and airy West Town spa, located in a former printing factory, lives up to its name. Spa-goers here forego a traditional night out for booze-inspired massages, facials and nail treatments. The Stomping of the Grapes Pedicure ($48) includes an exfoliating grape seed scrub and a foot mask made from wine and honey. Try the Facial Cocktail ($95), which begins with a hand and arm massage, and is followed by heated mittens. This spa also caters to the under-21 crowd, with treatments like the Kiddie Cocktail facial ($65)—at 45 minutes, a shorter version of the grown-up Facial Cocktail. Before you leave, buff your back with the "Backside" treatment ($70). This "facial for your back" includes a massage and volcanic mud mask.

SHOPPING

MACY'S

LEADING THE CHARGE

Surely you've heard of Chicago's Michigan Avenue. You can find the latest of pretty much everything in the mixed bag of department stores and upscale shops that line the legendary strip. Step beyond this dowtown drag and you'll also happen upon unique boutiques with one-of-a-kind finds. Just be fore-warned that at press time, Chicago was saddled with the nation's highest sales tax—10.25 percent—which doesn't seem to deter the many shoppers who flood Michigan Avenue on weekends. If you live in an area with a better tax rate, ask about having your purchases shipped to you to avoid the extra tariff.

GOLD COAST/STREETERVILLE

BARNEYS NEW YORK

15 E. Oak St., Gold Coast, 312-587-1700; www.barneys.com

The new Barneys harkens back to a time when visiting a department store was special, where you wore your best and prepared for a full-day event. This gleaming six-story building with marble floors and geometric staircases is full of beautiful clothes, shoes, purses, fragrances and cosmetics. Clerks dressed in black are ready to point you to the latest designer items, or you can take your sweet time pouring over the racks of Prada, Marc Jacobs, Lanvin, Diane von Furstenberg and Theory. Afterward, plan to spend a few blissful, lazy hours giggling over your purchases and sipping bubbly at Fred's, the store's penthouse restaurant complete with a lakeview terrace.

Monday-Saturday 10 a.m.-7 p.m., Sunday 11 a.m.-6 p.m.

BLAKE

212 W. Chicago Ave., Gold Coast, 312-202-0047

A boutique with no sign, no posted hours and no Web site? What is this, a nightclub? Well, it's almost as exclusive—the only way to get in is by ringing a lone doorbell outside (it's a weird system, but go with it), and it's so sparse in its interior design, you may mistake it for a gallery, save for the suspended racks teeming with an immaculately assembled collection. Blake caters to no-nonsense fashionistas who appreciate French, British, Italian and Belgian designers like Dries van Noten (the boutique has the largest collection in the city), Marni, Louise Goldin, Rick Owens and Maurizio Pecoraro. Accessories are displayed neatly on white islands throughout the museum-like space, and much like a museum, the pieces—like a Chloé violet-gray snakeskin purse—are almost works of art.

Monday-Friday 10:30 a.m.-7 p.m., Saturday 10:30 a.m.-6:30 p.m.

IKRAM

873 N. Rush St., Gold Coast, 312-587-1000; www.ikram.com

In 2001, Ikram Goldman took what she learned from being a salesperson for 10 years at the venerated Ultimo and opened up her own store. It must have been one heck of an education in designer fashion, because to this day, Ikram remains a favorite among Chicago and national élite. (First Lady Michelle Obama is a fan.) Inside the contemporary-European-styled store, bathed in a gentle cream-and-gold palette, you'll run into an eye-popping collection of designers like Alexander McQueen, Jean Paul Gaultier and Junya Watanabe. To the right of the store, near a well-edited and carefully assembled vintage collection, is the shoe selection, which almost solely consists of sharp-looking Azzedine Alaïa and Jimmy Choo pumps.

Monday-Saturday 10 a.m.-6 p.m. and by appointment.

IKRAM

JAKE
939 N. Rush St., Gold Coast, 312-664-5553; www.shopjake.com
This small and beautiful boutique is a favorite for local fashionistas. The space, one of the two that Lance Lawson and Jim Wetzel co-own and operate, is light on décor (expect a pair of zebra-print chairs here and palm stems there but not much else) but heavy on of-the-moment designers. Usual suspects for girls and guys include Philosophy Di Alberta Ferretti, Habitual, Ernest Sewn and Alexander Wang, though if you're not certain about what you're looking for, you can be sure that the highly trained and amicable staff will trot you out looking like a fashionable urbanite, a cross-breed of cosmopolitan New Yorker and effortlessly cool Angeleno.
Monday-Friday 10 a.m.-7 p.m., Saturday 10 a.m.-6 p.m., Sunday noon-6 p.m.

ULTIMO
116 E. Oak St., Gold Coast, 312-787-1171; www.ultimo.com
"Ultimo" means "the latest" in Spanish and Italian, and the latest you will find inside this intimate, three-floor walk-up. The store, a bit of an institution in Chicago at 40 years old, carries the very latest from runway superstars like Roberto Cavalli, Giambattista Valli, Stella McCartney and Michael Kors, which you'll find throughout neat but full racks on the first and second floors. The formidable Manolo Blahnik collection is gasp-worthy, as is the formal gown collection on the top floor, which has the look and feel of a Parisian closet as it glows under a white-linen skylight-cum-canopy.
Monday-Saturday 10 a.m.-6 p.m.

LOOP
MACY'S
111 N. State St., Loop, 312-781-1000; www.visitmacyschicago.com
When Federated Department Stores (the owner of Macy's) decided that it was not going to retain Marshall Field's name and image after it bought the legendary Chicago department store in 2005, the announcement

WHAT IS THE FASHION SCENE LIKE IN CHICAGO?

In cultivating homegrown designers and expanding sample sales and trunk shows, Chicago is finally trading in the sweatshirts and Zubaz for something a little more stylish.

Chicago isn't historically a fashion-forward city. In that respect, it usually fulfills the stereotypes of the pragmatic Midwest. Yet in the past few years, style is slowly starting to creep into the city's fabric. Witness, for example, the success of sample sales that take place all over the city each month. Long a fixture in New York and L.A.'s fashion scenes, these events present the opportunity to own designer pieces for a fraction of the price. The catch is that the garments are either seasonal one-off test pieces—i.e., samples— that fashion houses produce to present to buyers, stylists and media, or simply overstock. Check **Beta Boutique** (*2016 W. Concord Place, 773-276-0905; www.betaboutique.com*)—which started off as a once-a-month sale but now has a charming permanent storefront tucked away in Bucktown— and **Thread Lounge** in Lincoln Park (*918 W Armitage Ave., 773-281-0011; www.threadlounge.com*).

Likewise, trunk shows are put on by designers to introduce a new collection to boutique owners and a select group of shoppers before they're available in stores. Usually, the designer is on hand to answer any questions about the garments. While big department stores (like Nordstrom and Saks) and smaller boutiques regularly host these events, the best way to find out about an upcoming trunk show is by signing up for newsletters—*Chicago* magazine's **Sales Check** (*www.chicagomag.com/Radar/Sales-Check*) has a reputable one.

Sometimes, finding undiscovered gems is more than half the fun, and to that end, it's best to turn to the city's emerging designers. Local menswear designer **Kent Nielsen** (*www.kentnielsen.com*) has gotten big enough to sell out of boutique mini-chain Jake, and **Vatit Itthi** (*www.vatititthi.com*) outfits bold businesswomen with gracefully structured separates—not to mention Chicago darling **Lara Miller** (*www.laramiller.net*) and her deconstructed, multipurpose garments. A slew of even younger designers are also defining Chicago style. Watch for the architecturally informed concoctions of **Apparatchik** (*www.apparatchikdesign.com*) and **Agga B.** (*www.aggab.com*), and the punk-rock aesthetic of **Bruiser** and **Brazen Judy** (*www.wolfbaitchicago.com*). Check out **Chicago Fashion Resource** (*www.chicagofashionresource.com/designers*) charts emerging designers as well, so sign up for its newsletter. They also put on the four-day annual **Fashion Focus Chicago** in October featuring fashion shows, free events, seminars and more. If you're in town in May, see the fashion program graduate shows at the **School of the Art Institute of Chicago** (*www.saic.edu*) or **Columbia College Chicago** (*www.colum.edu*)—risk-taking style mavens will love the heady hybrid of art and fashion that head down the runway.

To find unique designs, visit boutiques like **Habit** (*1951 W. Division St., 773-342-0093; www.habitchicago.com*) and **Renegade Handmade** (*1924 W. Division St., 773-227-2707; www.renegadecraft.com*), which do all the work for you by gathering local talent and showcasing their work. While the former features ethereal but wearable wares, the latter cultivates a strictly homegrown, indie style in the store and its annual Renegade Craft Fair (held in September). It's about time the Second City showed New York a thing or two about fashion.

JAKE

launched high-pitched outcries from locals. Despite all the commotion—and the wishes of disgruntled Field's loyalists who vowed never to set foot in Macy's—this State Street building is worth a visit regardless of who sells what inside. Opened for business in 1907 by Marshall Field & Company, the State Street store is pure nostalgia, with its soaring atrium, a gorgeous Tiffany stained-glass ceiling and the historic "great clocks," which are still suspended on the corner of State and Washington and State and Randolph streets. Not much has changed inside, either—Macy's kept Field's favorites like the Merz Apothecary boutique on the ground floor and the exclusive 67-year-old 28 Shop on the third, which features a wide swath of designers, from Yves Saint Laurent to Marc Jacobs, as well as private elevator access and valet. You can still sit around the fountain in the historic Walnut Room restaurant, although a trip to the new food court next door is also definitely worth a visit. The upscale food court, Seven on State, features gourmet food stations from Rick Bayless (of Frontera Grill) and Marc Burger (from chef Marcus Samuelsson).
Monday-Saturday 10 a.m.-8 p.m., Sunday 11 a.m.-6 p.m.

LINCOLN PARK
BARNEYS CO-OP
2209-11 N. Halsted St., 773-248-0426; www.barneys.com
If you regularly worship at the altar of Phillip Lim and Marc Jacobs, then Barneys New York's quirkier baby sister needs no introduction. Cult-brand devotees religiously come to this concrete-and-metal loftlike space to find the usual urban-chic suspects—that'd be the aforementioned (Lim constantly puts out Barneys-exclusive items), Alexander Wang and Acne jeans for ladies, and PS by Paul Smith, Prada Sport and J Brand jeans for men. The salespeople—who sport trendsetting haircuts and clothes that scream "amazing staff discounts"—are helpful and not cloying, especially around the well-stocked beauty bar, massive denim wall and tightly selected shoe collection. Folks with handbag addictions should head to the gritty-girly bags by Marc Jacobs, soft leather slouches by Sissi Rossi and

VOSGES HAUT-CHOCOLAT

classic bowlers by Jas M.B., which are on display near the floor-to-ceiling windows up front.

Monday-Friday 11 a.m.-7 p.m., Saturday 11 a.m.-7 p.m., Sunday noon-6 p.m.

CYNTHIA ROWLEY

810 W. Armitage Ave., Lincoln Park, 773-528-6160; 1653 N. Damen Ave., Bucktown, 773-276-9209; www.cynthiarowley.com

It's only fitting that this designer's eponymous shop is in the heart of one of Chicago's hottest boutique-studded neighborhoods. Rowley—an Illinois native who sold her first collection while still a senior at the School of the Art Institute of Chicago—rolls out dynamic dresses, separates and sweaters without sacrificing girliness (achieved by using bold satins, soft leathers and sheer fabrics). Her quirky take on femininity translates into the boutique's pink-and-black motif and velvet monogrammed chairs. Head to the back for handbags and shoes, or make a beeline for Rowley's Bucktown store, which opened in late 2007 in response to that neighborhood's ever-growing shopping options.

Monday-Saturday 11 a.m.-7 p.m., Sunday noon-5 p.m.

LORI'S DESIGNER SHOES

824 W. Armitage Ave., 773-281-5655, Lincoln Park; www.lorisshoes.com

Don't even think of setting foot here on a Saturday or the first day of a major sale (often twice a year, at the end of summer and fall). The no-frills store—sales racks organized by shoe size line the perimeter of the space—has a large selection of footwear, from traditional brands like Calvin Klein, Franco Sarto and Charles David to funkier lines like Jeffrey Campbell and Irregular Choice, for less than you'd find them anywhere else (sometimes up to 50 percent off). Don't expect much attention from the sales staff, either; the no-return policy on sales items is strictly enforced.

WHERE IS THE BEST SHOPPING ON MICHIGAN AVENUE?

On the Magnificent Mile's double-wide sidewalks, wide-eyed tourists mix with fashionistas, while businessmen duck into department stores and iPod-plugged hipsters navigate around the many street performers. Start on the southernmost point of the Mag Mile, where Michigan Avenue meets the Chicago River.

Your first stop is the **The Shops at North Bridge** *(520 N. Michigan Ave.)*, which is anchored by **Nordstrom**. As any shopaholic with a sole addiction can tell you, the four-story department store has a huge shoe selection.

Cross Michigan Avenue and head inside the Midwestern flagship of **Gap** *(555 N. Michigan Ave.)*, where you can find the chain's signature dependably comfortable clothes. Cross back to the left side of Michigan, where you can get soft fleeces and all-purpose khakis at **Eddie Bauer** *(600 N. Michigan Ave.)* and timeless denim at **Levi's** *(600 N. Michigan Ave.)*.

At Ontario Street, boutiques such as **Cartier** *(630 N. Michigan Ave.)* and **Burberry** *(633 N. Michigan Ave.)* stand on either side of Michigan, while just down the block are jeweler **Van Cleef & Arpels** *(636 N. Michigan Ave.)*, Italian fashion houses **Ermenegildo Zegna** *(645 N. Michigan Ave.)* and **Salvatore Ferragamo** *(645 N. Michigan Ave.)*. Chicago-based housewares giant **Crate & Barrel** *(646 N. Michigan Ave.)* has its flagship on this block. Zip across the street to explore the colossal **Niketown** *(669 N. Michigan Ave.)* and the ultramodern cube that is the **Apple Store** *(679 N. Michigan Ave.)*, where hands-on displays let you play with the latest gadgets.

The next block includes **Brooks Brothers** *(713 N. Michigan Ave.)*. For an even larger selection of men's garments, stop in **Saks Fifth Avenue Men's Store** *(717 N. Michigan Ave.)*; inside, you'll find everything from elegant silk ties and suits to deluxe grooming lines. For more of the same but for ladies, cross Michigan Avenue to **Saks Fifth Avenue** *(700 N. Michigan Ave)*.

On the following block north, gaze in the window at the imposing **Tiffany & Co.** *(730 N. Michigan Ave.)* before you're distracted by the goods just up the block: **Banana Republic** *(744 N. Michigan Ave.)* and **Ralph Lauren** *(750 N. Michigan Ave.)*. For another kind of grandeur, go across Michigan to **Neiman Marcus** *(737 N. Michigan Ave.)*; just don't forget your Neiman's credit card, AmEx or cash, as the legendary designer department store doesn't take checks or other credit cards.

On the last leg of the Mag Mile, you'll want to check out the approachable and increasingly fashionable **Water Tower Place** *(835 N. Michigan Ave.)*, a shopping center that houses everything from **Custo Barcelona** to Neiman Marcus offshoot **Cusp** to kid cult favorite **American Girl Place**. Across the street from Water Tower is **Escada** *(840 N. Michigan Ave.)*, which is the first in a series of markedly more upscale stores in the northernmost reaches of this shopping strip. North of Escada, on the east side of Michigan, you'll find sharply cut variations of the traditional white blouse at **Anne Fontaine** *(909 N. Michigan Ave.)*; beautiful baubles from **Bulgari** *(909 N. Michigan Ave.)*; classic-chic options from **St. John** and **J. Mendel** *(919 N. Michigan Ave.)*; the ubiquitous monogrammed handbag and more at **Louis Vuitton** *(919 N. Michigan Ave.)*; and the classic wool suit, fragrances and eyewear at **Chanel** *(935 N. Michigan Ave.)*.

From here, cross the street and double back half a block to check out **The 900 Shops** *(900 N. Michigan Ave.)*, a shopping center bookended by **Bloomingdale's**, and which also houses **MaxMara**, **Gucci**, **L'Occitane** and **Lululemon Athletica**.

INTERMIX

Monday-Thursday 11 a.m.-7 p.m., Friday 11 a.m.-6 p.m., Saturday 10 a.m.-6 p.m., Sunday noon-5 p.m.

THREAD LOUNGE
918 W. Armitage Ave., 773 281-0011; www.threadlounge.com
Traditionally, "sample sales" have been relegated to New York or the Web. Thankfully, Thread Lounge, which used to travel around the country, has set up a permanent shop. Located on trendy Armitage Avenue in Lincoln Park, this shop is full of designer goods at discount prices. Grab everything from Trina Turk to Joe's Jeans to Milly at discount prices. The shop also carries a few accessories, including sunglasses and jewelry, and there's a nice selection for men.
Monday-Saturday 11 a.m.-8 p.m., Sunday noon-6 p.m.

VOSGES HAUT-CHOCOLAT
951 W. Armitage St., 773-296-9866, Lincoln Park;
www.vosgeschocolate.com
It's curious how a space so cozy and homey could whisk you to so many exotic locales. But that's just what happens inside this pretty, purple-hued chocolate-shop-cum-retail boutique. Owner and chocolatier Katrina

---

WHAT ARE THE BEST BOUTIQUES?
Blake *(page 122)* The shop caters to no-nonsense fashionistas who appreciate international designers like Dries Van Noten (the boutique has the largest collection in the city), Marni, Louise Goldin, Rick Owens and Maurizio Pecoraro.

Ikram *(page 122)* Ikram remains a favorite among Chicago's élite—First Lady Michelle Obama is a fan.

Ultimo *(page 123)* At 30-plus years old, Ultimo is an institution in Chicago. You can always count on finding the very latest off-the-runway styles.

WHERE IS THE BEST SHOPPING IN WICKER PARK/BUCKTOWN?
You've heard all about the great local boutiques and hip designer shops in the Bucktown and Wicker Park neighborhoods. Don't know where to start?

We recommend starting at the "six corners"—the intersection of North, Milwaukee and Damen avenues. (The CTA Blue Line Damen stop is right there, and a cab ride from downtown is $15 or less.) Begin with **Niche | City Soles**, which is on the southwest corner of that intersection. Head north on Damen Avenue and you'll hit **P.45**, **Pagoda Red**, **Apartment Number 9** and **Robin Richman** within six blocks. Double back to the six corners again (that is, head south again on Damen); at the six corners, head southeast on Milwaukee Avenue to hit **Eskell**, plus tons of other indie shops, salons, restaurants and bars. When you come across Ashland Avenue, make a right (so head south) and another quick right—you'll then be facing west on Division Street. Keep walking the double-wide sidewalks of Division, and you'll happen upon more cafés, boutiques and bakeries. As soon as you pass the intersection at Damen, you'll come across **Gamma Player**. Wrap up your shopping tour with a drink or a nibble at one of the area's many restaurants and bars.

Markoff—a Chicagoan trained at Le Cordon Bleu—has made waves across the nation with her surprising combinations, such as smoked bacon and milk chocolate (Mo's Bacon Bar); Mexican chiles, Ceylon cinnamon and dark chocolate (Red Fire Bar); and ginger, wasabi, sesame seeds and dark chocolate (Black Pearl Bar). Indulge in any of her signature truffles, or opt for gourmet ice cream from the dessert bar in the back.
Monday-Wednesday 10 a.m.-8 p.m., Thursday-Saturday 10 a.m.-9 p.m., Sunday 11 a.m.-6 p.m.

BUCKTOWN/WICKER PARK
APARTMENT NUMBER 9
1804 N. Damen Ave., Bucktown, 773-395-2999;
www.apartmentnumber9.com
It's almost impossible to leave this somewhat-removed Bucktown boutique without looking dashing and polished—at least if you're a guy. The store is dedicated to styling men, and to do so, it mixes the classic with the cutting-edge. Expect to find crisp dress shirts by John Varvatos, Paul Smith and Dries van Noten mingling in the racks with Splendid Mills T-shirts and Fred Perry sweaters. Clean up your act with John Allan's grooming products or the solid selection of ties and belts that hang out in the back.
Tuesday-Friday 11 a.m.-7 p.m., Saturday 11 a.m.-6 p.m., Sunday noon-5 p.m.

ESKELL
1509 N. Milwaukee Ave., 773-486-0830, Wicker Park; www.eskell.com
Nostalgia is a beautiful thing. Just ask local designers Kelly Whitesell and Elizabeth del Castillo, the designers behind Eskell. Their penchant and passion for vintage resulted in a line that masterfully incorporates retro prints into remixes of '60s- and '70s-inspired dresses, trousers, shorts and tops, as in a recently spied pretty, gathered-at-the-waist Louise blouse in a silk print with tiny rocking horses. Eskell's frocks hang side by side with other indie lines like Lorick, Samantha Pleet and In God We Trust. There's also an excellently curated rack of affordable vintage clothes near the fitting

WHERE ARE THE BEST HOME STORES AND GALLERIES?

It turns out style can be bought—at least for your home. The River North neighborhood houses some of the most established galleries in the city, sleekest interior-décor shops and one colossal home-design warehouse.

In the mid-'70s, a group of upstart galleries started to move into store-fronts along Franklin, Wells, Superior and Huron streets—then a desolate, industrial part of town. More than 30 years later, this block boasts one of the largest concentration of galleries in Chicago, regardless of the fact that the fare generally leans on traditional work and media. **David Weinberg Gallery** (*300 W. Superior St., 312-529-5090*) showcases fine art and photography with a socially conscious inclination, while **Ann Nathan Gallery** (*212 W. Superior St., 312-664-6622*), exhibits contemporary realist sculptures and paintings. For a taste of the nontraditional, visit **Judy A. Saslow Gallery** (*300 W. Superior St., 312-943-0530*)—the gallery specializes in outsider/intuit and folk art, like the eerily endearing works of Michel Nedjar or cartoonish portraits by David Lee Csicsko.

Next, take a stroll down Franklin Street and stop in at **Luminaire** (*301 W. Superior St., 312-664-9582*) and **Orange Skin** (*223 W. Erie St., 312-335-1033*). Both feature supremely slick furnishings, though the former also includes bathroom and kitchen fixtures and a housewares area, while the latter focuses on importing achingly chic Italian furniture. Standouts along Wells Street include the quirky home and personal accessories store **Elements** (*741 N. Wells St., 312-642-6574*); **Mig & Tig** (*540 N. Wells St., 312-644-8277*) for lusciously upholstered sofas and chairs; and **Hästens** (*430 N. Wells St., 312-527-5337*) for gotta-sleep-on-it-to-believe-it beds whose price tags run as high as $60,000.

At the southern end of River North is the Art Deco-style **Merchandise Mart**—a building so big, it had its own zip code for 45 years. Unfortunately, the Mart is by and large an industry-only design playground above the ground-floor **LuxeHome** showrooms. (Which is no mean feat, mind you: You can find just about anything at LuxeHome, from custom, hand-finished antique reproductions at Birger Juell Architectural Woodwork to the latest in bathroom hardware at Kohler.) If you're really that curious about the goings-on upstairs, visit during **Artropolis**, the city's international art fair in late April and early May, which takes over multiple levels of the Mart and allows plebeians on the premises to gawk.

rooms and a good selection of jewelry and purses throughout the store. *Tuesday-Saturday 11 a.m.-7 p.m., Sunday 11 a.m.-5 p.m.*

GAMMA PLAYER
2035 W. Division St., 773-235-0755, Wicker Park;
www.gammaplayer.com

Legendary techno DJ Jeff Mills and his wife, Yoko Uozumi, opened this razor-sharp boutique in spring 2007. The clothing is unpredictably edgy and decidedly high fashion, so shop with an open mind and an even more open wallet. Women, check out the risky designs by Tatsuya Shida, Jean Pierre Braganza, Veil, JSP and Firma. You might see a shape-shifting, spider-web-inspired vest by the latter. Guys get equal double-take-nabbing pieces from brands such as Obscur, Julius and Odeur. If you happen to catch Mills at the store, stick around—you may just get a taste of his taste in tunes. After

PAGODA RED

all, a shop that's named after one of his forward-thinking techno tracks has got to have hot music by design.
Tuesday-Saturday 11 a.m.-7 p.m., Sunday noon-6 p.m.

NICHE | CITY SOLES

1566 N. Damen Ave. or 2001 W. North Ave., 773-489-2001, Wicker Park; www.citysoles.com

Hipsters with cash migrate in droves to this über-trendy footwear store with a double-barreled name. Either side of the store—which occupies one of the Six Corners in buzzing Wicker Park—features fresh designer footwear for men and women, with American, European and Japanese brands such as Camper, Audley, Sendra, Biviel and Tsubo. The sales corridor in the Niche side offers hot discounts from last season's footwear, which, considering how fashion-forward the shoes here are, will probably hit mainstream appeal in the current seasons. (You might see a pair of mile-high Due Farina suede platform heels that look like they just walked off the Prada catwalk.) Accessories like sunglasses, colorful handbags and jewelry by local artists are also moderately represented, though the heart of the store centers on the soles. If you want to shop all night, call and ask when the next midnight madness sale is taking place.
Monday-Saturday 10 a.m.-8 p.m, Sunday 11 a.m.-6 p.m.

WHICH BOUTIQUE HAS THE MOST UNIQUE ITEMS?
Robin Richman *(page 133)* Richman sells small quantities of limited-production wares by emerging designers under the belief that items should be one-of-a-kind. Richman also sells her own hand-knit sweaters and there is even an in-house workshop.

WHERE IS THE BEST SHOPPING ON OAK STREET?

Michigan Avenue is all well and good for High Street fashions, but for high fashion, there's nothing like Oak Street. Start your walk of this beautiful boutique road at Michigan Avenue and Oak. On the south side of the street, make a stop at **Tod's** *(121 E. Oak St., 312-943-0070)* for gorgeously handcrafted leather handbags, shoes and accessories. Across the street, you'll find celebrated local shop **Ultimo** *(page 114)*. A couple of doors down is Chicago's only outpost of **Hermès** *(110 E. Oak St., 312-787-8175)*, the prestigious French couture house made famous for its leather goods and silk scarves.

As expected, there's no shortage of gems and jewelry on Oak Street, so cross to the south side of the street again for a look-see inside **Trabert & Hoeffer** *(111 E. Oak St., 312-787-1654)* — if the gemstones inside don't make your heart skip a beat, then not to worry. **Graff Diamonds** *(103 E. Oak St., 312-604-1000)*, **Lester Lampert** *(57 E. Oak St., 312-944-6888)* and **David Yurman** *(40 E. Oak St., 312-787-7779)* are all just down the road.

Young girls will want to pop into **Juicy Couture** *(101 E. Oak St., 312-280-1637; www.juicycouture.com)*. Otherwise, back to mid-Oak: Make a stop at **Kate Spade** *(56 E. Oak St., 312-654-8853)* for ladylike touches, such as beautifully embossed thank-you cards or Martha's Vineyard-worthy wallets, then nip across Oak Street where shoe lovers can indulge in **Jimmy Choo**'s *(63 E. Oak St., 312-255-1170)* elegant, sexy heels. Lovers of everything streamlined and understated must stop in at **Jil Sander**'s *(48 E. Oak St., 312-335-0006)* museum-like digs, and makeup mavens would do well to stock up on **M.A.C.** *(40 E. Oak St., 312-951-7310)* cosmetics, which often collaborates with high-end designers (McQueen, Ungaro) on limited-edition makeup lines. Make sure you stop in at **Loro Piana** *(45 E. Oak St., 312-664-6644)* for luxurious knitwear.

End your walking tour with three formidable houses of style: **Vera Wang** *(34 E. Oak St., 312-787-4696)*, **Prada** *(30 E. Oak St., 312-951-1113)* and **Barneys New York** *(25 E. Oak St., 312-587-1700)* — the latter which just recently moved into its gleaming new digs and now includes an outpost of the beloved eatery Fred's. While Vera Wang's Chicago shop specializes in wedding gowns and Prada is an ode to all things artistic, Barneys is all about cutting-edge designers and beauty lines in a casual environment.

DETOUR: WALTON STREET One street south, parallel to Oak Street, you'll find heaven for North Shore teens and college students. Here, you'll find West Coast-style purveyor **Samantha** *(64 E. Walton St., 312-951-5383)*, snowboarding outfitter **Burton** *(56 E. Walton St., 312-202-7900)*, the culty **AG Adriano Goldschmied Jeans** *(48 E. Walton St., 312-787-7680)*, basics giant **American Apparel** *(46 E. Walton St., 312-255-8360)*, trendy **Urban Outfitters** *(935 N. Rush St., 312-640-1919)* and **Diesel** *(923 N. Rush St., 312-255-0157)*.

DETOUR: RUSH STREET Starting at Chicago Avenue and walking north, you'll find luxury-clothing den **Ikram** *(page 113)*; stylist fave **Intermix** *(40 E. Delaware Place, 312-640-2922)*; Australian boots-maker **Ugg** *(909 N. Rush St., 312-255-1280)*; athletic gear at **Adidas Originals** *(923 N. Rush St., 312-932-0651)*; ladylike cardigans at **Anthropologie** *(1120 N. State St., 312-255-1848)*; and travel accessories at **Flight 001** *(1133 N. State St., 312-944-1001)*.

SPROUT HOME

P.45

1643 N. Damen Ave., 773-862-4523, Bucktown; www.p45.com

The "p" in p.45 might just stand for "pioneer." When Bucktown was an up-and-coming neighborhood mainly populated by artists and musicians in the '90s, this upscale store was among the first fashion boutiques to open. To this day, it offers simple and chic sleeveless tops, skirts, dresses and jewelry. Find 3.1 Phillip Lim and Laila Azhar on the roster of designers here, all of whom have one thing in common: understated cool elegance.

Monday-Saturday 11 a.m.-7 p.m., Sunday noon-5 p.m. Open Thursday until 8 p.m. in November and December.

ROBIN RICHMAN

2108 N. Damen Ave., 773-278-6150, Bucktown;
www.robinrichman.com

Richman opened her eponymous boutique in 1998 to showcase her own hand-knit sweaters. A little over a decade later, her boutique buzzes with a creative vibe, thanks to an in-house workshop. Richman sells small quantities of limited-production wares by emerging designers under the belief that items should be one-of-a-kind. To that end, you will find dip-dyed pieces by Marc le Bihan, jewelry made from leather and metals by Tuscan designer Riccardo Goti, and handmade wooden heels by Marsèll.

Tuesday-Saturday 11 a.m.-6 p.m., Sunday noon-5 p.m.

PAGODA RED

1714 N. Damen Ave., Bucktown, 773-235-1188; www.pagodared.com

You probably won't have the space to carry a pair of original Qing-era courtyard doors home with you, but there are so many gorgeous pieces of furniture and artifacts at this large Asian home décor showroom you're bound to come home with something. Many of the items—like a simple stool we recently saw replicated in a Crate & Barrel catalog or framed Chinese drawings depicting sexy, saucy vignettes—hold up surprisingly well to the test of time and taste. The pretty, Zen entrance alone is a free

WHAT ARE THE BEST SHOPS IN THE SOUTHPORT CORRIDOR?

Just a few blocks from Wrigley Field, this Northside strip of Southport Avenue incorporates a healthy blend of vintage homes, specialty boutiques and scrumptious restaurants. By the sheer number of strollers on the block at a given time, you'd think the corridor was lost to children's shops and mom-wear retailers, but Chicago's Northsiders don't take their shopping casually, and it shows with a plethora of stores offering upscale designer clothes at upscale prices.

Women seeking either casual outfits or chic eveningwear will find it a challenge to leave **Krista K** *(3458 N Southport Ave, 773-248-1967; www.kristak.com)* without a shopping bag in hand. The well-edited collection includes designers such as Botkier, Theory and Twelfth St. by Cynthia Vincent. The downstairs denim selection is second-to-none on the Northside, thanks in part to an informed—and honest—sales staff. A sister store, Krista K Maternity, is just down the block, providing great quality wear for moms-to-be and a few cute baby gifts.

One of the newest boutiques on the block is the very chic **Perchance** *(3512 N. Southport Ave., 773-244-1300; www.perchanceboutique.com).* The long, narrow space uses black and white displays and wall accents to promote the limited, but exceptional designer pieces. Pick up a sexy floral dress by Shoshanna and a cute MZ Wallace clutch to match, or prepare for winter with a stellar pair of Loeffler Randall boots. Don't be shy if you need a little fashion help; the staff is warm and eager to play dress up.

If you're looking for intimate apparel or swimwear that fits like a glove, walk right into **Trousseau** *(3543 N Southport Ave, 773-472-2727).* The stock ranges from racy lace get-ups to buttoned-up one-piece suits, as well as everything in between—including the ever-popular Hanky Panky panties. You'll be spending a little more than you would at a department store, but the quality craftsmanship and custom fittings are worth it.

Women's boutiques aren't the only big business on the Southport Corridor. Along with a slew of bars and restaurants catering to both young families and energized Cubs fans, there is **Southport Grocery and Café** *(3552 N Southport Ave, 773-665-0100; www.southportgrocery. com).* Lines run around the block come Sunday morning for the famed brunch, but as the name dictates, it's also a grocery, with tasty offerings including specialty olive oils, hand-made pastas, artisanal cheeses and wine, and some of the best cupcakes in the city.

lesson in feng shui, if too many options (or airline weight restrictions) leave you empty-handed.
Monday-Saturday 10 a.m.-6 p.m., Sunday noon-5 p.m.

UKRAINIAN VILLAGE/WEST TOWN
SPROUT HOME
745 N. Damen Ave., Ukrainian Village, 312-226-5950;
www.sprouthome.com
You know that feeling you get when you wish you could just move into the prettiest store you know? Slap a bed in the middle of this housewares emporium and nursery, and you're home. The poured-concrete floor and wood accents give Sprout a sleek look, while the neat shelves contain playful accessories for your home and garden: lampshades made of thin

sheets of wood, mouth-blown glass bird feeders and ultra-modern dinner chairs you'd never guess were made from recycled plastic. Take a stroll in the nursery, where urban gardeners get their pick of rare plants (passion flowers, anyone?), herbs and ornamental trees.

Monday-Friday 10 a.m.-8 p.m., Saturday-Sunday 10 a.m.-7 p.m.

REBAR

ON THE TOWN

Whether you're in the mood for lounging or dancing, Chicago's nightlife scene won't disappoint. Once darkness falls, dance floors light up with everything from Top 40 tunes to cutting-edge house and techno. If you prefer your music mainly for atmosphere, there are chic bars and lounges that put the focus on expertly mixed drinks, top-notch service and views. So raise a glass to the varied nightlife options—after a long day of meetings or sightseeing, you're going to need them.

GOLD COAST/STREETERVILLE

LE PASSAGE

937 N. Rush St., Gold Coast, 312-255-0022; www.lepassage.com

Any place that makes it this hard to find (you'll have to walk down a hidden brick alley, down a steep stairway and through a corridor) is bound to be a bit persnickety about who gets in. But once inside, you'll be glad for those hurdles, because they keep the riff-raff out and let a stylish crowd in. The slick space, outfitted in dark wood and potted tropical plants, gets its amber glow from dim lighting, and folks smart enough to reserve a table sit back and watch the action unfold on the dance floor. Don't feel like playing VIP? Hop up and get your own drink from one of the two bars—just make sure to bring sharp elbows, especially on weekends, when recent college grads descend on "Le Pas" to shake it to Top 40 hits and hip-hop beats.
Thursday-Friday 10 p.m.-4 a.m., Saturday 10 p.m.-5 a.m.

OLD TOWN/RIVER NORTH/RIVER WEST

BULL & BEAR

431 N. Wells St., River North, 312-527-5973; www.bullbearbar.com

What used to house a home goods store in the River North gallery district is now a popular and stylish sports bar, thanks to a makeover in 2009 that saw the addition of oversized windows to let light stream in and an abundance of flat-screen TVs, which makes the bar popular with Chicago's sports-worshipping after-work crowd. You'll have to reserve well in advance to be seated at one of the booths outfitted with table taps, which let you pour your own draft beer—a meter keeps track of your consumption and charges your tab accordingly. Otherwise, slide into one of the hightops in the cozy, brick-walled space and order up one of seven different kinds of sliders (turkey sloppy joe, kobe beef, etc.), spicy chicken wings or an gruyère-topped bowl of onion soup from the comfort food-heavy menu.
Daily 11 a.m.-2 a.m.

DISTRICT

170 W. Ontario, River North, 312-337-3477;
www.districtbarchicago.com

Experience the best of several worlds at District. Many patrons are not sure if this new River North hot spot is a restaurant, a sports bar or a nightclub. It has been described as a "contemporary tavern," that promises to show every game that airs on television. While 40 flat screens in the dining room are usually tuned in to ESPN, District's menu reflects more of an upscale dining experience than you would find at a typical sports bar. Forget cheese sticks and marinara sauce; the mozzarella log is topped with arugula, shaved fennel and sweet pickled red onions, served alongside smoked

tomato fondue. Some of the specials include half-priced appetizers, half-priced bottles of wine and Sunday brunch. District's unique private event room is tucked away behind a secret bookcase entrance, giving you the feel of stepping into an underground speakeasy.
Monday-Friday 11 a.m.-2 a.m., Saturday 11 a.m.-3 a.m., Sunday 10 a.m.-2 a.m.

ENGLISH
444 N. La Salle Blvd., River North, 312-222-6200;
www.englishchicago.com
With its dark, vaguely Victorian décor, this River North bar hints at the experience of drinking in an English pub. An open kitchen, menu of solidly American comfort food and oversized high-top tables, however, shifts the direction to this side of the pond, as does the preponderance of flat-screen TVs throughout the space. But whatever the influences, English is a comfortable space to settle in for an evening, just as you would at a proper British pub. On weeknights after work, the bar is perpetually packed with a young and stylish crowd who come to sip Pimm's Cups and take a turn on the pool table while listening to DJs spinning British rock.
Monday-Friday 11 a.m.-2 a.m., Saturday 4 p.m.-3 a.m.

HOWL AT THE MOON
26 W. Hubbard St., River North, 312-863-7427;
www.howlatthemoon.com
At Howl at the Moon, dueling pianists play Billy Joel, Elton John and more, while encouraged the audience to sing along. It might sound hokey but the place is wildly popular—especially with a young crowd on weekends, who often wait upwards of an hour to get in. Signature drinks are comically named: X-Boyfriend, Double Agent Martini and Tradewind Punch. After a long wait, you'll need one. The place tends to attract raucous bachelorette parties on weekends.
Monday-Friday 5 p.m.-2 a.m., Saturday 5 p.m.-3 a.m., Sunday 7 p.m.-2 a.m.

J BAR
James Hotel, 610 N. Rush St., River North, 312-660-7200;
www.jameshotels.com
Leather booths and mirrored walls skirt the periphery of the tiny, rectangle-shaped bar, and small, candlelit tables hold it down for high rollers (and the models who love them) with bottle service, especially on weekends, when the space reaches capacity well before midnight. If you can't manage to get a table, head to the bar, where trendy twenty- and thirty-somethings order up the potent and delicious cocktails, including the signature James Martini (a blend of raspberry vodka, elderflower liqueur, lime and fresh raspberries). Resident DJs spin house and dance music, but if beautiful-people-watching gets old, readjust your vision by watching video art installations on small plasma TVs embedded in the walls.
Wednesday-Friday 6 p.m.-2 a.m., Saturday 8 p.m.-3 a.m. Closed Sunday.

LASALLE POWER CO.
500 N. Lasalle Blvd., River North, 312-661-1122;
www.lasallepowerco.com
New to the River North neighborhood, rock bar and music venue Lasalle Power Co. brings a fresh scene to Chicago, with three floors of dining and music. Exposed brick walls, dark lighting and dim red candles make for a warm setting. You can catch both indie bands as well as national acts

RINO

here, which have included the Chelsea Girls and Matthew Santos. Drinks are affordable ($4-6), while the menu features comfort foods from breakfast (served all day), to a slider menu, as well as sandwiches and small plates. Check out the bathrooms—with quotes painted on the walls from rock legends like Keith Richards and Mick Jagger—to get you into the rock'n'roll frame of mind.
Monday-Friday 11 a.m.-2 a.m., Saturday 11 a.m.-3 a.m.

MANOR
642 N. Clark St., River North, 312-475-1390; www.manorchicago.com
You may not be a VIP, but you'll be treated like one with this club's focus on hospitality. The staff's been known to provide a hotel-like concierge service for anything from making dinner reservations or calling a car service to arranging accommodations for patrons at local hotels after one too many drinks. Of course, if it were up to us, we'd just sneak in a nap at one of the cushy booth-like benches that also serve as a storage area to hide your belongings (the dark wood and bordeaux accents of the place are so warm and cozy).
Thursday-Friday 10 p.m.-2 a.m., Saturday 10 p.m.-3 a.m.

NV PENTHOUSE LOUNGE
116 W. Hubbard St., River North, 312-329-9960;
www.nvpenthouselounge.com
If you think you have nothing to be envious about, you probably haven't seen Chicago's skyline from the terrace of this eighth-floor penthouse. Inside the stylish, minimalist space—adorned simply with black, white and green accents—you'll find a designer-clad crowd. The special packages of bottled spirits are all named after the seven deadly sins and are beguilingly strong and delicious. In warmer months, the staff throws open the doors of the small terrace, where you can sip drinks and take in the sparkling skyline from an even better vantage point.
Wednesday, Thursday-Friday 9 p.m.-2 a.m., Saturday 9 p.m.-3 a.m.

WHAT ARE THE BEST BREWHOUSES?

For every stereotype that Chicago tries to shrug off, there's an ounce of truth. And when it comes to beer, it's more like there's a pint of it. Chicagoans' love affair with beer is not a recent infatuation.

In fact, it's serious business that goes way back, from the Lager Beer Riot of 1855 (caused by then-mayor Levi Boone targeting German and Irish immigrant businesses by passing harsh liquor laws) to the debut of Pabst beer at the World's Columbian Exposition in 1893. Though most major breweries are located in Milwaukee or St. Louis, there have always been plenty of drinkers in the region to keep up demand for the stuff—witness the various turn-of-the-century buildings that bear the old Schlitz Brewing Company's logo in a concrete relief on their facade. You'll see early evidence of beer-related advertsing on buildings such as **Schubas Tavern** (page 156), or an apartment building on 21st Street and Rockwell Avenue or at Damen and Grand avenues. (Coincidentally, Milwaukee's Schlitz only began to succeed in Chicago after the Great Fire of 1871, which destroyed many of the city's breweries and left the field open for aggressive tavern tie-ins and marketing schemes.)

Of course, if you want to combine an afternoon of bending elbows with a classic Chicago experience, there's no need to run around town looking for old buildings. Head to the lower level of Michigan Avenue, to the **Billy Goat Tavern** (430 N. Michigan Ave., 312-222-1525; www.billygoattavern. com). Legend has it that the Billy Goat's original owner, Bill Sianis, is the one who put an ironclad curse on the Chicago Cubs, but most people recognize this greasy spoon from John Belushi's Saturday Night Live lampooning of its hamburger-flipping counter guys. (Order a double "cheezborger," no fries, chips.) Duck in after 5 p.m., have an Old Style, and you might overhear reporters from the Tribune and Sun-Times discuss the latest sports news, city gossip or decrees from the mayor.

For a more contemporary taste of history, head to Wicker Park's **Rainbo Club** (1150 N. Damen Ave., 773-489-5999), where Miller High Life is cheap and local lore plentiful. After all, the dingy dive used to be the haunt of author Nelson Algren, and it's said that rocker Liz Phair's breakout Exile in Guyville album cover was shot in the Rainbo's photo booth.

Serious beer geeks with a taste for more than just mass-produced ales should reach for a bottle of Chicago's biggest local brewer, **Goose Island Beer Company and Brew Pub** (3535 N. Clark St., 773-832-9040; www. gooseisland.com). Since 1988, Goose Island has been putting out popular craft brews like the crisp and creamy 312 Urban Wheat and a biting, English Bitter-style Honker's Ale. In recent years, other independent brewers—such as Half Acre Beer Company and Two Brothers Brewing Company—have followed in Goose Island's footsteps in producing quality ales and lagers.

Chicago is also no slouch when it comes to beers brewed beyond the city limits, and for proof, tipplers should head to **Hopleaf** (5148 N. Clark St., 773-334-9851; www.hopleaf.com), a local favorite for its constantly rotating and expertly curated selection of Belgians; **Map Room** (1949 N. Hoyne Ave., 773-252-7636; www.maproom.com), which boasts 200 types of American and international beers; and **Sheffield's** (3258 N. Sheffield Ave., 773-281-4989; www.sheffieldschicago.com) a local institution for its North American beers as much as for its tremendous alfresco beer garden. Sun and suds—two things Chicago can't get enough of, yet luckily, you can find the latter around the city all year long.

J BAR

REBAR

Trump International Hotel and Tower, 401 N. Wabash Ave., River North, 312-588-8100; www.trumpchicagohotel.com

Everyone knows that the word "subtle" is not in Donald Trump's vocabulary, and Rebar, the glitzy mezzanine-level bar at the Trump Hotel, falls right in line. Here, soaring 30-foot-tall windows overlook the Chicago River and Michigan Avenue Bridge, and the low lighting and even lower seating make for a sexy post-work or pre-dinner destination. Delicious cocktails include the Wild Orchid, made of Trump vodka, sauvignon blanc and St. Germain garnished with a mini orchid and lime slice—a refreshing tipple for enjoying the pretty views.

Monday-Wednesday 4 p.m.-midnight, Thursday-Friday 4 p.m.-1 a.m., Saturday 1 p.m.-1 a.m., Sunday 1 p.m.-midnight.

RINO

343 W. Erie St., River North, 312-587-3433; www.rinolounge.com

Pronounced like the horned animal and named after the River North territory in which it's set, RiNo is where the late-night party animals stampede to when the other clubs close. (RiNo is one of the few clubs to have the coveted 4 a.m./5 a.m. Saturday closing-time license; most bars and clubs in the city close at 2 a.m./3 a.m. Saturdays.) Sectioned-off leather seating

---

WHAT BARS HAVE THE MOST UNIQUE DÉCOR?

The Violet Hour *(page 148)* The elegant white and blue interior with high-backed seating, crystal chandeliers and parquet floors in a herringbone pattern is the perfect backdrop for the pre-Prohibition cocktails.

Map Room *(page 147)* Maps cover the walls and bookshelves are stocked with guidebooks at this quirky local favorite that boasts more than 200 brands of beer.

surrounds the main floor next to windows giving perfect views of who's coming in and who's getting a drink at the bar. DJs spin everything from Ice Cube mash-ups to the Pussycat Dolls. Bottle service is one way to survive the 2 a.m. swell of late-night partiers, but if you'd rather sit at the bar—made from a 200-year-old tree's midsection—one of the specialty martinis, like the potent Dirty Rino with vodka and olive juice, should tide you over for the night/morning.

Wednesday-Friday 10 p.m.-4 a.m., Saturday 10 p.m.-5 a.m.

SOUND-BAR

226 W. Ontario St., River North, 312-787-4480; www.sound-bar.com

Flashing lights, velvet ropes and lines down the block to get in? Though Sound-Bar can seem a little passé to jaded clubgoers, it's popular for a reason. The massive space features nine bars with two lounges, a minimalist design, the occasional platform go-go dancers, three DJ booths and, most important, a beast of a sound system (hence the name). While resident DJs Billy the Kid and Bobby D hold down the fort on the lower level with hip-hop beats, the main floor belongs to dance, electronic and house music, and often hosts touring DJ acts like JD Davis. Just watch out for the intense "state-of-the-art" dance floor light displays—they can be obnoxiously blinding.

Friday 10 p.m.-4 a.m., Saturday 10 p.m.-5 a.m.

SUNDA

110 W. Illinois St., River North, 312-644-0500; www.sundachicago.com

This sexy, urbane bar and restaurant is the latest offering from the local nightlife impresario Billy Dec. The name refers to the Sunda Shelf, the water-covered landmass that stretches across and connects Southeast Asia, and with a menu (created by L.A.'s "Food Buddha" Rodelio Aglibot) that spans so many different Asian cuisines, it's appropriate. The room, dreamed up by renowned restaurant designer Tony Chi, is vast and visually dramatic, with plays on light and dark through the pairing of blond and black lacquered woods and splashes of bright colors. The four-sided sushi bar is crowned with a milky-way tangle of faux antlers, while a glossy, black bar hides the front lounge and its low candlelit tables. The main dining room is a mass of communal tables paired with comfy, persimmon settees that are perfect for lingering on through dessert (which should definitely be liquid, in the form of a lychee martini).

Sunday-Thursday 5 p.m.-midnight, Friday-Saturday 5 p.m.-1 a.m.

THE UNDERGROUND

56 W. Illinois St., River North, 312-644-7600;
www.theundergroundchicago.com

This supposedly secret spot isn't so secret—after all, Jeremy Piven and David Schwimmer frequent the place. (If you need help finding it, just look for bouncers dressed in army fatigues.) Head downstairs to the military bunker-style main room, where dance, house and hip-hop music thunders from the speakers louder than an F-16. Two bars serve a crushing crowd, or you can lounge on low leather seating with bottle service. Unlike the club's entrance, people here desperately want to be seen—but you won't mind the scene after downing a Bunker Blues, made with raspberry and blueberry vodka, Pama Liqueur and pomegranate and cranberry juice.

Thursday-Friday 9 p.m.-4 a.m., Saturday 9 p.m.-5 a.m., Sunday 10 p.m.-4 a.m.

SUNDA

ZED451

739 N. Clark St., River North, 312-266-6691; www.zed451.com

A one-stop shop for an evening of fun, ZED451 pretty much has your night planned from A to Z. Start off by making reservations for dinner. You'll find that even on a weekday, this bi-level restaurant and lounge fills up fast. But the big draw is the rooftop lounge that overlooks the downtown skyline; the queue can form as early as 5 p.m., but the views and no-pretense scene are worth the wait. If you prefer to stay indoors, the lower-level bar is a cozy spot, where you'll find business types mixed with young trendsetters sipping cocktails by the fireplace.

Sunday-Thursday 4:30 p.m.-midnight, Friday-Saturday 4:30 p.m.-2 a.m.

LOOP/WEST LOOP

BON V

1100 W. Randolph St., West Loop, 312-829-4805;
www.bonvchicago.com

Bon V is a take on the French phrase meaning "good life." So what else would you expect but plush décor and attentive service? This bi-level nightclub is 7,500 square feet of lavishness, filled with chandeliers and a red-carpet welcome. With all the well-dressed dames and dapperly dressed men dancing to dance and disco tracks, you'd expect a snooty attitude from the staff. Amazingly enough, that's not the case. That's probably because Casey Urlacher—Chicago Bears football player Brian Urlacher's brother—is one of the owners, and he doesn't want to disappoint.

Thursday-Friday 9 p.m.-2 a.m., Saturday 9 p.m.-3 a.m.

FULTON LOUNGE

955 W. Fulton Market, West Loop, 312-942-9500;
www.fultonlounge.com

Looking for an intimate place for conversation and socializing over funk and acid house? Tucked away in the Fulton Market District, this hidden gem caters to a sophisticated after-work and post-dinner crowd that relaxes on

FULTON LOUNGE

Mid-Century Modern settees and lounge chairs along a brick wall background. Set in a 100-year-old building, formerly home to a book-binding business, the fireplace makes a cozy environment with bookcases lining a nearby wall. Munch on pizza baked in a wood-burning oven, or sip seasonal drinks such as the Fulton essence made with passion fruit vodka, watermelon syrup, homemade sour and fresh lime juice. That group of smartly dressed guys and gals at the next table? Probably Oprah's staffers taking a break after work; it's a frequent Harpo hangout.
Tuesday-Friday 5 p.m.-2 a.m., Saturday 5 p.m.-3 a.m.

LUMEN

839 W. Fulton Market, West Loop, 312-733-2222;
www.lumen-chicago.com

At a glance, you'd wonder why anyone would venture down the dark, cobblestone streets of the industrial Fulton Market at night. But true to its name, Lumen illuminates this dingy area, both literally and figuratively. Featuring clean lines and an elevated VIP area, this lounge keeps it simple with one bar, great LED lighting effects and a sexy crowd. Since it opened in 2007, Lumen's made a name for itself as the home for fashion shows and must-go events with celebrity appearances, so make sure to dress your best. The finishing touch is at the bar: the Casablanca cocktail (vodka, a splash of sweet and sour, and white grape juice).
Tuesday 10 p.m.-2 a.m., Friday 9 p.m.-2 a.m., Saturday 9 p.m.-3 a.m.

WHICH LOUNGE HAS THE BEST VIEWS?

Rebar *(page 141)* Everyone knows that the word "subtle" is not in Donald Trump's vocabulary, and Rebar, the glitzy mezzanine-level bar at the Trump Hotel, falls right in line. Soaring 30-foot-tall windows overlook the Chicago River and Michigan Avenue Bridge, and the low lighting and even lower seating make for a sexy post-work or pre-dinner destination.

WHAT ARE THE BEST PLACES FOR MUSIC?

Lasalle Power Co. *(page 138)* New to the River North neighborhood, rock bar and music venue Lasalle Power Co. brings a fresh rock 'n' roll scene to Chicago. Booking mostly rock and alternative bands, you can catch both indie bands as well as national acts here, which have included the Chelsea Girls and Matthew Santos.

The Underground *(page 142)* International and celebrity DJs like DJ Momjeans (a.k.a. Danny Masterson) perform here on a regular basis, as do musicians such as Ne-Yo, Jermaine Dupri and Snow Patrol.

MARKET
1113 W. Randolph, 312-929-4787; www.marketbarchicago.com
Market is not your average sports bar. For starters, it's co-owned by White Sox GM Kenny Williams, and the space boasts a chic, industrial décor. There are still plenty of TVs though—both inside as well as out in the beer garden—as well as a 92-inch projection screen. The Sidewalk Café is a great place to catch a quick bite, while the Rooftop Lounge provides an upscale experience with its cabanas and views of the city. The food is also more dressed up—you can still order sliders but here you could opt for braised beef and barbequed pork. A second-floor event room is equipped with its own bar, balcony and private restrooms.
Monday-Friday 11-2 a.m., Saturday 11-3 a.m., Sunday 11-1 a.m.

VICTOR HOTEL
311 N. Sangamon St., West Loop, 312-733-6900;
www.victorhotelchicago.com
When you see the neon sign at the end of a dark, dead-end street, you may be wondering what you've gotten yourself into. But inside this West Loop club, the scene is chic, sleek and sophisticated. Sky-high ceilings and a black-on-white color scheme look straight out of film noir, and curtained-off rooms are gorgeous, with red walls and Mid-Century Modern furniture. You can sample sushi and mini-burgers while you sip your drink at the floor-to-ceiling bar.
Wednesday-Friday 8 p.m.-2 a.m., Saturday 8 p.m.-3 a.m., Sunday 9 p.m.-2 a.m.

UKRAINIAN VILLAGE/WEST TOWN
DARKROOM
2210 W. Chicago Ave., Ukrainian Village, 773-276-1411;
www.darkroombar.com
While it promises to serve up tasty cocktails and frothy brews, the Darkroom's main focus, as the name suggests, is to feature local photographers. The bar was built as a photographer's light up box and the tabletops boast old film negatives to tie the whole concept together. Lit mostly by soft candle glows, the bar's dark décor is enhanced by red undertones. Local bands appear every so often and guest DJs spin the hottest music to get you moving on the spacious dance floor.
Sunday-Friday 9 p.m.-2 a.m. Saturday 9 p.m.-3 a.m.

THE VIOLET HOUR

SONOTHEQUE
1444 W. Chicago Ave., Ukrainian Village, 312-226-7600;
www.sonotheque.net

Know how some clubs' sound systems are so jacked-up that you can't hear anything beyond booming bass? The heaven to their hell is this chilled-out lounge, meticulously designed by audiophiles to create a pitch-perfect sonic environment. It's no surprise, then, that the shoebox-shaped space—all sleek lines and shades of gray punctuated with neon blue accents, with a long bar running its length—draws music nerds of all stripes, from babyfaced club kids and hip-hop aficionados to seasoned indie rockers too jaded to dance. Still, it's not like the talent on the decks don't try: resident DJs lean toward underground electronic and soul tracks, and international guests (which often include big-name musicians playing surprise post-show gigs) bring in a diverse mix of IDM, dancehall and jungle. Club-weary traveler, this place is music to your ears.
Sunday-Friday 7 p.m.-2 a.m., Saturday 7 p.m.-3 a.m.

LINCOLN PARK/BUCKTOWN/WICKER PARK
CANS BAR AND CANTEEN
1640 N. Damen Ave., Wicker Park, 773-227-2277;
www.cansbar.com

Kick it back to the "old school," as they call it, at Cans Bar in Wicker Park. With a beer in hand, play those video games you loved as a kid like Tetris and Ms. Pac Man. Feel like watching a cult classic? The bar has *The Breakfast Club* and *Fast Times at Ridgemont High* on hand. You can even enjoy your favorite childhood foods; snack on some flavorful mac n' cheese, a classic PB & J sandwich or a greasy grilled cheese. As its name suggests, Cans Bar offers 34 canned beers, as well premium spirits, wine and bottled beer.
Monday-Friday 4 p.m.-2 a.m., Saturday 10 a.m.-3 a.m., Sunday 10 a.m.-2 a.m.

CHAISE LOUNGE
1840 W. North Ave., Bucktown, 773-342-1840;
www.chaiseloungechicago.com

This restaurant/lounge strives for a South Florida vibe via an alfresco patio, an all-white dining room and a rooftop terrace complete with cabanas. Make a beeline to the latter when you're in the mood for a well-made cocktail (try the Queen Anne, a mix of vodka, lychee purée and a splash of champagne), inoffensive ambient house music and a great view of the Wicker Park action below. Once you finally nab a cabana and the sun is dipping into the horizon, there's not much of a difference between the Windy City and South Beach.
Monday-Friday 5 p.m.-2 a.m., Saturday 5 p.m.-3 a.m., Sunday 2 p.m.-4 p.m. (opens at 11 a.m. for brunch on Sunday during winter).

MAP ROOM
1949 N. Hoyne, Bucktown, 773-252-7636; www.maproom.com

The map room bills itself as a "travelers tavern." Indeed, this is the place to come to make plans for your next trip, or simply dream of seeing the world as you choose from the more than 200 brands of beer at this cozy spot. The bar proudly boasts that it represents 36 different brewing styles. Locals love the selection (and the free WiFi).
Sunday-Friday 11 a.m.-2 a.m., Saturday 11 a.m.-3 a.m.

THE VIOLET HOUR
1520 N. Damen Ave., Wicker Park, 773-252-1500;
www.theviolethour.com

If you're not paying attention, you'll breeze past this lounge with its unmarked wood-paneled entryway. The bar's name is a literary reference to T.S. Eliot's *The Waste Land*, as well as Bernard DeVoto's *The Hour*. The interior is hushed, relaxed and just as beautifully baffling as Eliot's poem: High-backed seating plays tricks on your eyes, while crystal chandeliers and parquet floors in a herringbone pattern are dizzyingly delightful. Even more mind-bending enjoyment comes courtesy of hand-mixed cocktails. Mixologists focus on pre-Prohibition libations, meticulously measuring the ingredients in jiggers. It's difficult to choose just one of these classics, but we recommend another literary nod: the Juliet & Romeo, made with gin, mint, cucumber and rose water.

Sunday-Friday 6 p.m.-2 a.m., Saturday 6 p.m.-3 a.m.

LAKEVIEW/WRIGLEYVILLE

KINGSTON MINES
2548 N. Halsted St., Lincoln Park, 773-477-4646;
www.kingstonmines.com

If you can't make it to Buddy Guy Legends on the South Side, stop into this famed bar in Lincoln Park for a healthy dose of Chicago blues. Live bands occupy two stages every night of the week, while barbecued ribs from Doc's Rib Joint and bottles of Old Style set the tone for an evening of revelry. There is nothing fancy about the space—think dark and slightly dingy—but the dance floor is expansive and the music rarely stops. It can get crowded on weekends so aim for a visit midweek.

Sunday-Thursday 8 p.m.-4 a.m., Friday 7 p.m.-4 a.m., Saturday 7 p.m.-5 a.m.

UNCLE FATTY'S RUM RESORT
3530 N. Clark St., Wrigleyville, 773-327-0868;
www.wildharemusic.com

As theme bars go, this one is a sure fit for Chicago. When winter weather turns the city into a polar ice cap, everyone is looking for a bit of tropical fun. And Uncle Fatty's delivers. The bar's bright décor features tiki bars, cabana seats, fishing nets and palm trees to get you in the island frame of mind. For further convincing, Uncle Fatty's offers a bevy of summery cocktails using Kahlua, Malibu and Bacardi O and mixed with fresh fruit juices like pineapple, papaya and cranberry. Beer drinkers also have plenty of options too, and groups can request their very own beach cooler filled with up to 36 bottles.

Wednesday-Friday 5 p.m.-2 a.m., Saturday noon-3 a.m.

THE WILD HARE
3530 N. Clark St., Wrigleyville, 773-327-0868;
www.wildharemusic.com

This bright escape claims to be America's Reggae Capital, and judging by the droves of Jamaicans that crowd the place on a regular basis, we couldn't disagree. The Hare works hard to earn that title, too, with bright sunshine yellow walls, a wide dance floor, two bars and an elevated sound stage where international artists such as Julian Marley and Jah Roots play

THE UNDERGROUND

to a packed place. Although it isn't necessary to bring your sunglasses and passport, you'll certainly forget that you're in Chicago once you step inside, especially with the fake palm trees next to the bar.
Sunday-Friday 8 p.m.-2 a.m., Saturday 8 p.m.-3 a.m.

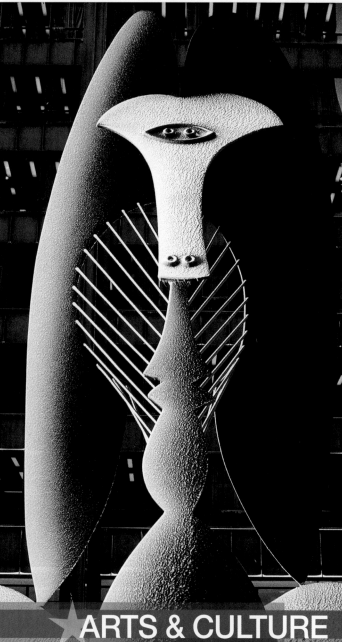

ARTS & CULTURE

PICASSO

ON WITH THE SHOW

Some locals theorize that Chicago's arts and culture community owes a debt to the city's toe-freezing winters. How so? If the ground weren't frozen over for about half of the year, then artists, musicians, athletes and DJs wouldn't have the time to hone their skills and elevate Chicago's arts to new heights. It's just a theory, though, and going by the quality work coming out of this city—from powerful plays by the Steppenwolf Theatre Company to powerhouse hits at the Friendly Confines and the Cell—we'll chalk it up to raw talent.

WHAT ARE THE BEST PLACES TO SEE ART?

AROUND THE COYOTE

1817 W. Division St., Wicker Park, 773-342-6777;
www.aroundthecoyote.org

The Around the Coyote Festival started in 2000, when Wicker Park and Bucktown were "developing" areas with cheap rent where artists congregated. Nothing has changed much since then (except maybe the rents); the festival, which now happens three times a year, is an interdisciplinary celebration of visual and performance art and music, with scheduled shows and open artists studios for the curious to wander through. In case you miss one of the big bashes, check out the gallery, which is open year-round and holds monthly art exhibitions for emerging talent.
Gallery: Monday-Friday 10 a.m.-4 p.m., by appointment only.

CHICAGO ARTS DISTRICT

18th and Halsted streets, Pilsen; www.chicagoartsdistrict.org

The South Side doesn't see much action when it comes to art, but this rapidly gentrifying area of Pilsen is an exception to the rule. (The others are the Bronzeville Art District around 35th Street and South Martin Luther King Drive and the nascent Bridgeport Art District around Morgan and 32nd streets.) Don't miss out on Pilsen stalwart Vespine *(1907 S. Halsted St.; www.vespine.org)*, an artist-run gallery. If you're the type to nab 'em while they're young and still starving, visit the Chicago Art Department *(1837 S. Halsted St., 312-226-8601; www.chicagoartdepartment.org)*—the gallery doubles as an art school.
Every second Friday of the month, the district's galleries and studios open to the public to showcase work or unveil new shows.

MONIQUE MELOCHE

2154 W. Division, West Town, 773-252-0299;
www.moniquemeloche.com

After cutting her teeth at the Museum of Contemporary Art, Monique Meloche decided to open her own gallery in the then-up-and-coming warehouse district just west of the Loop in 2001, before moving to her current location in West Town. The gallery focuses on contemporary artists—an eclectic bunch from Chicago, the U.S. and around the world—that showcase installations, mixed media pieces and paintings with a decidedly hip vibe. You might see anything from Kendall Carter's classic takes on street art to Carla Arocha's large-scale plexiglass creations.
Tuesday-Saturday 11 a.m.-6 p.m.

AUDITORIUM THEATRE

RIVER NORTH GALLERIES
Franklin, Wells, Superior and Huron streets
Don't let the location under the El fool you—this slightly industrial strip is home to some of Chicago's most cutting edge galleries. The focus ranges from contemporary photography and outsider art to original masters' work and sculpture pieces.
See page 117 for more information.

TONY WIGHT GALLERY
119 N. Peoria St., West Loop, 312-492-7261;
www.tonywightgallery.com
This spot—which used to be called Bodybuilder & Sportsman gallery—is the oldest in a building that also houses several other galleries and work studios (so make sure to wander around). Tony Wight features quirky, conceptually challenging pieces with a wisp of DIY aesthetic, such as Jason Salavon's digital prints and light and video installations or Scott Fife's cardboard-and-screws severed heads of Jackson Pollock.
Tuesday-Saturday 11 a.m.-5 p.m.

WHAT ARE THE BEST COMEDY SHOWS?
IO CHICAGO
3541 N. Clark St., Wrigleyville, 773-880-0199; www.ioimprov.com
Formerly Improv Olympics (the place was forced to change its name after the International Olympic Committee cried foul), this is the place for Chicago improv. Alumni include Mike Myers, Andy Richter and Amy Poehler, and talented improvisers still cut their teeth here on a nightly basis. The iO's signature show—created by one of the founding fathers of improv comedy, the late Del Close—is the long-form improvisation "the Harold," in which an improv team creates hilarious and often-convoluted "plots" with just one audience suggestion. However, it'd be a shame to miss the various other improv and sketch comedy shows at the Cabaret Theater or the Del Close Theater. The iO opened a Los Angeles branch a few years ago, a testament

to its growing success on the stage as well as in Hollywood.
Admission: $5-$18. Various show times; check Web site for details.

THE SECOND CITY
1616 N. Wells St., Old Town, 312-337-3992; www.secondcity.com
It's no joke: The Second City means serious funny business. How else could the theater have remained a top tourist attraction and a requisite for local comedians honing their skills (on stage and in workshops) since it was established in 1959? The Second City's brand of political and social satire still smarts, both on the mainstage and the gutsier e.t.c. stage next door—and even on TV (on shows like *Saturday Night Live* and *The Daily Show*) and film, as evident by famous, whip-smart grads such as Bill Murray, Steve Carell and Amy Sedaris. Donny's Skybox, the cabaret theater, serves as a performance space Thursday to Saturday for students.
Admission: $15-$25 depending on show. Various show times; check Web site for details.

WHAT ARE THE TOP DANCE COMPANIES?
HUBBARD STREET DANCE CHICAGO
1147 W. Jackson Blvd., West Loop, 312-850-9744;
www.hubbardstreetdance.com
Founded in 1977 by Lou Conte, the HSDC is arguably the city's foremost dance company, specializing in contemporary modern dance. Under the leadership of current artistic director Glenn Edgerton (following Conte's retirement in 2000 and artistic director Jim Vincent's departure in 2009), the company moved from its jazz-centric beginnings into a worldlier repertoire, and is now known for brilliantly performing works by choreographers Nacho Duato, Toru Shimazaki and Jorma Elo. HSDC established the Hubbard Street Dance Center in 2006, which houses and administers the main company, along with Hubbard Street 2 (a company of young dancers), Lou Conte Dance Studio and HSDC's educational and community programs.
Check Web site for details.

JOFFREY BALLET
10 E. Randolph St., Loop, 312-739-0120; www.joffrey.com
This is one of the country's preeminent ballet companies, and it's not hard to see why. Since its founding in New York City in 1956 by Robert Joffrey and Gerald Arpino (it moved permanently to Chicago in 1995), the company has built a reputation for supporting and staging contemporary American ballet pieces and choreographers, such as Twyla Tharp and Alvin Ailey. To balance out its modern tendencies, it also leans heavily on the Ballet Russes tradition, so expect some works in that style, as well as more classic ballet pieces.
Show times and ticket prices vary. Check Web site for details.

WHAT ARE THE BEST VENUES FOR LIVE MUSIC?
BUDDY GUY'S LEGENDS
754 S. Wabash Ave., Loop, 312-427-1190; www.buddyguys.com
Chicagoans had a bit of a scare in early 2007 regarding the possible move of the South Loop stomping ground of blues icon Buddy Guy. Thankfully, the venue will remain on this quiet corner for the time being, but call just in case before heading out. Once inside, you'll be rewarded with classic, electrifying Chicago blues, sometimes courtesy of Guy himself. (He's in

HUBBARD STREET DANCE CHICAGO

town the month of January, and on and off the rest of the year in between touring engagements.) There's a free acoustic blues set on Fridays from 5:30-8 p.m. and Saturdays from 6-8:30 p.m.; the full-on jams, however, start around 9:30 p.m. nightly, usually for a $10-$15 cover.

Monday-Friday 11 a.m.-2 a.m., Saturday 5 p.m.-3 a.m., Sunday 6 p.m.-2 a.m.

EMPTY BOTTLE
1035 N. Western Ave., Ukrainian Village, 773-276-3600; www.emptybottle.com
Consider yourself warned: This place is a dive. But this dark bar showcases some of the best up-and-coming bands in the country, whether it's straight-up rock, free jazz or experimental DJs, to a hipsterati crowd of twenty-somethings who are there first and foremost for the music. Occasionally, you'll get notable emerging international acts, too—for example, feisty UK rapper Lady Sovereign performed here a good four months before she was featured in *The Independent*. It's well worth the risk of braving the sticky floor to be able to say you saw the next big thing play here first.

Monday-Wednesday 5 p.m.-2 a.m., Thursday-Friday 3 p.m.-2 a.m., Saturday noon-3 a.m., Sunday noon-2 a.m.

GREEN MILL
4802 N. Broadway, Lakeview (Uptown), 773-878-5552; www.greenmilljazz.com
The Mill's legend goes beyond the fact that Al Capone and his cronies used to hang out at the bar in the '20s. After a brief decline in the '70s, current owner Dave Jemilo bought it in 1986 and restored its speakeasy décor, cool-cat vibe, and '30s- and '40s-inspired jazz sounds. On any day of the week, you can find discerning jazz fiends of all stripes: middle-aged suits be-bopping their heads alongside fresh-out-of-college hipsters. But if you're lucky, you'll show up on the day of the week when resident and internationally

recognized jazz vanguard Patricia Barber takes the stage. The Sabertooth Quartet still jams from midnight through 4 a.m. on Saturday nights, while the Uptown Poetry Slam showcases verses on Sunday nights.
Daily noon-4 a.m.

HOUSE OF BLUES
329 N. Dearborn St., River North, 312-923-2000; www.hob.com
Never mind the name: The only blues you'll find here is usually relegated to the small Back Porch Stage and presented in the form of Guy King and Jimmy Burns. What you'll find on the main stage is a cocktail of musical acts, including the likes of Wolf Parade, Common, Peter Frampton, Roger Daltrey and Jay-Z. It doesn't hurt that the Chicago outpost of this national chain is also smack-dab in the middle of the city and housed in a building that resembles a giant turtle shell—and it's even cooler for its lush sound system. Go ahead and splurge on balcony seats—the view of the stage is unbeatable, and it's a small price to pay to make sure you don't get accidentally swept into the thick standing-room-only crowd that rushes the stage downstairs.
Show times and ticket prices vary. Check Web site for details.

JAY PRITZKER PAVILION
Millennium Park, Loop, 312-742-1168; www.millenniumpark.org
When the Pritzker Pavilion opened to much fanfare in 2004, there were murmurs that it would be Ravinia's undoing. A Frank Gehry-designed alfresco bandshell with mostly free programming in the heart of the city? Ravinia seemed like a distant memory. Luckily, both are coexisting just fine, although the Pritzker's dramatic look and sound are nothing to scoff about. The trellis over the lawn is laced with concert hall-quality speakers, so not an inch of the 7,000-capacity Great Lawn goes hard of hearing. (There are 4,000 permanent seats near the stage, which usually work on a first-come, first-served basis for free shows.) Though regular fare includes world music (Seu Jorge, Bajofondo Tango Club), jazz (Sonny Rollins), classical (Pinchas Zukerman) and experimental (Andrew Bird, Calexico), the Pritzker is also the summer home to the Grant Park Orchestra *(www.grantparkmusic festival.com)*.
Concerts run from June to September. Check Web site for details.

LINCOLN HALL
2424 N. Lincoln Ave., Lincoln Park, 773-525-2501;
www.lincolnhallchicago.com
Though it's the newest addition to the live music scene, Lincoln Hall isn't without its share of Chicago history. After opening in 1912 as the Lincoln Theater, the building gained fame in 1934 when FBI sharpshooters positioned themselves on the roof to prevent John Dillinger's escape from the Biograph Theatre across the street. Dillinger didn't survive the night, but the hall did and has hosted everything from a garage to an arts cinema. Today, the bi-level, exposed brick space affords a surprisingly intimate arena for live bands such as The Walkmen and Ted Leo and the Pharmacists. The full bar and small plates menu round out the offerings.
Sunday-Friday 11 a.m.-2 a.m., Saturday 11 a.m.-3 a.m. See Web site for shows.

LYRIC OPERA

Civic Opera House, 20 N. Wacker Drive, Loop, 312-332-2244;
www.lyricopera.org

Considered one of the most classical opera houses in the country—when we say "classical," we're referring to its repertoire, Art Deco digs, resident orchestra and ornate costumes—the Lyric stages eight productions per season. In recent years, these have included Mozart's *The Marriage of Figaro* and Puccini's *Tosca*. Maybe it's a sign that Chicagoans like to stick to the basics, but the Lyric sells out to 95 percent capacity for all runs, so make sure to get your tickets early.

Show times and ticket prices vary. Check Web site for details.

METRO/SMARTBAR

3730 N. Clark St., Wrigleyville, 773-549-0203;
www.metrochicago.com; www.smartbarchicago.com

For rock 'n' rollers and dance-music geeks, Metro and Smartbar have been delivering a deliciously deadly one-two punch for more than 25 years. Rock out upstairs at the worn-but-who-cares Metro, where the likes of R.E.M. and The Smashing Pumpkins played their earliest shows. (The caliber here remains—The White Stripes, Kanye West and Fall Out Boy were just a few of the headliners in recent years.) House-heads take it downstairs, where the focus is on Chicago, Detroit and international DJs (such as Jeff Mills, Derrick Carter, Green Velvet and Telefon Tel Aviv) who play gigs to pulsating crowds hopped up on liquor and/or good vibes. And though Smartbar is in the basement, it's hardly a dungeon; a massive redesign in 2006 left in its wake one of the slickest specimens on the North Side, complete with the bombastic Funktion One sound system. Prepare to be blown away.

Metro: Show dates and times vary; check Web site for details. Smartbar: Wednesday-Friday, Sunday 10 p.m.-4 a.m., Saturday 10 p.m.-5 a.m.

RAVINIA FESTIVAL

Ravinia Park, Green Bay Road, Highland Park, 847-266-5100;
www.ravinia.org

This seasonal festival is one of the few things worth a trip into the suburbs if you're a strapped-for-time visitor. What began as the summer home for the Chicago Symphony Orchestra—still at the heart of Ravinia's programming— now showcases an outstanding repertoire of diverse acts. (Case in point: the 2009 season featured Carrie Underwood, Tom Jones, Joe Cocker, John Legend and Gipsy Kings.) But the music and the immaculate acoustics can hardly speak for the overall landscape. The expansive, tightly manicured lawn is the stuff of a Pottery Barn garden catalog, as are the picnics that patrons bring in (some replete with antique candelabras and free-flowing wine). The pricier seats of the 3,200-seat Ravinia Pavilion aren't shabby, either. Smaller acts (like chamber music groups and youth concerts) take place at the Martin Theatre and Bennett-Gordon Hall.

Season runs June-September; check Web site for details.

SCHUBAS TAVERN

3159 N. Southport Ave., Lakeview, 773-525-2508; www.schubas.com

Chicago has a healthy indie-rock music scene, and Schubas is one of the best places to witness it first-hand, whether it's local acts or touring ones. Thankfully, it's not all indie navel-gazing and forlorn lyrics; the roster runs

BROADWAY IN CHICAGO

This production company has made a name for itself by bringing in big-ticket showstoppers like *Mamma Mia!*, *Rent* and, of course, *Chicago*. Most of the touring productions Broadway in Chicago brings in hit the stages of the **Bank of America Theatre** *(18 W. Monroe St., Loop, 312-986-6821)*—formerly the Shubert Theatre—and **Cadillac Palace Theatre** *(151 W. Randolph St., Loop, 312-986-5853)*. The **Ford Center for the Performing Arts, Oriental Theatre** *(24 W. Randolph St., Loop, 312-986-6863)* housed *Wicked* since its Chicago debut in June 2005 until January 2009, and it's the highest-grossing Broadway musical in the city to date. (*The Producers* with Nathan Lane and Matthew Broderick—which debuted in February 2001 for its pre-Broadway test launch—is the one that got away.) And though *Wicked* is no more and *Jersey Boys*, at the Bank of America Theatre, wraps up in January 2010, the 2010 roster is full of sure-to-be hits: *Annie*, *Dreamgirls*, and *Billy Elliot: The Musical*.

Even if you don't make a show, try to make some time for the Broadway in Chicago walking tour, which covers two of the three theaters on Saturday mornings. During the tour, you'll learn how Judy Garland got her stage name at the Oriental and how the Cadillac Palace chandeliers avoided being drafted during World War II, in addition to the history behind the vintage opulence of these working relics of a bygone era. Theater tours are $10 and depart from the Oriental Theatre at 11 a.m. on Saturday mornings; visit the Web site for details *(www.broadwayinchicago.com)*.

Many shows sell through Ticketmaster *(www.ticketmaster.com)*, though hefty fees add to the price, so you're probably better off calling theater box offices directly. The **League of Chicago Theatres** *(www.chicagoplays.com)* has a comprehensive online guide to what's on and at what time; it also administers **Hot Tix** *(www.hottix.org)*, where you can buy half-off tickets to select shows. Buy through the Web site or at two locations *(72 E. Randolph St. and at the Chicago Waterworks Visitor Center, 163 E. Pearson St.; closed Monday)*.

the gamut from honky-tonk and country to pop and jazz. Among those to have graced the stage include Neko Case, Dave Matthews Band and Sufjan Stevens. But if for some reason the backroom main stage isn't filling you up, check out the photo booth at the bar up front or head next door to the Harmony Grill for reliably good comfort food.

Monday-Friday 11 a.m.-2 a.m., Saturday 9 a.m.-3 a.m., Sunday 9 a.m.-2 a.m.

SYMPHONY CENTER
220 S. Michigan Ave., Loop, 312-294-3000; www.cso.org

In early 2008, the Chicago Symphony Orchestra named a new director, Riccardo Muti, after its ninth one, Daniel Barenboim, left in 2006. Still, we've yet to see whether a new director signals a new direction: Muti's five-year contract starts with the 2010/2011 season, which means that until then, classical music fans will probably get more of the CSO's deep and brassy signature sound. It also doesn't hurt that the cavernous Symphony Center was renovated in 1997 and—though the CSO plays every weekend and certain weekdays except in the summer months—that it also serves as a concert hall for touring orchestras and organizations it runs, including the Civic Orchestra of Chicago and the Youth Symphony Orchestra.

Admission: $12-$200 depending on show. Various show times; check Web site for details.

WHAT ARE THE CITY'S SPORTS TEAMS?

CHICAGO BEARS
Soldier Field, 1410 S. Museum Campus Drive, South Loop (Museum Campus), 847-295-6600; www.chicagobears.com

Perhaps no other team is so loved across the city as "da Bears," which call Soldier Field home. Nobody will soon forget the glory days of the '80s, when the Super Bowl shuffle, William "Refrigerator" Perry and Mike Ditka made it all the way to the top. After a dry spell in the 1990s and early 2000s, the Bears made a comeback in 2007 (getting all the way to the Super Bowl before losing to the Indiana Colts) with formidable defense and a promising team of young players like Brian Urlacher, Matt Forte and Devin Hester.

CHICAGO BULLS
United Center, 1901 W. Madison St., West Loop, 312-455-4000; www.nba.com/bulls

Basically immortalized across the globe by Michael Jordan, the Bulls are no longer that dream team from the '90s: they've suffered through years of losing seasons, but the late-2000s saw a batch of rookies (Ben Gordon, Tyrus Thomas and Joakim Noah), changing the face of the team. Games now are fast-paced affairs that, although lacking the wow factor of the Jordan years, demonstrate just as much heart and action.

CHICAGO CUBS
Wrigley Field, 1060 W. Addison St., Wrigleyville, 773-404-2827; www.cubs.mlb.com

The curse of the billy goat. Poor trades. And then there's the 2003 Steve Bartman fiasco. Since 1908, when the Cubs last won the World Series, the gods of baseball seem to conspire against these "lovable losers." (Though they came awfully close in 2008, only to be swept in the first round of play-offs.) Still, going to watch the "Cubbies" is a summertime rite of

SOLDIER FIELD

MUSEUM CAMPUS

passage, one in which at least fans come out winning—just being inside the ivy-festooned, historic Wrigley Field is a stirring experience. (Wrigley was built in 1914, and it still boasts a manual scoreboard; it installed lights to play night games only in 1988.) Try to get tickets in the bleachers, where drinking, sunning and socializing is just as important to some Cubs fans as the team finally winning a pennant would be. Can't get into the stadium? Celebrate in any of the dozens of watering holes around the Friendly Confines—thousands of fans tend to make game days all-day benders at popular bars like Cubby Bear (1059 W. Addison St., 773-372-1662; www.cubbybear.com) and Murphy's Bleachers (3655 N. Sheffield Ave., 773-281-5356; www.murphysbleachers.com).

CHICAGO WHITE SOX

U.S. Cellular Field, 333 W. 35th St., Bridgeport, 312-674-1000;
www.whitesox.mlb.com

The pride of the South Side, the Sox are often considered the Second City's second team, at least outside the confines of the city limits. Though the Sox's 2005 World Series victory seems to be turning the tides of popularity outside of Chicago, for fervent, lifelong fans here at home, it's business as usual. That means standing behind captain Paul Konerko, heavy hitters Jermaine Dye, A.J. Pierzynski and Carlos Quentin, and jovial but foul-mouthed manager Ozzie Guillen as they try to keep the momentum going. The corporate-sounding name of the Sox's home, U.S. Cellular Field, is a good indication of what the stadium looks like—modern (it was completed in 1991), massive, in the middle of a sea of concrete, and by all counts a bit impersonal, especially in comparison to Wrigley. Still, fans have made "the new Comiskey" a bit friendlier by nicknaming it "the Cell". If that isn't cute and cuddly enough for you, head to Schaller's Pump (3714 S. Halsted St., 773-376-6332), where the heart of the franchise—die-hard fans—gather for a pre-game drink.

WHAT ARE SOME OF THE BEST THEATERS?

AUDITORIUM THEATRE
50 E. Congress Parkway, Loop, 312-902-2110;
www.auditoriumtheatre.org

Opened in 1889, this gorgeous Louis Sullivan and Dankmar Adler-designed theater—a National Historic Landmark—regularly hosts dance, music and theater events, thanks in part to its splendid acoustics. It has hosted the Bolshoi Ballet, Alvin Ailey American Dance Theater and Kirov Ballet, and Chicago's Joffrey Ballet has a permanent home here. But it's not just about dance. The theater is no stranger to musicals and jazz shows. The gold-leaf interior, nature-landscape murals and soaring arch above the stage are reason enough to pay the entry fee.
Show times and ticket prices vary. Check Web site for details.

THE CHICAGO THEATRE
175 N. State St., Loop, 312-462-6300; www.thechicagotheatre.com

Before "The Bean" and Navy Pier, and before the ritzy entertainment hub that was State Street hit the skids in the late '70s, this French Baroque-style theater with a colorful marquee was the stuff of postcards. Luckily, it is once again, thanks to the Loop's recent Theater District revival. On any given night, catch anything from national touring musicals and *So You Think You Can Dance* auditions to concerts by Steely Dan and Erykah Badu, and comedy shows by hometown gal Kathy Griffin—that is, if you're not too busy ooh-ing and ahh-ing at the lavish chandeliers and grand staircase.
Show times and ticket prices vary. Check Web site for details.

THE GOODMAN THEATRE
170 N. Dearborn St., Loop, 312-443-3800; www.goodmantheatre.org

Under Tony Award-winning artistic director Robert Falls, this theater company—one of Chicago's most venerable at 80-plus years old—has put on classics (*Death of a Salesman*) and cutting-edge spins on classics (Mary Zimmerman's version of *The Odyssey*). That's not to say that the work here is stuffy: The Goodman also focuses on ethnically diverse lineups, staging works by African-American playwrights and a notable (but, sadly, only biennial) Latino theater festival. If you're the sentimental sort, don't miss its annual staging of *A Christmas Carol*; it's what every holiday production hopes to be.
Show times and ticket prices vary. Check Web site for details.

HOUSE THEATRE OF CHICAGO
Chopin Theatre, 1543 W. Division St., Wicker Park, 773-251-2195;
www.thehousetheatre.com

For a taste of the future of Chicago theater, do not miss a production by this rough-and-tumble storefront troupe. Expect lots of pop-culture references, rapid-fire delivery and action-film moves. The trilogy of plays that put this group on the map spanned several centuries and took place in the Wild West, feudal Japan and 1920s gangland Chicago.
Show times and ticket prices vary. Check Web site for details.

STEPPENWOLF THEATRE COMPANY
1650 N. Halsted St., Lincoln Park, 312-335-1650;
www.steppenwolf.org

Everyone has heard of The Steppenwolf's famous co-founder, Gary Sinise,

CHICAGO BLUES FESTIVAL

HOW DID CHICAGO LEARN TO SING THE BLUES?

It all started in a small, lopsided former automobile parts factory at 2120 S. Michigan Ave., an address immortalized by the Rolling Stones in their bluesy instrumental of the same name. The building was purchased by the Chess brothers, and, from 1957 to 1967, it operated as the home of Chess Records, the recording studio that gave the world the sad, edgy sound of the "Chicago blues."

All the greats recorded here, or wanted to: Muddy Waters, Koko Taylor and Etta James. Junior Wells, whose harmonica playing—"harps," as it was called—influenced countless blues greats, including Junior's longtime friend and partner, Chicago legend Buddy Guy.

In the early days, Buddy was a red-hot backup musician. But as the years wore on, he became a showman, a flamboyant stylist who would hit his guitar against a microphone to get an acoustic sound, pluck its strings with his tongue, or hit the strings with a belt or drumstick to get a tone. He could coax any sound he wanted out of that thing, they said. Buddy made his guitar talk to you, they said. They said other things, too. Eric Clapton called him the greatest blues guitar player in the world and asked Buddy to play with him at Royal Albert Hall. The accolades inspired Guy's ironically titled album, Damn Right I've Got the Blues, the first of his four albums to win Grammys. Clapton wasn't the only rock star influenced by Guy, nor was he the first. The Rolling Stones asked Buddy and Junior Wells to open for them on their 1970 tour.

In 1989, Buddy opened a club on Chicago's South Side, **Buddy Guy's Legends** *(page 153)*, so that blues artists would have a home in the Windy City. For 20 years, the venue has drawn blues fans from across the globe, eager to hear the gritty soulful sound of Chicago's up-and-coming blues artists and revered mainstays. If you're lucky, you might even see the legend himself, though his club drop-in's are becoming less frequent. Recently, there has been talk of the club closing, but for now, it's as busy—and bluesy—as ever.

and its legendary ensemble (John Malkovich, Joan Allen, Martha Plimpton, John Mahoney, et al). But this company—which started in the basement of a suburban church, with blokes and tough guys as prime subject matter— hasn't let fame, nor a slick space in Lincoln Park, go to its head. It still produces thought-provoking work with bite, like ensemble member Tracy Letts' 2008 Pulitzer Prize- and Tony Award-winning play, *August: Osage County*.

Show times and ticket prices vary. Check Web site for details.

CHICAGO'S BEST FESTIVALS

Chicago's freezing winters mean only one thing—way too much to do during warmer months. Here's a primer to the city's best festivals.

FALL

Chicago Jazz Festival
Grant Park, Loop; www.chicagojazzfestival.us
This largely free fest features four full days of jazz courtesy of locals like Kurt Elling and genre luminaries like Sonny Rollins and Ornette Coleman. Bring a blanket and camp out in front of the Petrillo Music Shell or the Pritzker Pavilion, but be warned that this is the city's longest-running music fest (30 years and counting) and super popular, so show up early for a good spot. *Labor Day weekend*

SPRING

St. Patrick's Day
Downtown, Loop;
www.chicagostpatsparade.com
and South Side;
www.southsideirishparade.org
There are usually two big celebrations: downtown and on the South Side. The downtown one kicks off at 10:45 a.m. on the nearest Saturday to March 17 with the Chicago River being dyed a bright green hue, followed up with a parade. The South Side Irish St. Patrick's Day Parade—at Western Avenue and 103rd Street in the Beverly neighborhood—typically happens in early March and is a lot more authentic, but after the 2009 parade and much public drunkenness, the South Side Irish St. Patrick's Day Parade Committee decided to alter the annual parade for 2010. Stay tuned for smaller alternate events that celebrate the neighborhood's Irish heritage.
March

Gospel Music Festival
Millennium Park, Loop;
www.chicagogospelmusicfestival.us
Don't be surprised if you get goosebumps when you hear local musicians and seasoned performers belt out everything from classics to contemporary tunes. Past performers included Kirk Franklin, Maurice Griffin and *American Idol*'s Fantasia Barrino.
Late May/early June

Grant Park Music Festival
Jay Pritzker Pavilion, Millennium Park, Loop; www.grantparkmusicfestival.com
The country's only free, outdoor classical music series spans the city's warm months, and there's nothing like hearing Beethoven while sitting under the stars. Tickets for general seating aren't necessary (most concerts are free), and picnics are welcome and part of the fun.
June to mid-August

Chicago Blues Festival
Grant Park, Loop;
www.chicagobluesfest.org
There's some pressure for this festival—after all, this is Chicago, home of Muddy Waters and the electric blues, and that attracts more than half a million devotees to this event. Thankfully, its programmers do a consistently solid job with the lineup, which has included big acts like Grammy winner Buddy Guy and Mavis Staples and smaller local acts scattered over seven stages and venues.
First weekend in June

Old Town Art Fair
N. Lincoln and W. Wisconsin avenues, Old Town; www.oldtownartfair.org
You don't need to be an artist to appreciate the festivities at this juried fair, one of the oldest in the country. Come to see painting, sculpture, photography and ceramics by regional artists; stay to drink tall lemonades, chow down on food from nearby restaurants and listen to live music with the locals.
Second weekend in June

SUMMER

Chicago Pride Fest
Boystown, Lakeview;
www.chicagoevents.com
Chicagoans celebrate the LGBT community with this weekend of performances, arts & crafts and food vendors. The crown jewel of the three-day event is the Pride Parade on Sunday, which features some of the wackiest and boldest outfits and floats this side of Mardi Gras.
Fourth weekend in June

Taste of Chicago
Grant Park, Loop; www.tasteofchicago.us
At 10 days long and with 6 million visitors in attendance, this is the most bloated Chicago tradition. If you can navigate the molasses-thick crowds, you'll be rewarded with food from more than 70 city restaurants, and performances by the likes of Buddy Guy, Counting Crows, Ne-Yo and Barenaked Ladies.
Late June to early July

Independence Day Fireworks
Grant Park, Loop; www.tasteofchicago.us
The city's official Fourth of July fireworks display actually happens on the Third, around 9:30 p.m. The best views are near the Taste of Chicago grounds or by the lakefront. Locals stake out spots as early as that morning.
July 3

Chicago Outdoor Film Festival
Grant Park, Loop;
www.chicagooutdoorfilmfestival.us
Once a week at dusk during the summer, the City of Chicago screens classic films under the stars. Show up around 7 p.m. and stake out a spot with a picnic beforehand (it fills up fast so for the best spots, get there even earlier).
Tuesday, mid-July to late August

Venetian Night
Lake Michigan at Monroe Harbor, South Loop (Museum Campus);
www.cityofchicago.org
Why this event doesn't happen on the Chicago River is beyond us—after all, wouldn't that make it more like Venice?—but it's still worth a gander if you want to see privately-owned boats decked out in lights and parading down the lakefront

followed by a fireworks display. The parade usually starts around 8 p.m.
Last Saturday in July

Lollapalooza
Grant Park, Loop; www.lollapalooza.com
Lolla—the brainchild of Jane's Addiction's Perry Farrell—took root in Chicago in the summer of 2005, and it looks like it's here to stay, at least until 2011 when its contract with the city ends. The giant music festival brings in bigger-than-life acts like The Killers, Kings of Leon and Depeche Mode, alongside emerging indie fare of the local variety (Andrew Bird, Hey Champ) and international ones (Bat for Lashes, Gomez) spread out over three days. Stay hydrated—it gets hot.
First weekend in August

Bud Billiken Day Parade & Picnic
39th Street and S. King Drive to Washington Park, South Side;
www.budbillikenparade.com
This African-American parade started in 1929 by Chicago Defender founder Robert Abbott; it's now the largest of its kind in the nation. Held in honor of Chicago youth, the parade features more than 315 floats and has attracted celebrity participants such as Muhammad Ali, Oprah Winfrey, Michael Jordan and President Barack Obama. The parade meanders around the Hyde Park neighborhood and ends up with a barbecue at Washington Park.
Second Saturday in August

Chicago Air & Water Show
North Avenue Beach, Gold Coast;
www.chicagoairandwatershow.us
The U.S. Navy Blue Angels show off each summer with masterful aerial acrobatics. The best views are along North Avenue Beach. Actually, scratch that: The best views are from any of the skyscrapers facing Lake Michigan, so find yourself a friend with a condo on the lakefront.
Mid-August

BEYOND CHICAGO

INDIANA DUNES

MIDWEST BEST

Although there's an endless list of things to do in Chicago, the city's location along Lake Michigan and at the center of the tri-state area of Illinois, Indiana and Wisconsin makes it an ideal spot from which to tour some of the top parts of the Midwest. Just beyond Chicago's never-ending highway construction, you'll find beaches, art museums, concerts, festivals and, believe it or not, wineries, all within a 90-minute drive from the Windy City.

WHAT'S THE BEST WAY TO SEE NEARBY WINERIES?

For your grape escape, you'll want to follow the **Lake Michigan Wine Trail**, a ready-made tour denoted by blue and white signs along the roads. First, download the wine trail map from www.miwinetrail.com. Eleven wineries dot the route, several off Interstate 94, but if you're short on time (or designated drivers), instead of tackling all of the wineries, pick a couple of spots to savor.

St. Julian Winery *(716 S. Kalamazoo St., Paw Paw, Michigan, 800-732-6002; www.stjulian.com)* is Michigan's oldest winery and one of its best. After taking a free tour of the grounds, head to the tasting room and snag some delicious riesling. If reds are more your thing, visit **Lemon Creek Winery and Fruit Farm** *(533 E. Lemon Creek Road, Berrien Springs, Michigan, 269-471-1321; www.lemoncreekwinery.com)* to sample its cabernets. While you're there, check out the farm stand and buy some of southwestern Michigan's luscious, plump fruit, such as blueberries, raspberries or cherries (if they are in season).

Get your last drop of vino at **Tabor Hill Winery & Restaurant** *(185 Mount Tabor Road, Buchanan, Michigan, 800-283-3363; www.taborhill.com)*. After testing some vintages in the tasting room and taking the free tour of the grounds, eat a hearty meal to soak up the alcohol. The restaurant serves seasonal cuisine; pair the pecan breadcrumb-coated raspberry chicken and sweet potato succotash with demi-sec. As you dine in the honey-colored-wood dining room, be sure to drink in the beautiful view of the vineyard from the large windows before hitting your own trail back to Chicago.

How to get there: Taking your taste buds to southwest Michigan for a wine-tasting trip is easy. Harbor Country (www.harborcountry.org), an eight-town region that hugs Lake Michigan, is only a 70-minute drive from downtown Chicago. To get there, take Interstate 90 east, merging onto Interstate 94 east. Follow Interstate 94 through Indiana into Michigan.

WHAT IS THERE TO SEE AT THE INDIANA DUNES?

If you're tired of fighting for sand space on North Avenue Beach, head to **Indiana Dunes State Park** *(1100 N. Mineral Springs Road, Indiana, 219-926-7561; www.nps.gov/indu)* and make your monumental sand castle among the abundant sands of the dunes. Located 50 miles east of Chicago in Northwest Indiana, the park offers great hiking as well as year-round activities, from swimming and dune climbing in the summer to cross-country skiing and snowshoeing in the winter.

Before you go, visit **Ashkenaz Deli** *(12 E. Cedar St., Chicago, 312-944-5006)* in the Loop and order a box lunch (which comes with a sandwich, side, chips and a treat) to eat in the park during your hike.

Then hop onto I-90 east into Indiana and merge onto U.S. Highway east toward Porter. Your first stop should be at the recently built **Dorothy Buell**

MICHIGAN FRUIT

Memorial Visitor Center *(U.S. Highway 20 and Indiana Route 49, Porter, Indiana, 219-926-7561)*, where you'll receive an overview of the woodlands and beach areas, as well as directions to good picnic spots. Begin the day with a romp through the deep sands of the dunes, then settle down for a picnic lunch along the three-mile beach, West Beach, where the Chicago skyline is visible from the shore on a clear day. Hiking the huge desert-like sand dunes is the reason to come here; the largest is Mount Baldy, whose 126-foot climb is a challenge. Don't be surprised if, like the poet Carl Sandburg, who often visited the dunes, you find bliss in the park's quiet, punctuated by the calls and songs of its more than 350 bird species.

There's much to do nearby, too. The historic **Chellberg Farm** *(U.S. Highway 20 and Mineral Springs Road, Porter, Indiana)* and home shows what farm life was like back in the 1880s for the Chellbergs, an immigrant Swedish family who lived in the area. For something a little more 21st century, there's always one of the nearby riverboat casinos, the most-well known of which (thanks to its ubiquitous road-side signs) is **Hammond's Horseshoe Casino** *(777 Casino Center Drive, Hammond, Indiana, 866-711-7463; www.horseshoehammond.com)*, whose size more than doubled after a 2008 renovation. After betting the farm on the craps tables, empty the sand out of your shoes and head back to Chicago.

How to get there: If you're driving, get off at the U.S. 20/Indiana State Highway from Interstate 94 or the Indiana Toll Road. Or take the South Shore Line (there's a stop at Michigan Avenue and Randolph Street in downtown Chicago; www.nictd.com) to either the Miller, Portage/Ogden Dunes, Dune Park or Beverly Shores station in Indiana.

WHAT IS THERE TO SEE AND DO IN MILWAUKEE?

When Chicagoans want to unwind, they head to Milwaukee (just 90 minutes north of the city), where they can see groundbreaking art, take in amazing concerts and, most of all, just kick back with a frosty brew.

If you devoured Chicago's Art Institute in a day and are hungry for more eye candy, visit the **Milwaukee Art Museum** *(700 N. Art Museum*

Drive, Milwaukee, Wisconsin, 414-224-3200; www.mam.org), which was designed in part by world-renowned architect Santiago Calatrava. Against the backdrop of the lake, Calatrava designed a pedestrian bridge to the museum that looks like the sails of a boat leading to a one-story galleria, which evokes the shape of a wave. The collection of 20,000 works inside the building is outstanding, especially for fans of Wisconsin native Georgia O'Keeffe.

Milwaukee's lakefront also rocks with **Summerfest** *(200 N. Harbor Drive, Milwaukee, Wisconsin; www.summerfest.com)*, a massive annual concert that draws music fans from across the U.S. to hear acts as varied as Stevie Wonder, No Doubt, Kenny Chesney, Flogging Molly, Bob Dylan and Lupe Fiasco. The 11-day noon-to-midnight behemoth is Milwaukee's best festival, but it gets some fierce competition from **German Fest** *(200 N. Harbor Drive, Milwaukee, Wisconsin; www.germanfest.com)*, which celebrates the city's roots (and its beer)—Milwaukee didn't get the nickname Brew City for nothing. You can guzzle steins of suds and chow down on sauerbraten while watching lederhosen-clad musicians belt out traditional Teutonic tunes.

The city's known for its German heritage and the breweries German families started here, including Pabst, Schlitz and Miller. Now called **MillerCoors** *(4000 W. State St., Milwaukee, Wisconsin, 800-944-5483; www.millercoors.com)*, the company still offers the best brewery tour (it helps that the other mega-brewers have left town), which shows off how Miller started out at a small Plank Street property to become eventually the brand that fills out about half the commercials during any given football game. After the free hour-long tour, which looks at every stage of the brewing process, you're rewarded with some complimentary ale (for those over 21). For a taste of the smaller breweries bubbling up in the city, check out **Lakefront Brewery** *(1872 N. Commerce St., Milwaukee, Wisconsin, 414-372-8800; www.lakefrontbrewery.com)*. The brewery's tours are $6 and include a complimentary pint glass and four pours—yet more great reasons to plan a return trip to Cream City.

How to get there: Take Interstate 94 from Chicago into Wisconsin, or take Amtrak's Hiawatha line (www.amtrakhiawatha.com) out of Union Station (225 S. Canal St., Chicago) to the Milwaukee Intermodal Station.

WHERE CAN YOU SEE FRANK LLOYD WRIGHT'S ARCHITECTURE?

Oak Park is best known for having the highest concentration of homes and buildings designed and built by Frank Lloyd Wright, the preeminent American architect whose streamlined style took on the once-prominent and ornate Victorian standard. Bibliophiles also head to Oak Park to see the birthplace of Ernest Hemingway and the local museum dedicated to his life and work.

If you happen to be driving there, slow down on Chicago Avenue just east of Harlem Avenue—along the street, keep an eye out for houses numbered 1019, 1027 and 1031, all of which are Wright's not-so-exciting early works. They followed the Queen Anne-type designs that were popular before Wright created the style that would make him famous.

The **Frank Lloyd Wright Home and Studio** *(951 Chicago Ave., Oak Park, Illinois, 708-848-1976; www.wrightplus.org)* is a must-see for any fan of architecture. But you won't be able to peruse the museum on your own; entry is available with a 60-minute guided tour only (just be sure to reserve a ticket online beforehand since tours often sell out). The home served as Wright's workplace and residence for the first 20 years of his career. It's not his best work—he changed it frequently for practical purposes and it has little of the grace of sites he developed nearby—but the home shows off the evolution of his style as it changed to meet the needs of his growing family. In this house and the adjoining studio, Wright and his associates invented the Prairie School of architecture, designing 125 buildings along the way, including the **Unity Temple of Oak Park** (875 W. Lake St., Oak Park, Illinois, 708-383-8873), where as a congregant, Wright was asked to design a replacement for the previously burned-down church. The exterior of the building is cold and uninviting, but the interior is still exciting to see and maintains a contemporary feel more than a century after its design. Using simple angles and stained wood instead of paint, Wright managed to design a church that was both "democratic," as he set out to do, and magisterial, befitting its role as a place of worship.

Very different in architectural style is the **Ernest Hemingway Birthplace** (339 N. Oak Park Ave., Oak Park, Illinois, 708-848-2222; www.ehfop.org), a Victorian building refurbished to its turn-of-the-century style. The home contains some mementos from Hemingway's childhood and information about his birth and life here; understandably, it downplays the writer's characterization of Oak Park as a place of "wide lawns and narrow minds." A short walk away is the **Ernest Hemingway Museum** (200 N. Oak Park Ave., Oak Park, Illinois, 708-524-5383), which has photos and Hemingway artifacts, including his childhood diary and earliest writing. The museum features a short documentary on his life and covers in detail his teenage years—good grist for parsing the psyche of this complicated man.

Beyond the Wright and Hemingway homes, there is much to do in Oak Park, which takes pride in its attention to the arts. Local art galleries show off some of the best works in the Chicagoland area. Check out **Ridge Art** (21 Harrison St., Oak Park, Illinois, 708-848-4062; www.ridgeart.com), which carries unusual Haitian pieces. With tree-lined streets and amiable proprietors of charming cafés and bakeries—take a final pit-stop at **Petersen's** (1100 Chicago Ave., Oak Park, Illinois, 708-386-6130, www.petersenicecream. com), for some lip-smacking old-fashioned ice cream sundaes—you'll find Oak Park a nice treat after your taste of Chicago.

How to get there: Just ten miles due west of downtown Chicago, Oak Park is easily accessible by car (or you can hop on the El's Green Line to the Oak Park stop). Take I-290 west to Harlem Avenue (Route 43). Turn north, and drive 1.5 miles to Chicago Avenue.

WHAT IS THERE TO SEE AND DO IN KOHLER, WISCONSIN?

There is a lot more to Wisconsin than delicious cheese and beautiful lakes. The small city of Kohler, located two and a half hours north of Chicago on the shores of Lake Michigan and the Sheboygan River, just happens to be the Midwest's golf mecca.

One of the nation's first planned communities, designed with the help of the Olmsted Brothers firm of Boston, Kohler began as a garden at the factory gate and headquarters for the country's largest plumbing manufacturer. Today, the city is all about recreation. The four world-class golf courses within **Blackwolf Run** and **Whistling Straits**, both designed by legendary Pete Dye, are challenging and scenic with 40-foot high dunes and miles of coastline. (The Straits course is slated to host the 2010 and

MILWAUKEE ART MUSEUM

2015 PGA Championships and the Ryder Cup in 2020.)

The John Michael Kohler Arts Center *(608 New York Ave., Kohler, 920-458-6144; www.jmkac.org)* is a nice alternative to hitting the links, with changing contemporary art exhibits, galleries and a theater, dance and concert series. A must-see for nature-lovers, the **River Wildlife** *(411 Highland Drive, Kohler, 920-457-0134)* is considered a "country club in the woods" with horseback riding, canoeing, fishing, hiking and camping all on a private 500-acre wildlife preserve.

Of course, you don't need to camp. One of the nation's most luxurious resorts is right here. **The American Club** *(419 Highland Drive, Kohler, 920-457-8000; www.americanclub.com)* epitomizes country chic, offering upscale accommodations and warm customer service. The rooms are elegantly simple with wood-beamed ceilings, white duvets and Kohler bathrooms (of course). The Kohler Waters Spa is the centerpiece of the resort and sets a happy, relaxing atmosphere. You'll find guests padding around in spa robes throughout the day and into the evening, when everyone mingles in the lobby over wine, cheese and other tasty nibbles.

For a more complete meal, try **The Immigrant Restaurant and Winery Bar** *(419 Highland Drive, 920-457-8888)*. No expense was spared when it came to creating the space, originally remnants of Walter J. Kohler Sr.'s boarding house. Divided into six rooms, each of which represents the nationalities that populated Wisconsin in its early days—Dutch, German, Norman, Danish, French and English—the restaurant is elegant and cozy. You can't go wrong anywhere on the menu, which is why the tasting menu is a popular choice, offering such delicacies as olive oil-poached black cod in an orange emulsion and braised organic pork belly and New England lobster. For a more casual dining experience, try **Cucina** *(725 E. Woodlake Road, Kohler, 920-457-8888)*. The pastas are hearty and the view of Wood Lake is spectacular regardless of the season.

While the summer is the most popular time to visit, the fall can be equally enjoyable, thanks to vibrant changing foliage and special events. The **Kohler**

FRANK LLOYD WRIGHT'S MOORE-DUGAL HOUSE, OAK PARK

Food and Wine Experience *(11 Upper Road, Kohler, 800-344-2838; www. destinationkohler.com)* is another good excuse to avoid the crowds and come in October, when the community is aflutter with cooking demonstrations, food and wine tastings and seminars. Or see how Wisconsin does winter, as the Traditional Holiday Illumination puts Kohler aglow with more than 200,000 lights on trees surrounding the Kohler village.

How to get there: Kohler is about 2 1/2 hours from Chicago. Take Interstate 94 West from Chicago into Wisconsin; continue onto Interstate 43 North for 50 miles; Exit at 123 for Interstate 28 toward Sheboygan/Sheboygan Falls; Take that to Co Road A, and go right, then left at Co Road PP/Lower Road/ Lower Falls Road; then take the first right onto Highland Drive.

KNOW BEFORE YOU GO

WILLIS TOWER

WHAT IS THE BEST WAY TO ARRIVE AND DEPART?

Two international airports serve Chicago: **O'Hare International Airport** (ORD) and **Midway International Airport** (MDW). O'Hare *(773-686-2200; www.flychicago.com)* lies about 20 miles northwest of the city center, and it's used by more than 70 million passengers a year. The airport has four terminals: 1, 2 and 3 serve mostly domestic flights, while Terminal 5 serves international arrivals and departures. O'Hare can be a nightmarish beehive for the uninitiated, so make sure you show up at least two hours before your flight, and double-check that you're going to the right terminal. Airport architects were wise to build in a Starbucks at baggage claim, too—this area alone can be enough to test your patience.

The Airport Transit System (ATS) provides transit between all terminals, long-term parking lots and the Metra station. Passengers can also access the Chicago Transit Authority (CTA) Blue Line El train, which provides 24-hour service to downtown Chicago for $2.25 There are also taxi ranks outside the baggage claim area of each terminal; rides downtown cost about $40 with tip, and usually take 30 minutes with no traffic.

The recently renovated but smaller Midway International Airport *(773-686-2200; www.flychicago.com)* is 10 miles southwest of downtown. It serves mostly low-fare lines, in addition to a few major airlines, and though prone to busy periods, it's still a much smaller option than O'Hare, and thereby more manageable. You can access the CTA El train here as well; a $2.25 trip on the Orange Line to downtown takes about 35-40 minutes. Taxis are also available outside baggage claim and the 20- to 25-minute trip downtown costs $25-$35.

WHAT ARE THE PUBLIC TRANSPORTATION OPTIONS?

The **Chicago Transit Authority** (CTA) is the state-run organization responsible for most city buses and the "El" (short for "Elevated Track," this is the mass-transit train line that crisscrosses the city). Aside from being safe, if somewhat rickety and old, the train system is also a good way to get around the city if you're going the four cardinal directions, and if you're not in a hurry. (Constant track repairs and train delays are part of the experience.) Don't ask us why the El's planners place most of the system above ground, in a city that's so cold for a solid three months. Locals put up with it because it's the cheapest way to zip across town—plus, it's a great way to get a bird's-eye view of neighborhoods and, in the Loop, practically a free architectural tour.

Most of the eight color-coordinated lines meet downtown. You can get maps and information at CTA station booths or at www.transitchicago.com; the Web site also has added bonuses like a trip planner (an itinerary builder fueled by Google maps) and CTA Bus Tracker (which tracks buses with GPS technology).

Fare cards can be bought at automated machines within 144 rail stations; likewise, most stations have information kiosks, but non-CTA personnel occasionally man these, and they don't sell fare cards. At press time, fares using a Transit Card were $2 per one-way ride on buses and $2.25 on trains, and transfers (two additional rides within two hours after first boarding) were $0.25. Cash: $2.25 per ride for buses (you must have exact change and transfers are not issued when paying cash). You can also buy a Visitor Pass (one day, $5.75; three days, $14) and 7-Day Pass ($28) options. Just be mindful that the beleaguered CTA constantly battles budget shortages and service cuts, so prices are subject to change.

ARE TAXIS AVAILABLE?

Taxis are plentiful in highly trafficked areas (the Loop, River North, Michigan Avenue, Lincoln Park, Lakeview, Wicker Park), and less so in strictly residential neighborhoods and the suburbs. If a cab has its lights on, it means it's unoccupied and ready to be flagged; when the light is off, it means it already has passengers. Fares start at $2.25 and increase by $0.20 for each 1/9 of a mile; the first additional passenger is $1 (after that, each additional passenger is $0.50). There's no extra charge for your luggage, though a 15 to 20 percent tip at the end of your trip is expected.

DO I NEED TO RENT A CAR?

Locals love to say how Chicago is a very drivable city, but unless you're staying far away from any public transportation, you really don't need a car. Depending on where you're staying, you might end up paying more for parking than you would for your flight or your rental car. If you do need a car, major car rental firms are available outside O'Hare and Midway; they include **Avis** *(800-331-1212; www.avis.com)*, **Budget** *(800-527-0700; www.budget. com)*, **Hertz** *(800-654-3131; www.hertz.com)* and **Enterprise** *(800-261-7331; www.enterprise.com)*. Visitors accustomed to driving in unpredictable city traffic won't have a problem navigating Chicago's streets.

IS IT POSSIBLE TO WALK EVERYWHERE?

Walking is a great way to get to know this "City of Neighborhoods." That said, it's probably not the smartest idea to try to walk from one neighborhood to another, as these can sometimes be spaced quite far apart. (Eight city blocks equals roughly about a mile.) Use this as a rule of thumb in orienting yourself: Chicago is on a grid system, with north-south State Street and east-west Madison Avenue being 0; one block north of Madison Avenue on State Street is 100 North State, two west of State on Madison is 200 West Madison, and so on. Most street signs feature the name of the street and its numerical coordinate in this grid system.

HOW SAFE IS CHICAGO?

Though Chicago is a safe city, avoid potentially dangerous areas, such as the Near West Side and some portions of the South Side. Certain well-lit and well-trodden neighborhoods, like Streeterville, the Gold Coast, Lincoln Park and Wicker Park, are safe to walk around in at any time of the day, though in general, don't draw attention to yourself in public and leave valuables in your hotel safe (including credit cards—carry only one and cash for what you need).

No matter what neighborhood you're in, you're likely to encounter panhandlers, whether they're opening a convenient store's door for spare change in Wicker Park or sitting with a sign in the Loop. Whether you donate a buck or two is up to you, but one of the most constructive ways to give is by buying a *StreetWise* magazine ($2) from vendors working throughout the city. The weekly publication—sold by homeless or near-homeless men and women—features articles and art by vendors and an editorial staff. Vendors make a $1.25 profit per magazine sold, and you get to give knowing that it's for a good cause.

WHERE ARE THE CITY'S HOSPITALS?

Chicago is home to some of the foremost medical schools-cum-hospitals in the region. Among these institution-backed hospitals are **Northwestern**

DOWNTOWN CHICAGO

Memorial Hospital *(251 E. Huron St., 312-926-2000; www.nmh.org)*, **University of Chicago Medical Center** *(5841 S. Maryland Ave., 773-702-1000; www.uchospitals.edu)*, and **Rush University Medical Center** *(1653 W. Congress Parkway, 312-942-5000; www.rush.edu)*. The city's top-notch public hospital, **John H. Stroger, Jr. Hospital of Cook County** *(1901 W. Harrison St., 312-864-6000; www.cchil.org)*—a.k.a "County" to Chicagoans—treats emergencies as well, though the wait can stretch for hours.

WHAT ARE THE LOCAL MEDIA OUTLETS?

Chicago's major newspapers are the venerable *Chicago Tribune (www.chicagotribune.com)*—owned by media heavyweight Tribune Company—and the grittier *Chicago Sun-Times (www.suntimes.com)*.

Weeklies include *Chicago Reader (www.chicagoreader.com)*—a 38-year-old alt-weekly—and *Time Out Chicago (www.timeout.com/chicago)*. Both hit the streets on Thursday and obsessively cover local arts, theater, film, nightlife, restaurants and more. Other publications include the music-centric *UR Chicago (www.urchicago.com)* and monthly lifestyle magazine *Chicago* magazine *(www.chicagomag.com)*.

HOW COLD IS CHICAGO?

Chicagoans often suffer through bone-chilling, face-smacking winters. The coldest months are January and February, where the wind-chill factor can plunge into double digits below zero degrees Fahrenheit. Summers are on the other extreme—hot and humid. Despite any humidity, though, the city is a summer playground for locals who flock to the beach and the many street fests. Spring and fall are also very pleasant, if a bit short sometimes: Spring realistically falls somewhere between March and June (though it can be in the 50 to 60 Fahrenheit range through May), while autumn usually sweeps in from September to November.

★MAPS

CLOUD GATE

Chicago
Overview

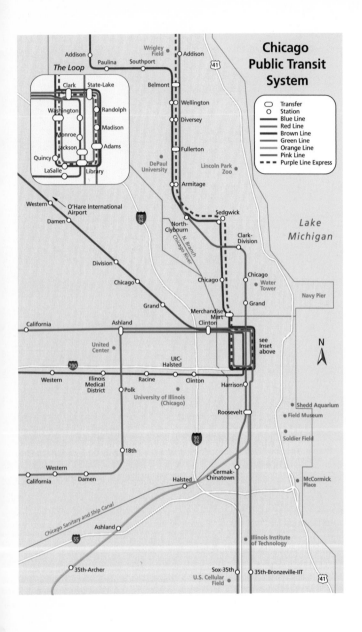

Chicago Public Transit System

The Loop

- Addison
- Paulina
- Southport
- Clark
- State-Lake
- Washington
- Randolph
- Monroe
- Madison
- Jackson
- Adams
- Quincy
- LaSalle
- Library
- Addison
- Wrigley Field
- 41
- Belmont
- Wellington
- Diversey
- Fullerton
- DePaul University
- Lincoln Park Zoo
- Armitage
- Sedgwick
- North-Clybourn
- N. Branch Chicago River
- Clark-Division
- Lake Michigan
- Western
- O'Hare International Airport
- 90 94
- Damen
- Division
- Chicago
- Chicago
- Chicago Water Tower
- Grand
- Navy Pier
- California
- Ashland
- Merchandise Mart
- Clinton
- Grand
- see Inset above
- United Center
- 290
- N
- Western
- Illinois Medical District
- Racine
- Clinton
- UIC-Halsted
- Harrison
- Polk
- University of Illinois (Chicago)
- Shedd Aquarium
- Field Museum
- Roosevelt
- Soldier Field
- 90 64
- 18th
- Western
- California
- Damen
- Halsted
- Cermak-Chinatown
- McCormick Place
- Chicago Sanitary and Ship Canal
- 55
- Ashland
- Illinois Institute of Technology
- 35th-Archer
- Sox-35th
- U.S. Cellular Field
- 35th-Bronzeville-IIT
- 41

Legend
- ⬭ Transfer
- ○ Station
- ▬ Blue Line
- ▬ Red Line
- ▬ Brown Line
- ▬ Green Line
- ▬ Orange Line
- ▬ Pink Line
- ┅ Purple Line Express

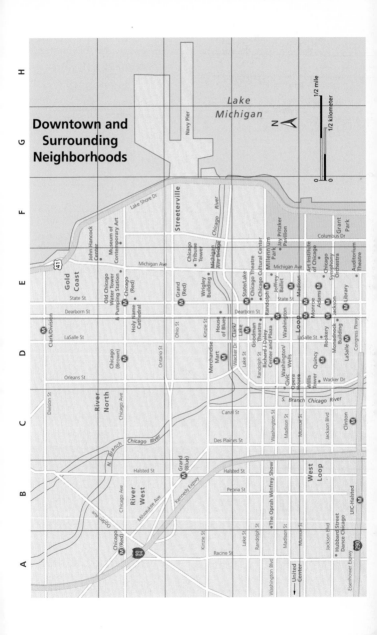

Downtown and Surrounding Neighborhoods

Lake Michigan

Navy Pier

N

1/2 mile
1/2 kilometer
0
0

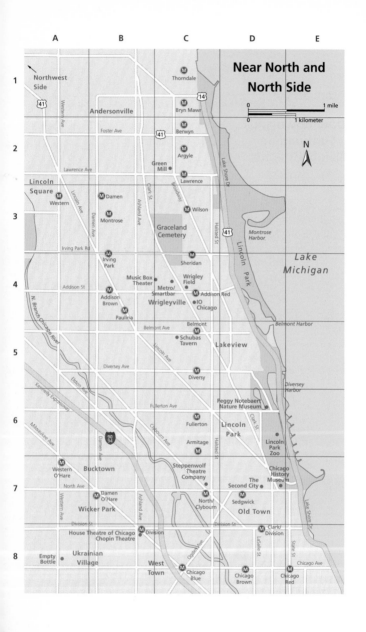

Near North and North Side

A B C D E

1 Northwest Side
Thorndale
Andersonville
41
Bryn Mawr
14
41
Foster Ave
Berwyn

2 Lawrence Ave
Argyle
Green Mill
Lawrence
N
Lake Shore Dr

Lincoln Square
Western
Damen
Montrose
Broadway
Clark St
Ashland Ave
Wilson
Sheridan

3 Irving Park Rd
Graceland Cemetery
Halsted St
41
Montrose Harbor
Lake Michigan

Irving Park
Music Box Theater
Addison St
Metro/ Smartbar
Wrigley Field
Addison Red
Addison Brown
Wrigleyville
IO Chicago
Paulina

4 Belmont Ave
Belmont
Belmont Harbor
Lakeview
Schubas Tavern
Lincoln Park

5 Diversey Ave
Diversy
Lincoln Ave
Diversey Harbor

6 Fullerton Ave
Kennedy Expressway
Elston Ave
Clybourn Ave
Fullerton
Peggy Notebaert Nature Museum
Milwaukee Ave
90 94
Armitage
Lincoln Park
Lincoln Park Zoo
Clark St
Halsted St

7 Western O'Hare
Bucktown
North Ave
Damen O'Hare
Wicker Park
Steppenwolf Theatre Company
Chicago History Museum
The Second City
Sedgwick
North/ Clybourn
Old Town
Lake Shore Dr

8 Division St
House Theatre of Chicago
Chopin Theatre
Division
Clark/ Division
LaSalle Dr
State St
Empty Bottle
Ukrainian Village
West Town
Ogden Ave
Chicago Blue
Chicago Brown
Chicago Ave
Chicago Red

0 1 mile
0 1 kilometer

182

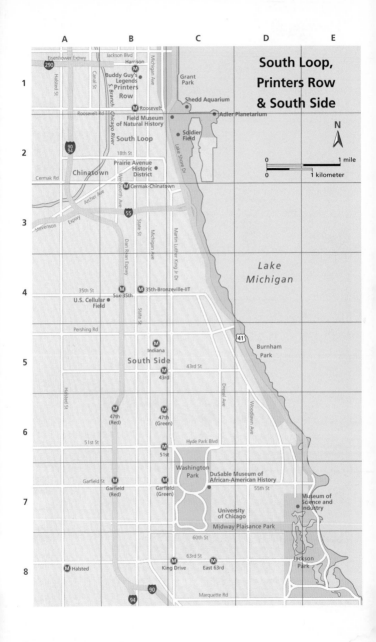

South Loop, Printers Row & South Side

N

0   1 mile
0   1 kilometer

Eisenhower Expwy
290
Jackson Blvd
Harrison
Buddy Guy's
Legends
Printers
Row
Michigan Ave
Grant
Park
Halsted St
Carol St
S. Branch
Roosevelt
Shedd Aquarium
Roosevelt Rd
Chicago River
Field Museum
of Natural History
Adler Planetarium
South Loop
18th St
Soldier
Field
90
94
Prairie Avenue
Historic
District
Lake Shore Dr
Cermak Rd
Chinatown
Wentworth Ave
Cermak-Chinatown
Archer Ave
55
Stevenson Expwy
State St
Michigan Ave
Martin Luther King Jr Dr
Lake
Michigan
Dan Ryan Expwy
35th St
Sox-35th
35th-Bronzeville-IIT
U.S. Cellular
Field
State St
Pershing Rd
41
Burnham
Park
Indiana
South Side
43rd St
Halsted St
43rd
Dresel Ave
Woodlawn Ave
47th
(Red)
47th
(Green)
51st St
Hyde Park Blvd
51st
Washington
Park
DuSable Museum of
African-American History
Garfield St
Garfield
(Red)
Garfield
(Green)
55th St
Museum of
Science and
Industry
University
of Chicago
Midway Plaisance Park
60th St
Jackson
Park
Halsted
King Drive
East 63rd
63rd St
94
90
Marquette Rd

183

WATER TOWER

CHICAGO RIVER

CHICAGO SKYLINE

ART CREDITS

Taste of Chicago: © Chicago
    Convention & Tourism
    Bureau (CCTB)
Navy Pier: © Cesar Russ RE-
ALVIEWS™ Photog-
raphy
Empty Bottle: Empty Bottle
Buckingham Fountain: ©
    CCTB
Millennium Park: © CCTB
Chicago Theater Sign: ©Istock
City Skline: © Cesar Russ
    REALVIEWS™ Photog-
raphy
Watertower at Night:©Istock
Urban Garden: ©Istock

El Train: © Cesar Russ REAL-
VIEWS™ Photography
Pilsen: ©Istock

Chicago Skyline: © Cesar
    Russ REALVIEWS™
    Photography
Navy Pier: © Chicago Conven-
tion & Tourism Bureau
Cloud Gate: © City of Chicago
Lakefront Recreational Park:
    ©Istock
Field Museum of Natural His-
tory: © CCTB
Shedd Aquarium: Shedd
    Aquarium
Pritzker Pavillion: Millennium
    Park
Michigane Avenue Bridge: ©
    CCTB
Air Show: © CCTB
Graceland Cemetery: ©istock
Museum of Science and
    Industry: Museum of
    Science and Industry
El Train: ©istock
Robie House: ©istock

NoMi: Park Hyatt
Seasons: Seasons
Chicago Hotdog: ©RF123
Tru: Tru/Mark Ballog
Avenues: The Peninsula Hotels
Naha: Naha Restaurant
Otom: Otom Restaurant/Dan
    Dry
Sixteen: Sixteen Restaurant
The Publican: The Publican
Everest: Everest Restaurant

3 1170 00821 4540